Advance praise for

Surviving Economic Crises through Education

"The recent huge hiccup of capitalism ('global financial crisis') and its continuing gurgles of pain have profound implications for education, teacher training, and the role of knowledge for human betterment (given that claims to knowledge and expertise were no protection from the cataclysm itself). This collection shows us why this is so, framing an imperative for rethinking education as a process of self-knowing and empowerment in a period of enormous economic and ontological insecurity. David R. Cole has brought together a significant set of theorists whose empirical evidence flows through to insights and indications of what is to be done. One hopes, as some of the authors propose, it is the very depth of the crisis that may force the shedding of the most deeply entrenched (mis)beliefs about education, enabling thereby a new if wobbly space for innovation and growth."

–*Andrew Jakubowicz, Professor of Sociology, Director of the Institute of Cultural Diversity, University of Technology, Sydney*

"In times of economic crisis politicians often present their policies by claiming that 'there is no alternative.' This book unmasks such claims by providing critical readings of the politics of contemporary crisis talk and by presenting a range of generative educational responses that provide real alternatives for educational thought and action. This is a timely and inspiring collection that affirms the crucial role of education in the struggle for democracy in uncertain times."

–*Gert Biesta, Professor of Education and Director of Research, School of Education & Laboratory for Educational Theory, University of Stirling*

"This book represents a kaleidoscope of views on the roles of education in a world rapidly changing since the 2008 financial crisis and the collapse of the Western world economies. Ideas mushroom from each chapter challenging the role of education in a capitalist society. A must-read for those from various disciplines who care about education."

–*Arnaud Chevalier, Senior Lecturer in Economics, Royal Holloway, University of London*

Surviving Economic Crises through Education

GLOBAL STUDIES IN EDUCATION

A.C. (Tina) Besley, Michael A. Peters,
Cameron McCarthy, Fazal Rizvi
General Editors

Vol. 11

The Global Studies in Education series is part of the Peter Lang Education list.
Every volume is peer reviewed and meets
the highest quality standards for content and production.

PETER LANG
New York • Washington, D.C./Baltimore • Bern
Frankfurt • Berlin • Brussels • Vienna • Oxford

Surviving Economic Crises through Education

Edited by David R. Cole

PETER LANG
New York • Washington, D.C./Baltimore • Bern
Frankfurt • Berlin • Brussels • Vienna • Oxford

Library of Congress Cataloging-in-Publication Data

Surviving economic crises through education / edited by David R. Cole.
p. cm. — (Global studies in education; v. 11)
Includes bibliographical references and index.
1. Education—Economic aspects. 2. Business and education.
3. Recessions. 4. Critical pedagogy. I. Cole, David R. (David Robert).
LC65.S865 338.4'7374013—dc23 2011046127
ISBN 978-1-4331-1479-3 (hardcover)
ISBN 978-1-4331-1478-6 (paperback)
ISBN 978-1-4539-0523-4 (e-book)
ISSN 2153-330X

Bibliographic information published by **Die Deutsche Nationalbibliothek**.
Die Deutsche Nationalbibliothek lists this publication in the "Deutsche Nationalbibliografie"; detailed bibliographic data is available on the Internet at http://dnb.d-nb.de/.

Cover art by Justin Bower

The paper in this book meets the guidelines for permanence and durability of the Committee on Production Guidelines for Book Longevity of the Council of Library Resources.

29 Broadway, 18th floor, New York, NY 10006
www.peterlang.com

Printed in the United States of America

• CONTENTS •

Part Two: Case Studies of Argentina

Part Three: Educational Theory and Economic Crisis

• FOREWORD •

Crisis and Attentiveness

Stephen J. Ball

One central feature of contemporary global education policy, and I use the phase advisedly, is the fundamental antagonism and, at the same time, mutual dependency between markets and states. Indeed, a global education policy is being constituted at the nexus between regulation and midwifery (Blackmore, 1999). That is, the role of the state in setting limits to the market, while at the same time, creating conditions within which the market can flourish and expand. Furthermore, the financial crisis of 2008 is now decisively entrenched within that nexus. What might have been a moment at which dominant interpretations of political reality were fundamentally tested (Gamble, 2010) has provided new opportunities and 'justifications' (Jones, 2010) for a neoliberal assault on public education and public educations. Cuts, contestability and contracting out are all very attractive or 'necessary' responses by governments seeking to address private sector failures by making the public sector 'pay'! There is a bitter irony here, inasmuch that the public sector is to be subject every more minutely to the values and methods which produced the financial crisis. All of this is well and good, all of this is true, but Ken Jones is right when he draws on Rogoff's work to say:

> Irit Rogoff (2008) notes that the discussions of academics and cultural professionals tend to constitute an 'eternal lament of how bad things are: how bureaucratised, how homogenised, how understaffed and underfunded'. Though 'not without its justifications...this voice of endless complaint serves to box education into the confines of a small community'. How can education become more, Rogoff asks, 'than this site of shrinkage and disappointment?' Part of her answer involves thinking about 'the principles we cherish in the education process', in particular attentiveness to the complexities of meaning-making, desire and curiosity, intellectual challenge. (Jones, 2010, pp. 797-98)

This book is an example of that 'attentiveness' and of thinking about crisis from the bottom up. As David R. Cole says in his introduction, 'This book signifies a search for the breaks and rupture points between economic crises and education'. It is about seeing the gaps rather than the closures, and this is addressed in a variety of ways–good and bad. The gaps are virtual, in common spaces on the internet, they are financial, in entrenched precarity and new opportunities for profit, they are material, in struggles over the ownership of common spaces, in schools and in the community, and they are moral, in struggles between citizenship and consumption, and over the meaning of professionalism. What the contributions do is both map the profundity of changes in education over and against and in relation to the financial crisis and map the social and political landscape over which the struggle for survival, the survival of Education, that which we cherish, is taking place. This is not about the survival of institutions and structures; it is about the survival of particular forms of subjectivity, self-worth and moral purpose. All of this is 'in here' as well as 'out there'. Survival is a matter of who we are, what it means to be educated, what is means to be a teacher and a learner and a parent. Be prepared to be challenged and chastened; a lot is at stake. As Gamble (2010, p. 708) concludes, the financial crisis of 2008 will "shape current debates and future projects for the international political economy as well as for domestic politics, and these debates may test the robustness of many democracies, and the way in which these conflicts are resolved will shape the context within which future education policy is determined".

Stephen J. Ball
London, July 2011

References

Blackmore, J. (1999). Localization/globalization and the midwife state: Strategic dilemmas for state feminism in education? *Journal of Education Policy*, vol. 14(1), 33-54.

Gamble, A. (2010). Introduction: After the crash. *Journal of Education Policy* Vol. 25, No. 6, 703–708.

Jones, K. (2010). Crisis, what crisis? *Journal of Education Policy*. Vol. 25, No. 6, 793–798.

Rogoff, I. (2008). *Turning. e-flux*, November: http://www.eflux.com/journal/view/18

• PREFACE •

This collection of chapters on education and economic crises comes at a time of increasing anxiety about the repercussions of financial instability and the probability of widespread market volatility. The educators and researchers represented here have considered these factors deeply when constructing their responses to prevailing economic conditions. The result is a book of varying political, social, educative and cultural views. These views guide the reader through economic crises as a mode of survival and as a means to deploying education at its most meaningful and intense.

The book is organised into three parts. The first part focuses on educational responses to the crises. There are chapters on public education and the promise of open science; education for resilience and resistance in the big society; facism and capitalist crisis; teachers' reflections on economic crises and the prospects for technology-enhanced learning in times of crisis. The first part of the book serves to show how economic crises permeate current educational practice as a permanent alarm factor. The second part of the book presents three case studies set in the educational system of Argentina. The first case study analyses the effects of the 2001 crisis on the Argentinean education system in terms of the results in international education ratings; the second case study examines agency and struggle in Argentinean schools; the last study looks at education and governmentality in degraded urban territories. Part three of this book focuses on educational theory. The chapters look at work as a reflection of 'the other'; the crisis of mutative capitalism; the current dynamics of professional expertise; educating the person for democratic participation; remachining educational desire; and the endless vertigo of capitalist education.

This volume offers a new approach to surviving economic crisis through education. The approach aligns practice with theory and takes the empirical evidence from these studies as a means to determining the economic influence on education. For example, the Argentine studies show how the educational system in Argentina has been depleted of resources since the 2001 economic collapse. Yet the inhabitants of this system have not given up hope or become less educated. On the contrary, one could argue that the striving for educational excellence has increased; the importance of education is vindicated and sharpened by cutbacks.

I would like to thank Andrew Jakubowicz (UTS), Michael A. Peters, Chris Myers and Sophie Appel for facilitating the publication of this important book.

David R. Cole
Sydney, September 2011

CHAPTER ONE

Introduction to Surviving Economic Crises through Education

David R. Cole

> It's a sad Everyplace, where citizens are always getting fired from their jobs at the 7-Eleven and where kids do drugs and practice the latest dance crazes at the local lake, where they also fantasize about being adult and pulling welfare-check scams as they inspect each other's skins for chemical burns from the lake water. (Coupland, 1991, p. 45)

Introduction

This quote from the novel *Generation X* is a provocation for some educationalists, who might perceive their job to be a corrective one in terms of the social ills as listed above. However, Coupland (1991) describes an aspect of reality in which we now find ourselves. The point that will be advanced in this book is not to valorize or negate such social realities, but to understand how these interconnected phenomena are comprehendible from a perspective where social life is not categorized or othered through the imposition of ideal (educative) thought. On the contrary, this book examines social life from the perspective of complex and entwined material practices–sometimes unconscious. This means that one cannot cordon off aspects of social life because one finds them disagreeable, or because they do not correspond to the socialities of an educated and well-organized elite (Cole, 2010). The collection of essays that is represented here derive from responses to surviving economic crises through education that accept multifarious social activities and mores. Furthermore, the use of Justin Bower's cover image, called the Architecture of Infection, signals the ways in which this book will examine how one is conformed and compromised by present social tendencies, rather than presenting ideal solutions in terms of learning, education, or by ignoring the negative underbelly in contemporary society. This book suggests that one survives economic crises through education by closely examining the breaks and rupture points through which new tendencies in society are disclosed and made apparent (Deleuze & Guattari, 1984). First, we must analyze the key terms of survival narratives, economic crises, and education, before we may understand how these notions come together through the chapters of this book.

Survival Narratives

In Reza Negarestani's (2008) *Cyclonopedia: Complicity with Anonymous Materials*, a connection between the survival narratives that currently riddle globalized culture and society and the present state of world affairs is drawn. To understand the proliferation of survival narratives, one must delve into the connections between 'petropolitics', as Negarestani puts it, and the occult codex of historical data that we have about conflictive societal tendencies. For example, the 'war on terror' is the prime mover of techno-military resourcing, design and capabilities in countries such as the United States, UK or Australia. If one delves further into the expanse of militarization that exists beneath the panoply of the 'war on terror', one encounters a clear, yet treacherous and subterranean world of politics, oil, capital flows and views on Islam. The conflict point is obvious: Who controls the world's oil? Countries are scrambling to secure their supplies of this precious commodity, as economic and social mobility depends on its supply. Yet at the same time, the major conflict over oil unearths hidden and buried elements from such a pressurized and evolving point. The survival narratives relating to supplies of oil involve the belief structures of Christianity and Islam, as much of the oil is to be found in the Middle East, and this forces us to ask questions about absolute and relative value systems. For example, if the monotheistic worldviews of Christianity and Islam are truly in conflict (over oil), how could (one) God (given agency) allow this?

The secular response to the unearthing and proliferation of survival narratives is being fought over in an equally ferocious way. This huge tract in the forest of survival narratives takes millennial and global conflict and resolves them in terms of ecology, environment and global warming (Gough, 2004). The conflict changes from being 'East versus West' (theistic) to that which concerns poor versus rich, or First versus Third (or Fourth) world nations. The argument is that if we are to survive, rich countries need to take action and work to aid the planet (because they can afford to). Governments in rich countries are imposing carbon output limits, carbon taxes and restrictions on carbon dioxide. Yet beneath this feverish anti-carbon activity, the 'petropolitics' of the situation remains. The pipelines of oil have not been dismantled. Middle Eastern countries still rely on the riches that oil production has brought. Therefore a fundamental contradiction is lodged in the world's economy between oil production and reducing carbon dioxide emissions. On top of this contradiction, poorer countries, and the poor in first world countries, struggle to cope with the increased costs involved with switching to a carbon-free economy. Survival narratives are born out of these contradictions as stories are invented to explain such a riven context. These narratives serve to give hope and motivation to populations drowning beneath oceans of increased carbon bureaucracy, increased divisions in wealth and an accelerated pace of environmental uncertainty.

Yet the point from Negarestani (2008) is that these survival narratives are not part of the 'natural order' from whence they originate (the bacterial fluidics of oil), but are part of an overestimation in human consciousness. According to *Cyclonopedia*, we cannot simply make up stories about surviving the current era, and these threads will miraculously take us out of intractable conflict between opposing ideologies such as Christianity and Islam or climate skeptics and green ecologists. Rather, the survival narratives lead backwards to objects and symbols buried in the past, which are made prescient in the inertia of petropolitics. Contrariwise, petropolitics throws up a type of smokescreen, through which the truths of oil are made secret and are transcribed into the evolution of new strategies and practices in everyday life. For example, the Islamic notion of *Taqiyya*, or concealment in civil society for the purposes of war, crosses over and becomes other to itself and enters into commercial media channels as an intensification in the war on terror or a distrust of Islam. An anonymous, shifting cloud or blob called 'the outside' sits parallel to everything that we now do and relates as a complementary mechanism to the ways in which desires are codified and commodified by techno-capitalist digital technology (Cole, 2005). Survival narratives are lost and trivialized through the immense beating pulse of the blob and the strange new energies that are emerging on the Net. Trying to plot a survival path and narrative through the blob is like attempting to explain voodoo with reference to children's toys. The result is always the same: a blank screen, nihilism, the loss of self, powerlessness.

If one reads survival narratives such as Cormac McCarthy's *The Road*, the idealization of the father-and-son relationship and the overestimation of human consciousness in an ecologically ravaged planet are evident. The point here is not that survival narratives are wrong, but that one should look elsewhere to find the requisite energies to push through the current situation. With reference to economic crises, the relevant survival narratives are entwined within capitalist mechanisms and processes that drive the world economy. This entwinement is part of a technologically accelerated system that moves capital around the globe in order to make profit. There is very little human consciousness left in this process, as traders and investors rely on computerized programs, which plot economic activity and examine the ways in which emergent trends correlate to growth. The survival narratives therefore correspond to gradients on graphs and moments in which to invest and sell. Of course, there are still people overseeing the computers, and governments that try to influence the markets with their decisions, yet these intentionalities are but nothing compared to the cybernetic functions of the machines. The collective story of how we are to cross through and survive this period in history is therefore about computers and flesh, digitalization and belief, acceleration and community. Most of all, it is perhaps about trying to explicate the forms and penetrations of otherness, as they reveal new ways of being and becoming in the world. For this otherness connects with the politics of containment and restraint that maintains the current status quo, and, as Alberto Toscano (2010) has written:

> While scarcity is both produced and reproduced in ever new forms, and is not necessarily the cause for open conflict, it does mean that the relations of production are established and pursued in a climate of fear and mutual mistrust by individuals who are always ready to believe that the Other is an anti-human member of an alien species; in other words, that the Other, whoever he may be, can always be seen by Others as "the one who started it." (p. 12)

Petropolitics works in and through this climate of fear and as such devolves survival narratives through relationships with others, as the politics of production turns from types of labor exploitation and consolidation to the drives and apparatuses for adequate resourcing (Agamben, 2005). There is a strong ethical aspect to the educative relationships that one might invent and use in this situation, as oil resources dwindle beneath an expanding human population. Futurists, social scientists and demographers have speculated for many years about the ways in which the resource 'merry-go-round' may play out as the human population expands into the 21st century (e.g., Toffler, 1970). Petropolitics is currently bleeding and fusing into 'waterpolitics', 'foodpolitics', 'airpolitics', and so forth, as successive resource crises are translated into the world's economic functioning, price indexing and governmental responses to fewer resources per capita. The extrapolations of the world's population make the connective synthesis of political responses to resource shortages inevitable. In this situation, survival narratives are extracted at an accelerated pace from their hiding places amongst urban and country locations. These narratives are currently being reconciled through 'sustainability' and green initiatives. Yet notions of sustainability and the move to a green economy do nothing to halt the onward marching of the global population to catastrophic resource conflict. This is not the plot of a disaster or horror movie, but the path that we are currently taking. The only response that could adequately cope with the resource versus population doomsday equation is a universal and groundbreaking rethink about education and its place with respect to the future of economic crises (Pink, 2005). This book should be seen as a step towards this reformulation.

Economic Crises and Education

What are the survival narratives specific to economic crises and education? Education has been connected to the formations of the state and its citizens since at least Plato (1965 [360 B.C.]).[1] In these globally connected, accelerated times of instantaneous capital investment, the citizen is a product of consumerist values and state intervention in community affairs. Education is mandated to produce these citizens, and to do this, teaching and learning must presently inculcate: the requisite duties, speeds and repetitions of everyday life (in order to pay taxes), notions of services and product creation appropriate to market conditions (including efficiency markers such as linguistic and numerical skills), and robust self-building and resilience studies (effective affect-cognition, suitable for sales, interview situations and decision making under stress). Admittedly, there is another side to these through-lines in contemporary education, which have been neatly summarized by Negarestani (2011) and help us to link education with economic crises:

> As the event immanent to the polis, the citizen is the horizon whereby the trauma of the human organism is transplanted within the territorial trauma of the city and the state. (p. 15)

The notion of economic crisis is a traumatizing agency. In an accelerated economic situation, the likelihood of further crises and therefore increased trauma is amplified. One could, perhaps straightforwardly, relate these dispersed factors in the analysis of trauma to a type of non-representative affect relation, as Nigel Thrift (2004) has done in his analysis of cities. Yet, in order to effectively place education in the frame of an undulating economic curve of boom and bust, that perhaps goes back to the 1500s as Braudel (1967) suggests, one must take into account the machinery of citizenship. This machinery is laid out like an extended cage and shadows over and beyond the specific highs and lows of economic contextualization. For example, Renaissance Italy (1650–1750) was a time and place of extraordinary economic growth. This wealth helped advance the arts, literature, architecture, science, mathematics and learning in general. However, underneath and at the same time as the unity between wealth creation and education was apparent, there was the strong development of fierce political rivalries and officious, power-hungry institutions, such as the Catholic Church (see Peters, 2000). The idea of the citizen carried with it the traumas from these power and institutional elites, and this ultimately leads to the unraveling and containment of Italian power in the nineteenth century. Education does flourish under resource rich conditions (economic boom times), yet the apparatuses of social control are also able to proliferate, often in the guise of and through education (e.g., developing notions of citizenship).

The task of this book is therefore to link economic crises with education, without the masks of power-created apparatuses such as the citizen, with its requisite traumas, detracting from understanding the ways in which teaching and learning have altered due to the crises. The setup of containment strategies for the population by power elites, who had benefitted most from economic growth, unravels when the economic situation deteriorates (Scott, 1998). This means that educational mores, often conceptualized during the period of strong economic activity, carry on through resource retraction and may appear as a type of nostalgia for the golden times when progress, money and social cohesion had been easier to achieve. Italy still looks back to the Renaissance as a period of unrequited blossoming. This is excellent for the creation of tourist Italy, and the maintenance of the Vatican, yet does nothing to help enhance the current economic, political or educational situation. The continuation of the mythology of the Renaissance man in Italian life acts as a shield and retrogressive factor with respect to adaptation in terms of current global conditions, including the construction of adequate educational systems (Rullani, 2004). In the United States, the boom times of the 1990s and the 'dot-com' revolutions still resonate in terms of developing new economic, social and educative progress. Indeed, much of the global interest in new ways to educate comes directly from this period, with the exultation of information and communication technologies (ICT) solutions to social and educative problems touted as the most efficient ways to produce learning communities (Lauder, Brown, Dillabough & Halsey, 2006). Yet educators working in poverty-stricken communities know that installing interactive whiteboards (IWBs) in the classroom will not fix low educational expectations and achievement. Rather, one must look to the sources of the power imbalances (often institutionalized) and try to understand how and why they have become operative in the affective-cognitive practice of education over time.

> It is here that Nietzsche speaks of a break, a rupture, a leap. Who are these beings, they who come like fate?—Some pack of blonde beasts of prey, a conqueror and master race which, organized for war and with the ability to organize, unhesitatingly

> lays its terrible claws upon a populace perhaps tremendously superior but still formless–. Even the most ancient African myths talk to us of these blonde men. They are the *founders of the state.* (Deleuze & Guattari, 1984, p. 192)

This much quoted and misunderstood reference from Nietzsche that Deleuze and Guattari (1984) use in their analysis of the state is relevant to questions of education and economic crises. This is because the ways in which practices are conditioned and ingrained in populations over time comes from an originatory spark of life outside the practice (Cole & Hager, 2010). In the case of education, the spark has come from disciplinary, religious and military forms of organization. This is why it can be so difficult to initiate and sustain creative responses to learning and change in contemporary education, as the organizational forms that educational systems carry with them, such as timetabling and lesson planning, have been rigidly determined in advance and through history by state-controlled curricula mechanisms (Land, Meyer & Smith, 2008). These states also control disciplinary mechanisms, for example, prisons, laws, the police force, and the military, and have strategic alliances with large-scale religious organizations such as the Catholic Church. The answer to this problem of state control in educative systems is not to turn over the running of schools and universities to private ownership, as the corporate sector has equally inflexible systems and hierarchies that depend on capital flows, investment strategies and shareholder value (often dependent on merging, asset savings and future orientation). Rather, the ways in which the business of education should be run requires a new organizational mode to emerge, one that breaks with the state controls of the past and allows for differentiated and local concerns to determine the ways in which teaching and learning relate to the socius (Agamben, 2005) without falling back into 'economism'.

This book signifies a search for the breaks and rupture points between economic crises and education. The idea is that when an economic crisis such as the recent events of the global financial crisis (GFC) unfolded in 2008 in the United States, one is given the opportunity to question and examine normatively determined forms of living that may have carried on previous to the crisis. These forms of living entwine and become other in the context of a practice such as education (Cole, 2010). This means that the outside forces that may have started the practice such as military organization or religious belief become progressively hidden beneath the cloaks of educative values and stasis. In the context of an economic crisis, the cloaks will be unveiled, and the ways in which the entwinements have been knotted will be revealed. This happens because the resourcing systems of education depend on surplus capital flows, and the disequilibrium of an economic crisis forms tipping points whereby different directions in practice, such as the new modes of educative organization mentioned above, may become apparent. To this extent an economic crisis is an opportunity for reflection and change; it is a chance for educators, students and teachers to use this moment for the purposes of coming together, breaking the blinkers and limitations that have been set up for teaching and learning in the past, and designing a new path in education for the future.

The Chapters of the Book

This book represents an international collaboration of educators concerned with 'surviving economic crises through education' from the United States, UK, Australia, Canada, Argentina and Norway. The team of writers and researchers assembled here do not have a unified solution to the problems that result from economic crises in education, but they do provide cogent, well-considered responses to the connections between economic crises and education. The chapters are not homogeneous in terms of ideology, theoretical framing or methodology. Yet the writing here does resonate with the overwhelming message that education plays and will play a fundamentally critical role in steering paths through economic crises. This is because the world's economy is driven by the ways in which education can deliver human and social capital (Bourdieu & Passeron, 1990). This knowledge and affective/cognitive production depends on understanding how economic crises relate to education and what messages one may ascertain from this complex relation. As such, this book signifies a survival narrative for the present and future; it is a means to drawing disparate yet combinatory threads together about economics, teaching and learning, and the evolution of culture and society.

Educational Responses to the Crises

The first section of the book has been designated as representing the educational responses to the crises. There are enormous crossover themes that reverberate throughout the book, yet the foregrounding of education as a practice is vital to understand which specific elements of teaching and learning will endure and make a difference in times of economic retraction and potential collapse. The opening chapter, by Michael A. Peters, is called "'Knowledge Economy,' Economic Crisis and Cognitive Capitalism: Public Education and the Promise of Open Science." This chapter examines the relationships between the knowledge economy and education in times of cognitive capitalism. Peters argues for a reappropriation and development of the 'global knowledge commons' as a way of surviving economic crisis through education. To advance this theoretical construction, Peters outlines the theory of cognitive capitalism to focus on the question of immaterial labor as a framework within which to view a critical approach to surviving economic crises through education. Peters demonstrates that the survival of economic crises depends upon the promise of open science as both a link to the transformation of public education and as a means of reappropriating the global knowledge commons.

Chapter 3 is written by Jim Crowther and Mae Shaw and named "Education for Resilience and Resistance in the 'Big Society'". Whilst there are immediate concerns about the resilience of communities to withstand the consequences of the worst public expenditure cuts since the Second World War (in the UK), the authors argue that there is also a necessity to bring into focus the real causes of the current crisis. The authors identify two distinctive but interconnected discourses that are central to transforming the relationship between the state, the market and citizens: a moralizing discourse and an entrepreneurial discourse. In contrast, the authors argue that resilience and resistance are best understood as collective processes with both personal and political dimensions and that education has an important role in stimulating and resourcing community engagement in these terms as a means of resisting those powerful but disempowering discourses identified above. This chapter focuses on the survival of community and implications for educational purposes, processes and practices in times of economic crises and the subsequent cutbacks. Mike Cole has written the next chapter, "Capitalist Crisis and Fascism: Issues for Educational Practice". In times of capitalist crisis, given certain additional political, economic or social circumstances, the barometer of racism rises, both within mainstream political parties and at the fringes. In June 2009, two members of the fascist British National Party (BNP) were elected to the European parliament. The following years have also witnessed the appearance on the streets of various Islamophobic 'defence leagues'. These developments need to be seen in the context of a lurch to the right in British politics, unprecedented since the Thatcher years. In this chapter, Cole begins by considering the concept of a capitalist crisis per se, before moving on to a detailed examination of the rise and fall of the BNP. Throughout the chapter, the author addresses issues for Marxist educational practice: anticapitalist and antifascist education and education for socialism.

Chapter 5, "Teach for *What* America? Beginning Teachers' Reflections about Their Professional Choices and the Economic Crisis", is by Gustavo E. Fischman and Victor H. Diaz. Although the 2008 economic downturn in the United States has highlighted several of the flaws and contradictions in neoliberal economic policies, the responses within teacher education institutions to the constraints of the economic crisis appear to still be framed within a managerial, neoliberal model. One would imagine that in the throes of financial crisis, when very well-educated and highly credentialed people experience high levels of unemployment in spite of their education level, the redemptive power of schools would at least be brought into question. Yet, in this study of beginning teachers' reflections on their decision to become teachers through Teach for America, the authors found the opposite. After surveying forty-six beginning teachers in Teach for America (known in the program as corps members) and reading through their application materials for the program, the vast majority of these teachers do not seem to believe that the financial crisis over the past three years should create education responses, in the form of accommodations or modifications, that differ from the policies of the past. This chapter analyses the data of the corps members in terms of redemptive narratives, which complements the survival narratives as an 'othered' response to economic crisis. In the last chapter in the educational responses to crises, Patrick Carmichael and Kate Litherland have written about "Transversality and Innovation: Prospects for Technology-Enhanced Learning in Times of Crisis". While learning technologies and their role in higher education have been interpreted in broadly 'Deleuzian' terms, the argument that the authors advance here is that the current crises and lacunae in higher education present opportunities to put such ideas to work. This, Carmichael and Litherland suggest, can be achieved through the formation of, and work within, those 'transverse groupings', composed of students, staff and researchers, which Guattari suggests can "overcome both the impasse of pure verticality and that of mere horizontality" (1984, p. 18). The authors draw on writers and activists in the autonomist tradition to present an alternate view of how technological and pedagogical innovation might be initiated; where expertise lies; and how technology relates to pedagogical environments, activities and outcomes. In this chapter the authors present an account drawn from a recent research-and-development project in which the ideas of Guattari were framed and enacted in the development of new Web technologies—in the course of which teachers and students creatively appropriated elements of existing technologies in pursuit of pedagogical ends. This activity leads to the question: Can this kind of rethinking of the place of learning technologies reinforce the central role of pedagogy in higher education in times of economic and educational crisis?

Case Studies of Argentina

In 2001, the country of Argentina suffered the most extensive economic crisis in history. Part 2 is a study section based on this fact and is written by educational researchers working in the field. The first chapter in part 2 is titled "When the Sun Does not Shine after the Rain: The Effects of the 2001 Crisis on the Education System of Argentina", by Silvina Gvirtz and Ana Laura Barudi. This chapter aims to describe and analyze the effects of this crisis on Argentina's education system, considering three dimensions simultaneously. First, the focus is on the internal efficiency of the system within the basic educational levels, studying variations in enrolment, repetition and dropout rates. Second, data on academic performance is analyzed by evaluating student achievement in reading, mathematics and science through the Organisation for Economic Co-operation and Development's (OECD) Program for International Student Assessment (PISA). Finally, the chapter pays close attention to differences in teaching and learning conditions such as investment (in relation to public spending) and instructional time (based on the number of hours and days per year schools are open). The central hypothesis is that system performance measured through evaluation of internal efficiency, academic performance and teaching and learning material conditions significantly worsened after the 2001–2002 economic and financial crisis. Although Argentina's economy reactivated significantly after 2002, the education system recovered much more slowly, with noticeable signs of improvement observed only after 2005.

Chapter 8 is titled "Struggle for Agency in Contemporary Argentinean Schools", by Ana Inés Heras. This chapter reflects on what agency looks like when it is taken up by families at public, state-supported schools. In doing this, a tension between two different sets of ideas—*education as a right* versus *education as a commodity*—becomes apparent. When education is conceived of as a right, the guiding principle is *equal education for all.* This line of thought was prominent in Argentina over several decades, and the country had been known for its high literacy rates, high school attendance and high graduation rates. A different orientation has been pushed forward for more than two decades now and has sought to equate families to consumers and to frame education as being bought and sold within the market economy. This chapter argues that this logic is tied to the discourse on the benefits of globalization, which in Argentina was overtly taken up during the 1990s, yet was foregrounded prior to that decade, and still prevails. In the midst of this ideological conflict over education, there was the economic crisis of 2001, which deepened and inflated the divide between those who believe that education is a fundamental right and those who follow free market economics. Therefore, to survive economic crises through education one must bridge this divide and reconcile the rights of individuals to be educated with prevailing market conditions. The last chapter in the case studies of Argentina is titled "Education and Governmentality in Degraded Urban Territories: From the Sedimented to the Experience of the Actual", by Silvia Grinberg and Eduardo Langer. In this chapter, the authors discuss schools located in the areas of the Buenos Aires metropolitan area commonly called shantytowns, areas that have grown exponentially since the late 1970s. This writing draws largely from a research project currently under way in schools in these areas.

In the perspective of governmentality studies and in keeping with the work of Deleuze and Guattari, the authors describe forms of state regulation as well as noncodified flows of desire as they exist in these urban areas. In the words of Tamboukou, "Resistance is immanent in *dispositifs* of non-juridical models of *power...lines of* flight and *becoming* are immanent in *agencements*" (2010, p. 693). Thus, Grinberg and Langer undertake their reflection with a keen awareness of the population's potential for life and the way these subjects inhabit and exist in their neighborhoods and institutions. They are particularly interested in students, their concerns and desires, and the particular modes of regulation that are enacted in these schools. It is in this context that this chapter delves into the particularities of pedagogical devices in extremely degraded urban territories in the age of management during years marked by crisis, reform and counterreform. The authors address the ways that the school, after years of social and educational crisis, has become a place where students place their hopes and desires for the future. Incidents like a student jumping over the wall to get into his school express what the authors believe to be the complex fabric of school life in these urban spaces. How can we understand these situations? The authors suggest that in times of permanent crisis, the school, in the midst of and despite all the contradictions and tensions experienced therein, constitutes the most stable institution in these communities. And that is not a minor fact. The question, then, becomes how survival is possible and what remains of schools and subjects in contexts where crisis has become the norm. The authors offer first a brief conceptual reflection and then organize a discussion of the research.

Educational Theory and Economic Crisis

Part 3 expands and builds upon the first two sections by focusing on educational theory and economic crises. The authors in this section deem economic crises to be opportunities to evolve new theories of education that entwine with the survival narratives as enhanced ways to understand education and economic crises. The first chapter, by David R. Cole, is called "Doing Work as a Reflection of the Other: Notes on the Educational Materialism of Deleuze and Guattari". This chapter analyzes recent economic crises through a philosophical lens provided by the ideas of Gilles Deleuze and Félix Guattari. This lens allows us to focus on the 'regimes of work' associated with the crises and their connections to education as a practice. Regimes of work are increasingly being sieved and processed through the mechanics of a deterritorialising, post-industrial global capitalism. This digitized, 'machinic' influence reaches into the subjectivating heart of what it means to exist in regimes of work, how to escape if necessary, and how to formulate and sustain questions of freedom from within these regimes. This chapter analyzes such a multilayered situation using the connections to educational practice as a frame of reference and as a way of understanding how the forces at work are organized. This chapter includes understanding the immanent materialism that Deleuze and Guattari formulate through *A Thousand Plateaus* and relating this to the 'regimes of work' and interconnected educational practice. The work of high school English teachers will be given as an example of educational practice. The writing presented in this chapter takes the ideas of Deleuze and Guattari seriously as a philosophical means to explaining the ways in which capitalism currently functions and, with reference to this book as whole, helps us to understand how economic crises, exemplified by the GFC of 2008, has definite and lasting interpersonal effects beyond financial loss. This chapter also builds on previous work that explains literacies and multiple literacies, and functions to connect educational practice with regimes of capitally differentiated and digitalized work.

Chapter 11, "The Crisis of Mutative Capitalism: Holey Spaces, Creative Struggle and Educative Innovations", by Robert Haworth and Abraham P. DeLeon, looks at the mutative characteristics of capitalism, the economic crisis's brutal dismantling of public spaces, and why, even under most oppressive practices by corporations and the state, subjects desire to become what Deleuze and Guattari described as oedipalized subjects. The current and most ubiquitous political narrative is that the only solution to economic crisis is privatization, corporate populism, and, of course, more free-market values. By contesting desired neoliberal movements, the authors draw upon Deleuze and Guattari's work regarding the smith and nomad as potential subjectivities for transformation, not only in their capacities to contest capitalist mutations but also in their ability to create political and educational experiments or imaginaries outside of formations of global capitalism. The following chapter is by Torill Strand and is called "The Current Dynamics of Professional Expertise: The Movable Ethos, Pathos, and Logos of Four Norwegian Professions". Taking the fact that the dynamics of knowledge are going global, professional expertise and its theoretical representations now seem to undergo deep-seated transformations. But what are the characteristics of these changes? And to what degree are the transformations produced by the epistemic ruptures generated by the ways in which global-local symbolic economies now interact, converge, and convert? Strand addresses these questions by exploring findings from an extensive theoretical and empirical study on the altering expertise of Norwegian teachers and nurses over a span of eight years (2003–2010). It should be said, however, that these two Norwegian professions cannot be seen as representative of global survival narratives, since Norway has experienced a shallower recession than other countries. Norway has a productivity lead over most OECD countries, and the labor utilization is also high. Nevertheless, the shifting expertise of the two Norwegian professions does illustrate some dynamic exemplars that influence working life in most knowledge intensive societies.

Chapter 13 has been prepared by R. Scott Webster, and has the title "Educating the Person for Democratic Participation". Since John Dewey's time our current societies in the West have become predominantly capitalistic and corporate. Consequently the ontology of such societies, that is, the way of life that young persons are initiated into via their schooling and education, encourages them to primarily seek entry into an economic world. Dewey described this sort of ontology or individualism as a "perversion". Through sociocultural theories we can appreciate that human nature is indeed largely influenced by the cultural environment in which we find ourselves. In this chapter Webster draws mainly on the works of Dewey to explore this connection between culture and our nature in order to examine how a focus upon the ontology of education, that is, what sort of personhood is encouraged through educative experiences, addresses how education might contribute towards the prevention of such crises from reoccurring. The particular focus to be argued for is for a democratic way-of-being or character as the recommended ontology for education. The last chapter, "Remachining Educational Desire: Bankrupting Freire's Banking Model of Education in an Age of Schizo-Capitalism", by Jason J. Wallin. Wallin argues that the current economic crisis to which education is interminably wed is no longer recognizable according to the formulations advanced in Paulo Freire's groundbreaking *Pedagogy of the Oppressed.* On this point the stakes are clear; "inflating an obsolete target...could serve to misdirect critical and creative energies" (Conway, 2010, p. 2). It is this general provocation that will inform the trajectory of the chapter insofar as the author will use Freire's conceptualization of *banking education* in order to redeploy it in relation to the emerging forces of *integrated world capitalism*[2] (Guattari & Negri, 2010). Via this general tactic, Wallin attempts to accomplish *two tasks*. First, his chapter seeks to detect the unthought problematic education faces in the moment of economic crisis. In part, this tactic will require that the concept of *banking* be wrested from Freire in an effort to draw it more adequately into relation with the contemporary function of capitalism and its abstract contact point with education. Second, this chapter will redress the problem advanced at its outset. Specifically, how is it that those social impulses that refuse to join dominant processes of cultural production ostensibly fail to fulminate into a full-scale revolution of the educational apparatus?

The afterword of this collection is by Marcus Bussey and fittingly titled "When No Crisis Is the Real Crisis! The Endless Vertigo of Capitalist Education". Bussey rounds the chapters off by entertainingly commenting on the fact that financial crisis equates with capital crisis and this in turn becomes educational crisis as the ground for 'edu-anxiety', which demands the response of the system. This permanent reinvention of systems, the endless restlessness of formulations, as the reflection of an equally restless creator-market is currently framing education as a strata of the economic in which calculability, legibility and accountability are driving memes. Market failure, or learning failure, is punishable as an offence against order. Yet, the socioeconomic assemblage of capitalist modernity is in fact committed to the disorders of restless capital formations, in which the human is constantly transported to other parts of the system in order to maintain the sense of vertigo that underpins its maintenance. From this perspective, the real crisis would be for there to be no crisis at all.

Conclusion

In conclusion, this collection of chapters on 'surviving economic crises through education' develops a plane of understanding about education and economics. In this period of global interconnected economics, the ways in which investment strategies are organized and formulated with respect to education are paramount in the minds of many governments. This book does not give easy solutions or investment guides for governments, but it does show how the realities of economic crises play out in education. These realities join together and signify social-cultural trends for the future, as economic crises, connected to resource shortages and cybernetic investment functioning, accelerate and intensify. In such an environment, a reevaluation of education is essential; this reevaluation is perhaps our most important job and the prime survival narrative that confronts us:

> Capital is not an essence but a tendency, the formula of which is decoding, or market-driven immanentization, progressively subordinating social reproduction to techno-commercial replication. (Land, 1993, p. 480)

Notes

1. In *The Republic* education consists of music and gymnastics. These are the two formative aspects of Greek education.
2. Guattari's notion of integrated world capitalism might be briefly summarized in terms of its prioritization of production over both the state and the market. This model is distinct from both liberal capitalism's focus on the market and the privileged position of the state in state capitalism.

References

Agamben, G. (2005). *State of Exception*. Chicago: University of Chicago Press.

Bourdieu, P., & Passeron, J.-C. (1990). *Reproduction in Education, Society, and Culture*. London: Sage.

Braudel, F. (1967). *Capitalism and Material Life: 1400–1800* (M. Kochan, Trans.). New York: Harper and Row.

Cole, D. R. (2005). Reading in the Future: Literacy and the Time of the Internet. *Reconstruction*, 5 (2), EJ.

Cole, D. R. (2010, December). The Reproduction of Philosophical Bodies in Education with Language. *Educational Philosophy and Theory*, 42 (8), 816–829.

Cole, D. R., & Hager, P. (2010). Learning-practice: The Ghosts in the Education Machine. *Education Inquiry*, 1 (1), 21–40.

Conway, J. (2010). *Gilles Deleuze: Affirmation in Philosophy*. New York: Palgrave Macmillan.

Coupland, D. (1991). *Generation X: Tales for an Accelerated Culture*. London: Abacus.

Deleuze, G., & Guattari, F. (1984). *Anti-Oedipus: Capitalism and Schizophrenia* (R. Hurley, M. Steem & H. R. Lane, Trans.). London: The Athlone Press.

Gough, N. (2004). Living in a Material World. In W. A. H. Scott & S. R. Gough (Eds.), *Key Issues in Sustainable Development and Learning: A Critical Review* (pp. 236–240). London and New York: RoutledgeFalmer.

Guattari, F. (1984). *Molecular Revolution: Psychiatry and Politics*. Harmondsworth: Penguin Books Ltd.

Guattari, F., & Negri, A. (2010). *New Lines of Alliance, New Spaces of Liberty*. Williamsburg, Brooklyn, NY: Autonomedia.

Land, N. (1993). Machinic Desire. *Textual Practice*, 7 (3), 471–482.

Land, R., Meyer, J., & Smith, J. (2008). *Threshold Concepts within the Disciplines*. Rotterdam: Sense Publishers.

Lauder, H., Brown, P., Dillabough, J. A., Halsey, H. (Eds.). (2006). *Education, Globalization and Social Change*. Oxford: Oxford University Press.

Negarestani, R. (2008). *Cyclonopedia: Complicity with Anonymous Materials*. Melbourne: re.press (publishers).

Negarestani, R. (2011). On the Revolutionary Earth: A Dialectic in Territopic Materialism. Presentation at Kingston University of London.

Peters, M. A. (2000). *Orthos Logos, Recta Ratio*: Pope John Paul II and Postmodern Philosophy. *Journal for Christian Theological Research*, 5 (1), EJ.

Pink, D. H. (2005). *A Whole New Mind: Moving from the Information Age to the Conceptual Age.* New York: Riverhead Books.

Plato. (1965 [360 B.C.]). *The Republic* (A. D. Lindsay, Trans.). London: J.M. Dent & Sons Ltd.

Rullani, E. (2004). *Economia della conoscenza: Creatività e valore nel capitalismo delle reti.* Milano: Carocci.

Scott, J. (1998). *Seeing like a State: How Certain Schemes to Improve the Human Condition Have Failed.* New Haven, CT: Yale University Press.

Tamboukou, M. (2010, November). Charting cartographies of Resistance: Lines of Flight in Women Artist's Narratives. *Gender and Education,* 22 (6), 679–696.

Thrift, N. (2004). Intensities of Feeling: Towards a Spatial Politics of Affect. *Geogr. Ann.*, 86 B (1), 57–78.

Toffler, A. (1970). *Future Shock.* New York: Random House.

Toscano, A. (2010). Petropolitics as Retropolitics: Oil and the Geopolitical Imagination. Presentation at Goldsmiths' College, London.

• PART ONE •

Educational Responses to the Crises

• CHAPTER TWO •

'Knowledge Economy', Economic Crisis and Cognitive Capitalism: Public Education and the Promise of Open Science

Michael A. Peters

Introduction

In a recent paper, 'Forms of Knowledge Economy: Learning, Creativity, Openness,' I identified three discernibly separate but interrelated developmental strands of the 'knowledge economy' based around the notions of: (1) The Learning Economy, based on the work of Bengt-Åke Lundvall; (2) The Creative Economy, based on the work of Charles Landry, John Howkins and Richard Florida; and (3) The Open Science Economy, based on recent technological developments in promoting the openness of scientific communication (Peters, 2010a).[1] This conception has been part of an ongoing engagement with the discourse of the knowledge economy that views it as a structural transformation of Western capitalism, a third stage of development after *mercantile capitalism*, a doctrine that characterized the period 1500–1800 based on the the premise that national wealth and power were best served by increasing exports and collecting precious metals in return (Coleman, 1969; Miller, 1988), and *industrial capitalism*, that replaced the merchant as a dominant actor in the capitalist system with the industrialist and established a factory system of manufacturing based on a complex division of labor. David Hume and Adam Smith were among a new group of economic theorists that questioned the fundamental mercantile belief that the amount of the world's wealth remained constant and that a state could only increase its wealth at the expense of another state. Knowledge capitalism, by contrast, is another transformation of capitalism. The term 'knowledge capitalism' emerged only recently to describe the transition to the so-called knowledge economy. Knowledge capitalism and knowledge economy are twin terms that can be traced at the level of public policy to a series of reports that emerged in the late 1990s by the Organization for Economic Cooperation and Development (OECD) (1996) and the World Bank (1998), before they were taken up as a policy template by world governments in the late 1990s. In terms of these reports, education is reconfigured as a massively undervalued form of knowledge capital that will determine the future of work, the destiny of knowledge institutions and the shape of society in the years to come (Peters, 2003, 2007; Peters and Besley, 2006).

These three forms of knowledge economy and their associated discourses represent three recent related but different conceptions of the knowledge economy, each with clear significance and implications for education and education policy. They indicate that there have been different national policy constructions of the knowledge economy. I argue that the last conception based on openness provides a model of radically nonpropertarian form that incorporates both 'open education' and 'open science' economies and provides a radical alternative to neoliberal conceptions in providing a way to respond positively to the Great Recession by establishing and encouraging open science and education as part of the global knowledge commons. These developments of openness can be understood as an extension of arguments for the public good in a global context, of knowledge and education as global public goods, and as a necessary platform for the promotion of global civil society. In terms of the main theme and topic of this collection of essays—surviving economic crisis through education—this chapter makes a contribution by first providing the appropriate context of political economy of knowledge and education in which to view survival; second, it outlines a theory of economic development (cognitive capitalism) where education takes central stage as providing the new knowledge production systems required for both advanced and transitional economies; third, it chronicles the crisis of Western capitalism and the crisis of education as governments and states in the West cut back on education; fourth, it presents the opportunities of the historical moment for surviving the crisis through education by outlining 'open knowledge production' as an emerging alternative to neoliberalism in the forms of open science and open education that leads to the digital transformation of the public sphere and the development of good public science and education.

In this chapter I document and hypothesize emergent forms of knowledge capitalism before reviewing the rise and failure of neoliberal finance capitalism (as an aspect of knowledge capitalism) and the rollback of public education. In this context, in brief excursus, I comment on the related concepts of 'crisis' and 'transformation', drawing on the tradition of radical political economy and following the work of Marazzi and others, and I argue for a reappropriation and development of the global knowledge commons as a way of surviving the crisis through education. To advance this overall theoretical construction I outline the theory of cognitive capitalism to focus on the question of immaterial labor as the framework within which to view a critical approach to the main theme of the book. And finally, I demonstrate the promise of open science as both a link to the transformation of public education and a means of reappropriating the commons.

'Knowledge Economy' and Emergent Forms of Knowledge Capitalism

In the genealogy of knowledge economy it is important to distinguish a number of different strands and readings of the knowledge economy and important to do so because it provides a history of a policy idea and charts its ideological interpretations. The different strands of this discourse are radically diverse and include attempts to theorize not only knowledge economy but also the parallel term 'knowledge society', and also the attempts to relate these terms to wider and broader changes in the nature of capitalism, modernity and the global economy.

Theorists from different political perspectives and disciplines have simultaneously tried to analyze and describe certain deep-seated and structurally transformative tendencies in Western capitalism, society and modernity to move to a form of postindustrial economy that focuses on the production and consumption of knowledge and symbolic goods as a higher-order economic activity that encompasses and affects the entire economy and society. In these studies we should recognize certain long-term structural tendencies of increased *formalization* that transform both the production and consumption of symbolic goods. These are all tendencies toward increasing (in)formalization and abstraction centered on the sign, symbol and the image including a set of overlapping processes that transform knowledge production—informatization, mathematization, digitalization—together with process that transform consumption—culturalization and aestheticization. Most recently, capitalism has begun to exploit the reproduction of new synthetic life in terms of a set of biological processes. These are the leading processes transforming contemporary postmodern capitalism that rely on new forms of systems (cybernetic) capitalism based on design principles with the capacity to make new connections among old structures; to form areas of exquisitely precise specialization for recognizing patterns in information; and the ability to learn to recruit and connect information from these areas automatically.

Theoretical studies of U.S. 'knowledge economy' have proceeded from different assumptions, focusing on technological development, the economic value of knowledge, the role of information in the market and the emergence of postmodern global systems theory:

- 'Technological revolution' studies (e.g., Daniel Bell's [1973] *Postindustrial Society* and Alvin Toffler's [1980] *The Third Wave* predicted a radical break).
- Economic value of knowledge (e.g., Fritz Machlup [1962] *The Production and Distribution of Knowledge in the United States*).
- (Marc Porat [1977] *The Information Economy*).
- Role of information in market (e.g., Mark Granovetter [1985]—economic transactions are embedded in web of complex social relations; economic actions undertaken for economic and noneconomic reasons; institutions constraining economic interactions are socially constructed).
- Postmodern global systems theory (e.g., Manuel Castells [2000] emergence of networks as basic unit).

Jean-Francois Lyotard (1984/1979, p. 3) was one of the first to recognize 'postmodern capitalism' in his initial formulation: 'Our working hypothesis is that the status of knowledge is altered as societies enter what is known as the postindustrial age and cultures enter what is known as the postmodern age.' He writes of the significance of language-related developments as being essential and the leading technologies of the new capitalist system:

> For the last forty years the 'leading' sciences and technologies have had to do with language: phonology and theories of linguistics, problems of communication and cybernetics, modern theories of algebra and informatics, computers and their languages, problems of translation and the search for areas of compatibility among computer languages, problems of information storage and data banks, telematics and the perfection of intelligent terminals, to paradoxology. (p. 4)

He also warned us that economic powers have reached the point of imperiling the stability of the state through new forms of the circulation of capital that go by the generic name of *multinational corporations*.

Fredric Jameson, who wrote the foreword to Lyotard's work on the postmodern condition, remarked on the shift in ideological premises of these discourses:

> Theories of the postmodern—whether celebratory or couched in the language of moral revulsion and denunciation—bear a strong family resemblance to all those more ambitious sociological generalizations which, at much the same time, bring us the

news of the arrival and inauguration of a whole new type of society, most famously baptized "postindustrial society" (Daniel Bell).

> Often also designated consumer society, media society, information society, electronic society or high tech, and the like. Such theories have the obvious ideological mission of demonstrating, to their own relief, that the new social formation in question no longer obeys the laws of classical capitalism, namely, the primacy of industrial production and the omnipresence of class struggle. (Jameson, 1991, p. 55)

There have been different formulations that try to capture these tendencies including perhaps the most recognized as informationalism or *informational capitalism* that emerges from the work of Manuel Castells on the 'networked society.' Castells (2000) sees informationalism as a new technological paradigm (he speaks of a mode of development) characterized by "information generation, processing, and transmission" that have become "the fundamental sources of productivity and power" (Castells, 2000, p. 21). Christian Fuchs (2007) also writes of an informational capitalism of *self-regulation*, sometimes also referred to as the networked model of capitalism.

Another strand emphasizes *cultural capitalism* associated with the change of culture. This strand emerges from work in the 'new geography' and sociology and is epitomized by Richard Sennett's (2006) *The Culture of the New Capitalism*, Nigel Thrift's (2005) *Knowing Capitalism*, Boltanski and Chiapello's (2005) *The New Spirit of Capitalism*, and Paul du Gay and Michael Pryke's (2002) *Cultural Economy* (see Peters, Britez and Bulut, 2010).

With *biocapitalism*, "A new economic space has been delineated–the bioeconomy–and a new form of capital–biocapital" (Rose, 2007, p. 6). The term 'biocapitalism' recently has emerged to map the growing significance of the life sciences and biotechnology as an innovation within late capitalism that controls, changes and experiments with the material basis of life. Biocapitalism, or 'genomic capitalism' it has sometimes been called (Rajan, 2003), increasingly is seen as the new funding priority for public good science and the basis of the new genetic revolution symbolized by the significance and 'success' of the Human Genome Project (Peters and Venkatesan, 2011a, b).

Cognitive Capitalism is a theory that has become significant in the last few years for analyzing a new form of capitalism, sometimes referred to as 'third capitalism' *after* mercantilism and industrial capitalism. It is a term that focuses on the socioeconomic changes ushered in with the Internet as platform and new Web 2.0 technologies that have transformed the mode of production and the nature of labor. The theory of cognitive capitalism has its origins in French and Italian thinkers, particularly Gilles Deleuze and Felix Guattari's *Capitalism and Schizophrenia*, the work of Michel Foucault on the birth of biopower, and Michael Hardt and Antonio Negri's *Empire* and *Multitude*, as well as the Italian 'Autonomst' Marxist movement that had its origins in the Italian 'Operaismo' ('workerism') in the 1960s.

Finally, the term *finance capitalism* is associated with the dominance of neoliberalism and the deregulation of finance markets. Financialization describes the development over several decades of a form of capitalism leading up to the 2007–2010 financial crisis where accumulation strategy is based on profit making that occurs increasingly through financial instruments and derivatives rather than trade and commodity production, and financial markets dominate over traditional industrial economy.

Financialization and the Economic Crisis

'Financialization' is a term that describes an economic system or process that attempts to reduce all value that is exchanged (whether tangible, intangible, future or present promises, etc.) either into a financial instrument or a derivative of a financial instrument. The original intent of financialization is to be able to reduce any work product or service to an exchangeable financial instrument. It is an aspect of increased symbolization, mathematization and computerization of financial markets.

It is the first systemic and global crisis of neoliberal financial capitalism that began with the crisis of the Fordist model of accumulation and the consequent deregulation of the banking system during the 1970s. As the OECD (2009, p. 3) acknowledges:

> The current crisis is the first of this severity to hit OECD countries, since they have shifted to knowledge-based service economies where investment in intangible assets is of equal importance as investment in machinery, equipment and buildings.

Stephanie Blankenburg and José Gabriel Palma (2009, p. 532), writing for the *Cambridge Journal of Economics*, suggest, 'The current financial and economic crisis that has forced the likes of Greenspan to question the coherence of dominant conceptual frameworks is unprecedented in global reach and systemic gravity' and they go on to plot the dimensions of the crisis in the following terms:

> According to McKinsey's *Mapping Global Financial Markets* (October 2008), global financial assets rose from US$12 trillion in 1980 to US$196 trillion in 2007. The International Monetary Fund's *Global Financial Stability Report* (IMF, 2009a) estimate for the latter figure is considerably higher, at US$241 trillion. Global cross-border capital flows more than doubled between 2002 and 2007, with foreign investors holding one in four debt securities and one in five equities. While in 2000 only 11 countries had financial assets of more than 350% of gross domestic product (GDP),

> 25 countries had deepened their financial markets to the same extent by 2007. As early as 1990, money managers had increased their control of US corporate equities from 8% in 1950 to 60% (Porter, 1992, p. 6; Whalen, 2002, p. 402). Similarly, pension funds had extended their share of total business equities from less than 1% to just short of 39%, and their fraction of corporate debt from 13% to 50% (Ghilarducci, 1992, p. 117; Whalen, 2002, p. 402). In the period from 1986 to 2006, the US financial sector as a whole increased its share of corporate profits from 10% to 30%, while its outstanding debts grew from 20% of GDP in 1980 to 116% in 2007 (FED, 2009). According to Gillian Tett from the *Financial Times*, outstanding credit defaults swaps (CDS) today amount to no less than US$60 trillion, with the risk embodied after discounting mutually off-setting contracts still as high as US$14 trillion. (Tett, 2009, p. 264)

They also indicate that U.S. financial institutions have already written off US$1 trillion and are expected to write down at least another US$3 trillion to US$5 trillion. Predictions on the basis of this financial crisis and recovery suggest that a decline, especially in the Western world, is unavoidable with high and sustained levels of unemployment and rapid growth of inequalities.

Financialization and the Rollback of Public Education

Neoliberalism is an expression of the power of finance that gathered pace with the internationalization of capital and the globalization of markets. Some scholars suggest that neoliberalism and globalization are themselves expressions of finance, closely tied to the development of derivatives markets and the evolution of an international financial system where the international rentiers have managed to significantly increase their share of national income. The inherent nature of financial markets has a tendency to lead to speculation and the privatization of individual savings in the U.S. economy with investors seeking higher returns from riskier investments. The increasing role of institutional investors, the role of mutual funds, and the rise to power of large Wall Street firms has made the markets susceptible to misinformation and lobbying of financial agency design to regulate the system.

The advent of financial crisis and apparent collapse of financial capitalism had a large role to play in making Barack Obama's election possible and at the same time signaled a dramatic shift in U.S. federal government policies toward intervention and policies designed to stimulate the economy. Obama in his first term tried to take the initiative on restructuring the health system reforming to provide better public health. The conservative lead by the Tea Party movement has managed to displace job creation as a top priority and made reducing the debt and tax increases for the rich almost an unshakeable article of faith leading up to the next presidential election. The effect has been to popularize a debate on budget cuts across the board for public services provided at the state level with massive cuts to education in all aspects, attacks on collective bargaining, and the sacking of thousands of teachers. The extent of these cuts and their impacts on economic recovery has yet to be assessed but the conservative-led UK government under Cameron has made huge cuts to public universities in the order of 25 percent. Public sector works and public institutions are struggling to remain viable.

Yet these budget cuts come upon long-term changes in education including the wholesale adoption of the human capital policies and the shift from state and publicly funded human capital strategies to the encouragement of private-funded investment in human capital, especially at the university level. Starting with Gary Becker's (1964/2004) seminal work *Human Capital: A Theoretical and Empirical Analysis, with Special Emphasis on Education*, human capital theory comes to characterize American neoliberal discourse in the form of Chicago school economics as one that transforms the classical function of labor and *homo economicus* into an 'entrepreneur of himself' (Foucault, 2008), wherein the individual takes the risks and makes the investment in themselves through a form of actuarial rationality that in effect is forced upon university students (Peters, 2011a). The effect of many years of neoliberal discourse and policies has been to 'win' the argument concerning whether university is a public good and to force students into increased debt accumulation to finance their studies. Other forms of parallel privatization have accelerated the budget erosion of public universities, reducing forms of public and state support and forcing universities to increase tuition fees and to focus on research that wins funds or activities that provide a commercial return (Peters and Roberts, 1999; Roberts and Peters, 2008).

In an editorial titled 'The University of Finance,' the editors of *Ephemera*, Armin Beverungen, Stephen Dunne and Casper Hoedemaekers (2009, online) focus on the rise of the business school and turn to finances of the university, writing:

> Once we shift the focus of analysis in the direction of the university and financialization, we move beyond the content of university teaching, its curricula and pedagogies, and look at the form which university education takes today. In so doing, we proceed to ask how this very form is itself shaped by finance. And so we come to question why there is hardly a university left without a private equity club, a hedge fund society, or a trading room. While some insist on the learning experience and ethical aspects of trading, others note the ways in which these activities imbue a particular conservatism and opportunism, which deny the call for a critical engagement with finance (Jacobs, 2009)...Apart from finance as a subject of study, on the side of the students, there is student debt, which is rocketing so much so that in the US there is now talk of student debt as the next big bubble. (Samuels, 2010)

They plot 'the transformation of the University of Excellence (Readings, 1996) into the University of Finance, where it is the entrepreneurship of students and faculty, and their financial gravitas that seems to count most.'

After Nietzsche, philosophical critique of the Western university has developed along two interrelated lines: the first, pursued by Weber and continued by Heidegger, Jaspers, Lyotard and Bourdieu, emphasized the dangers of economic interest vested in the university through the dominance of *technical reason*; the second, initiated by members of the Frankfurt School and developed differently by Foucault, traces the imprint and controlling influence of the state in the academy through the apparatus of *administrative reason*. With the rise of the 'neoliberal university', these two forms of reason come together in a new way, first, through capitulation of norms of liberal humanism and the Kantian ethical subject to the main articles of faith underlying the revitalization of economic rationalism and *homo economicus*, and, second, through the imposition of structural adjustments policies of the IMF during the 1980s with devastating impacts of universities in the developing world. Neoliberal universities, with little self-reflection, have been harnessed in service to the 'new economy' under conditions of *knowledge capitalism* that raises issues of intellectual capital, the ownership of the means of knowledge production, and depends upon the encouragement of all forms of capitalization of the self. In the age of global terrorism, when traditional rights are being curtailed and eroded, the neoliberal university is content to pursue business as usual.

'Crisis' and Transformation

The concept of 'crisis' comes from the Greek noun *krisis* (choice, decision, judgment), deriving from the Greek verb *krinein* (to decide) and popular in Greek historical writing as the turning point in a decisionor argument. It reappears in the late eighteenth century as a catchall term for a crucial or decisive stage with reference to historical events, periods, or processes. Jacob Burckhardt developed the concept of crisis in relation to world history, especially the French Revolution and the European revolutions of 1848, and later conservative anxieties over the stage of European modernity. As a historian of the Renaissance and the rise of Christianity, Burckhardt was concerned with periods of rapid social, political, and cultural transformation accompanying the rise of industrial capitalism and mass politics which he viewed with suspicion. Karl Marx developed a different emphasis in his reflections on crisis articulating a theory of economic crisis centered on the economics of overproduction, specifically on the chronic disequilibrium between production and consumption under capitalism. Each crisis would be more severe than the last until a 'general crisis' occurred wherein the working class would rise against their exploiters. As Reinhart Koselleck (2006), the German historian, notes:

> Marx and Engels integrate the economic concept of crisis into their political and historical analysis. This is illustrated in the *Communist Manifesto*: 'For decades, the history of industry and commerce is but a history of the revolt of modern productive forces pitted against modern conditions of production, property relations that are the condition for the existence of the bourgeoisie and its domination...In these crises there breaks out an epidemic that in all earlier epochs would have seemed an absurdity—an epidemic of over production....How does the bourgeoisie overcome these crises? On the one hand, by enforced destruction of mass productive forces; on the other, by the conquest of new markets and by a more thorough exploitation of old ones. But how then does it do this. By paving the way for ever more extensive and devastating crises and by diminishing the means whereby crises are prevented.' On the basis of this economic interpretation, Marx and Engels could finally predict the foreseeable demise of capitalism. But this requires simultaneous political action by the proletariat, that 'death-bearing' class which the bourgeoisie itself had created. Incorporated into their social and political analysis, is the expectation of a final economic collapse, a 'global crash' as well as the certainty of revolution—or whatever other circumlocution Marx and Engels chose instead: 'A new revolution is possible only in the wake of a new crisis. But the one is as certain as the other.' Yet for Marx and Engels 'crisis' retained an essentially positive connotation, though on political rather than economic grounds. As Engels exults in 1857: 'The crisis will make me feel as good as a swim in the ocean.' (p. 354)

The widespread interest in and development of crisis studies that peaked by the early 1970s has in the wake of the current financial crisis experienced increasing use even although the term is often used without precise definition. The concept of 'crisis' has a long and complex genealogy employment to understand issues of order and change since at least the eighteenth century, following Marx's notion on the evolution of macrosocial developing as an object of inquiry in its own right to indicate transformative and structural change. Koselleck (2006) concludes his inquiry with the following assertion:

> From the nineteenth century on, there has been an enormous quantitative expansion in the variety of meanings attached to the concept of crisis, but few corresponding gains in either clarity or precision. 'Crisis' remains a catchword, used rigorously in only a few scholarly or scientific contexts...
>
> In all the human and social sciences, crisis appears as a key concept; in history, of course, to characterize epochs or 'structures.' Political science tries to operationalize the term and distinguish it from 'conflict.' From medicine the concept has spread to psychology and anthropology, ethnology, and the sociology of culture. Above all, it is the media which have inflated the use of the term. On the basis of current headlines, a list of 200 different contexts was compiled in which the term crisis appears as

> adjective (crisis-torn), as subject (mini-crisis, crisis of self-confidence) or as defining word (crisis expert, crisis bungler). Not only can 'crisis' be conjoined with other terms, it is easy to do so. While it can be used to clarify, all such coinages then require clarification. 'Crisis' is often used interchangeably with 'unrest,' 'conflict,' 'revolution,' and to describe vaguely disturbing moods or situations. (pp. 397–98)

In the tradition of Marxian radical political economy Christian Marazzi (2010) in *The Violence of Financial Capitalism* argues that the current financial crisis is a systemic crisis of the entire capitalistic system, which is today a 'cognitive capitalism,' based on interconnected global financial markets. This is a fundamental shift that represents the financialization of the reproductive sphere of life itself. Under this regime the monopolization and privatization of knowledge and education has proceeded rapidly. He suggests it is time to redress the balance between private and public knowledge goods at national and global levels through the promotion of 'super-multiplier' investments in global public knowledge infrastructures and the regulation of global knowledge intellectual monopolies and private science. As the blurb clarifies: 'He argues that the processes of financialization are not simply irregularities between the traditional categories of wages, rent, and profit, but rather a new type of accumulation adapted to the processes of social and cognitive production today. The financial crisis, he contends, is a fundamental component of contemporary accumulation and not a classic lack of economic growth.'[2] Mazzini is an Italian economist who works in the tradition of Italian Autonomous Marxism, coming from the tradition of Operaismo (Workerism) to theorize financialization as a crisis of accumulation of the new 'cognitive capitalism.'

As Francesca Bria (2009, p. 388) remarks, 'It is the first systemic and global crisis of neo-liberal financial capitalism that began with the crisis of the Fordist model of accumulation and the consequent deregulation of the banking system during the 1970s' and goes on to provide the following brief account of Marazzi's argument:

> The central thesis of Marazzi's book is that the dualism between the real economy (real money for tangible production) and the financial economy (production of money by means of money) no longer exists. Financialisation now has taken over and it encompasses the whole business cycle; what is really at stake in Marazzi's perspective is the very concept of capital accumulation. (p. 388)

In this context Marazzi argues for a project of *reappropriation* of the commons. Bria (2009, p. 393) expresses the point: 'The central issue is to recognize the question of *the right to social ownership of a common good* or in other words a *social rent*, as opposed to the only right recognized today, which is the right to private ownership.' He goes on to make the assertion:

> If the boundaries between education and production are porous and tend to be more blurred, when we criticised this socio-economic and financial system we are also criticising the educational system and thinking about alternative organisational and pedagogical models that can help us to move beyond this crisis (p. 394)...His analysis clearly shows that this crisis can be used as an opportunity to pursue radical changes and to open new terrains of conflict and sites of struggles, and it is only through struggles that we can identify common perspectives outside and beyond the crisis. This is an invitation to further enquiries into the role of knowledge in the production systems and its relationship with transformations in the capital/labour relation and the collective self-management of common goods. (p. 394)

Contemporary forms of knowledge capitalism have the arts and the sciences as their basis. They emphasize the role of creativity and designing intelligence in intellectual capital modes of production and promote informatization of subjectivity of workers through networks including flexibilization, part-time, competency-based, performance-related, continuous, contract work ('digital labor').

Cognitive Capitalism and Immaterial Labor

Knowledge capitalism involves an increasing and infinite substitution of capital for labor with the automation of secondary (e.g., fully automated factory) and tertiary knowledge activities. The discourse of the knowledge economy has largely ignored the concept of class or recommended its replacement by a specialized 'new class' of scientists or students as a new social movement. This new symbolic development involves a clear mathematization of knowledge with the new search algorithms and the development of an algorithmic capitalism (Peters, 2011a) with the attendant 'googlization of higher education.' For example, Siva Vaidhyanathan asks how Google's ubiquity is affecting the production and dissemination of knowledge:

Cognitive capitalism emerges as a global economic system based on the development of virtual (immaterial) economy ('third capitalism') focused on the increasing informatization (digitization) of production,[3] with increasing formalization, mathematicization and digitization of language, communication, and knowledge (especially journal systems). At the same time, and as a response to the same forces, there is the emergence of social media, social networking and social mode of production enhanced by Web 2.0 technologies and distributed knowledge and learning systems, including online publication and archives leading to *open knowledge production* systems including open science economy. The decreasing cost of network access, knowledge-sharing and transmission, and greater 'borderless' interconnectedness of knowledge spaces concomitantly gives rise to the emergence of the 'world brain'.

Distributive knowledge systems under cognitive capitalism leads to the eventual displacement of material production as core of the system with an emphasis on interactive and dynamical relations between material and immaterial sectors, and the digitization and systematization of value (rather than chains) where collective intelligence represents the core of exchange value and profit-making. Coproduction exists through 'just-in-time production' where the market precedes production and increasing through processes intellectual property private appropriation of global public knowledge goods takes place through the enforcement of patents, copyright and trademark, further increasing the capacity of computing, copying, file-sharing and storage to help enforcement of intellectual property rights. Externalities in complex systems now determine the general conditions of growth, investment and redistribution of revenue.

There is accorded a central role of innovation with a new sociotechnical 'cybernetic' paradigm of innovation based on 'hothouse' social networking and social media. Continuous endogenous innovation is increasingly focused on science as a leading part of the accumulation regime together with the promotion of new models of social and public entrepreneurship.

Fuchs (2010) provides an emerging typology of approaches from theorizations of cognitive capitalism on knowledge labor and class and reveals a variety of characterizations that serve as models for understanding intellectual labor within the school and the university:

- *Internet users as a new class*: Terranova (2000) notes that Internet users constitute a kind of free labor that is exploited by capital. Margonelli (1999) talks of 'cybersweatshops.'
- *Knowledge labor as a new class*: Ursula Huws (2003) says deskilling and delocalization lead to a new class of information-processing workers—'the cybertariat.' McKenzie Wark (2004) believes there is antagonism between the hacker class that produces information and the vectoral class that dispossesses the hacker class of its intellectual property by patents and copyrights. Franco Berardi speaks of the emergence of the 'cognitariat'— a 'new consciousness of cognitive workers' (2003, p. 4).
- *Knowledge labor as revolutionary class*: The multitude is a new class that is 'embedded in cooperative and communicative networks' (Hardt and Negri 2004, p. xv). Its labor is 'immaterial labour' 'that creates immaterial products, such as knowledge, information, communication, a relationship, or an emotional response' (Hardt and Negri, 2004, p. 108). Immaterial labor is collective and cooperative and that capital exploits the commons of so-

ciety for accumulating 'revolutionary processes of liberation determined by the multitude' (Hardt and Negri, 2000, p. 249).

- *Precarious knowledge labor as new class*: Nick Dyer-Witheford notes that "poorly paid, insecure, untrained, deskilled" (1999, p. 88) service workers constitute the 'new high-technology proletariat' (p. 96), the 'virtual proletariat' (p. 123). Andre Gorz sees those expelled from production by automation and computerisation, the underemployed, probationary, contracted, casual, temporary, and part-time labor as 'post-industrial neoproletariat' (1980, p. 69).
- *Knowledge labor as unproductive subsumed labor class*: Resnick and Wolff (1987) distinguish between fundamental class processes, in which surplus value is directly produced, and appropriated and subsumed class processes, in which already-appropriated surplus value or its products are distributed.
- *Knowledge labor and knowledge capital as one new class*: Florida (2002, p. 8) discusses the rise of a 'creative class' that is made up of a supercreative core.
- *Knowledge labor as petty bourgeoisie*: For Nicos Poulantzas, knowledge workers are part of 'the "new" petty bourgeoisie composed of nonproductive wage earners' (1973, p. 106).

The discourse of the knowledge economy points to the question of 'immaterial labor.' Networks and flows of immaterial labor are based on mass participation and collaboration rather than traditional Smithian division of labor that is nonlinear and comprise dynamical systems of labor. Learning economies reinforce autonomy and collective intelligence as the main source of value in the market with emphasis on codification and contextualization of practical and implicit knowledge. Situated, personal and implicit knowledge is not easily reduced to machine or to mere information (codified software or data). Creative learning economies emphasize 'right brain' ascendancy with an accent on a psychology of openness, meta-cognition and 'learning by doing'. The infinite substitution of capital for labor for 'left brain' logical and sequential tasks releases creative energies (Pink, 2006). Fundamental to what characterizes cognitive capitalism is the emergence of team or network as fundamental labor units in a new political economy of peer production ('Interneting') based on cooperation and collaboration rather than competition. There is an increasing importance of post–human network knowledge and learning practices based on mega-data bases and global portals.

The Promise of Open Science: Reappropriating the Knowledge Commons

Public education is in a state of crisis. After years of neoliberal policies that have reduced levels of public funding, school and university systems now are being forced to manage with less. At the same time, managerialist ideologies have impacted the administration of education. Public universities, in view of funding deficits, have been forced to increase student fees, and neoliberal policies have overridden the idea that knowledge is a public good to promote the wholesale commercialization of the production of knowledge or to develop a regulatory system that closely audits outcomes in the name of efficiency, productivity and accountability.[4] There are alternatives for the restoration of the public university based upon a model of deliberative democracy and empowered participatory governance that promotes a greater reflexivity and a new vision of the public university (Burowy, 2010; Calhoun and Rhoten, 2011).

There have been many attempts to elaborate the crucial importance of the close relationship between universities and the public good, emphasizing links between civil society, public discourses and deliberation, public culture, and the health of democracy. The notion of the public sphere lies at the heart of the liberal theory of civil society distinguished by an institutional setting characterized by openness in communication and the production of public goods (Calhoun, 2001, 2006). Habermas's (1989/1962) *The Structural Transformation of the Public Sphere* serves as the point of departure for the analysis of the formation of the bourgeois public sphere that depended upon the principle of universal access to constitute a realm characterized by critical-rational debate. The institutionalization of a fully political public sphere took place first in Britain during the eighteenth century and was preceded by a literary public culture that revealed the interiority of the self and emphasized a communicative, rational subjectivity that created a new phenomenon of public opinion and the basis for a new liberal constitutional social order. There have been critiques of Habermas's conception in terms of marginalized groups excluded from a universal public sphere (Fraser, 1990) and the way in which Habermas draws the distinction between public and private (Benhabib, 1992). Other scholars have sought to develop the concept of the public sphere emphasizing its discursive or rhetorical nature (Hauser, 1998). Habermas's work of the public sphere was written well before the age of the Internet, and some followers have developed his theories within the new public space of electronic and social media that, unlike traditional industrial one-way broadcast media, are open, interactive and characterized by a plurality of voices and the absence of a central control or authority (Bohman and Roberts, 2004). Against neoliberal theories that seek to privatize the public sphere, Hardt and Negri (2004,

2009), following Michael Foucault's (2008) biopolitics, suggest that in liberal political economy the very distinction between public and private spheres is founded upon a concept of private property in an economy of scarcity. With the postmodernization of the production of knowledge and a shift to the knowledge economy, Hardt and Negri (2009) see open source and open access as encouraging new forms of collaboration that no longer hold that economic value is founded upon exclusive possession but rather increasing depends upon new collectives based on the logic of networking that has the power to reconstitute the public sphere.

The global knowledge economy represents a set of deep structural transformations in the transition to a networked information economy that has the power to alter not only modes of economic organization and social practices of knowledge production but also the very fabric of liberal economy and society. As Yochai Benkler (2006, p. 2) expresses the point: 'Information, knowledge, and culture are central to human freedom and human development' and changes to the 'information environment' in advanced economies herald new freedoms and a more active role for individuals than was possible in the industrial economy. Benkler (2006) focuses on the effects of laws that regulate information production and exchange on the distribution of control over information flows, knowledge, and culture in the digital environment.[5] He talks about *freedom* in a practical sense,

> ...as a platform for better democratic participation; as a medium to foster a more critical and self-reflective culture; and, in an increasingly information dependent global economy, as a mechanism to achieve improvements in human development everywhere. (p. 2)

The new open communications environment has the power to reshape the university as a networked environment, allowing the emergence of radically decentred forms of social nonproprietarian and nonmarket models of academic production and exchange, alongside market and property forms, that will transform cultural production in general and the concepts of readership, scholarship and authorship that have ruled the academic economy. In the process, these changes will also alter the concept of the disciplines, disciplinarity and its cognate concepts of inter- and multidisciplinarity. The university is caught in an epic struggle between a neoliberal construction of knowledge capitalism as the latest phase of globalization based on what I have called the 'capitalization of knowledge', the 'deterritorialization of information' and the 'technologization of education' and 'knowledge socialism' based on the effective and large-scale collegial and peer production of information, knowledge and culture exemplified in the convergence of open source, open access and free science movements.

The debate concerning knowledge capitalism becomes one that increasingly turns on the economics of knowledge, the communicative turn, and the emerging international knowledge system where the politics of knowledge and information dominates. One issue concerns intellectual property, not only copyright, patents and trademarks but also the emergence of international regimes of intellectual property rights and the accompanying emphasis on human capital and embedded knowledge processes that now drive university management. In these debates, issues of freedom and control reassert themselves at the levels of content, code and infrastructure. The issue of freedom-control concerns the ideation and codification of knowledge and the new 'soft' technologies that take the notion of 'practice' as the new desideratum: practitioner knowledge, communities of practice, and different forms of organizational learning adopted and adapted as part of corporate practice.

Since Boyle's 'invisible college' and the birth of learned societies in the late seventeenth century modern science has always been the prototype of open scientific communication based on peer governance and review. There are some signs that the globalized privatization regime in science funding representing the end of 'big science,' shrinking budgets and the breakdown of scientific nationalism that define the Bush years has begun to recognize the new model of open science as an aspect of an emergent global science system structured by the forces of *networks*, *emergence*, *circulation*, *stickiness (place)*, and *distribution (virtual)*.[6] The decline of the U.S. economy relative to those of the rest of the world is facilitating the strengthening of science elsewhere with an evolving multipolar world economy leading to multiple centers of science. The increasing wealth of China, India and South Korea is enabling them to lure back many younger scientists trained abroad in the world's leading institutions. In this changing environment there has been a shift to international collaborative research with an accent on the virtual organization of global science teams.

Truly transnational open science alternatives are emerging in new research cultures that are no longer solely state- and university-oriented; although there is concomitantly rapid growth of corporate multinational research especially in new materials, biotechnology (genetics), pharmaceutics, information technology—growth of private science. This shift is accompanied by a change in funding regimes from public to private, state to global, and big science to applied science, science to technology. There is also a new role for humanities, performing arts and social sciences as 'soft' sciences and technologies concerned with new international values, legalities, global civic cultures, knowledge measurement, and knowledge management, together with recognition of the increasing importance of internationalization in education and research training and new forms of technology-led education on the basis of new architectures of participation and collaboration. Global science and research organization and cultures are emerging, extra-national organizations—NGOs, UN, UNESCO, ESF and other international science-based organizations and science portals—that aim as addressing cross-border problems beyond the resources of a single country.

The struggle is between new models of open science versus expanded protection of IP. Open source initiatives have facilitated the development of new models of production and innovation. The public and nonprofit sectors have called for alternative approaches dedicated to public knowledge redistribution and dissemination. Distributed peer-to-peer knowledge systems rival the scope and quality of similar products produced by proprietary efforts. The speed of diffusion of open source projects is a huge advantage, and there have been many successful projects in software and open source biology.

Open access science has focused on making peer-reviewed online research and scholarship freely accessible to a broader population (including digitized back issues). Open science demonstrates an 'exemplar of a compound of "private-collective" model of innovation' that contains elements of both proprietary and public models of knowledge production (von Hippel and von Krogh, 2003). Science 2.0 sites are beginning to proliferate; one notable example is the OpenWetWare project started by biological engineers at the Massachusetts Institute of Technology. Rich text, highly interactive, user-generated and socially active Internet (Web 2.0) has seen linear models of knowledge production giving way to more diffuse open-ended and serendipitous knowledge processes.

There have been dramatic changes in creation, production and consumption of scholarly resources—'creation of new formats made possible by digital technologies, ultimately allowing scholars to work in deeply integrated electronic research and publishing environments that will enable real-time dissemination, collaboration, dynamically-updated content, and usage of new media' (Brown et al., 2007, p. 4). Alternative distribution models including institutional repositories, preprint servers, open-access journals have also arisen with the aim to broaden access, reduce costs, and enable open sharing of content.

One might argue that the open science economy plays a *complementary* rather than an oppositional role with corporate and transnational science and implies strong roles for governments. Increasingly, portal-based knowledge environments and global science gateways support collaborative science (Schuchardt et al., 2007).[7] Cyber-mashups of very large data sets let users explore, analyze, and comprehend the science behind the information being streamed. The new Web 2.0 technologies and development of data sharing with cloud computing has revolutionized how researchers from various disciplines collaborate over long distances, especially in the life sciences, where interdisciplinary approaches are becoming increasingly powerful as a driver of both integration and discovery (with regard to data access, data quality, identity, and provenance).

The economic crisis of Western neoliberal capitalism brought about through the Great Recession has impacted the nature of public knowledge and education institutions, privatization education and monopolizing knowledge flows. Education and science have always been wedded to principles of free inquiry and to the academic freedoms that are necessary to sustain the open society and social democracy. The project for revitalizing and restoring the publicness of science and education is enhanced, especially in an era of severe budget cuts to public services through the utilization of new platforms of openness based on Web 2.0 technologies that promotes universal access to knowledge and economical forms of collaboration through file-sharing and the nested convergences in open access, open archiving and open publishing (open journals systems) that have the potential to reconstitute science and education as open and public institutions in the years to come.

Notes

1. For work on the knowledge economy and its different modes see Peters and Besley (2006), Peters (2007), Peters, Marginson and Murphy (2009), Marginson, Murphy and Peters (2010), Murphy, Peters and Marginson (2010), Araya and Peters (2010).
2. See http://mitpress.mit.edu/catalog/item/default.asp?ttype=2&tid=12084.
3. This is my compilation adapted and developed from Moulier Boutang (2007) with allusions to the work of Lyotard, Deleuze and Guattari; Foucault, Hardt and Negri; Castells; Benkler; Lessig; Bauwens; Tapscott; Fuchs; Howkins; Florida; Gorz; Pink; Lundvall; and others.
4. See the 'Universities in Crisis' blog of the International Sociological Association with more than fifty reports from some thirty-five countries. See also the UK-based 'Campaign for the Public University' at http://publicuniversity.org.uk/; 'University Politics–Universities as Public Goods' at http://universitypolitics.blogspot.com/; and the excellent Web site Transformations of the Public Sphere at http://publicsphere.ssrc.org/.
5. See Benkler's Web page at http://www.benkler.org/. The site contains a statement of his research interests as well as selected online papers on themes of the intellectual commons, intellectual property, open spectrum, democracy and information, and regulation of the Internet.
6. For my work on openness see Peters and Britez (2008), Peters (2009a; 2010a, b, c, d; 2011b), Peters and Roberts (2011).
7. See, for example, http://www.science.gov/

References

Araya, D., & Peters, M. A. (Eds.). (2010). *Education in the Creative Economy*. New York: Peter Lang.

Becker, G. (1962/2004). *Human Capital: A Theoretical and Empirical Analysis, with Special Reference to Education.*. Chicago, University of Chicago Press.

Bell, D. (1973). *The Coming of Post-Industrial Society: A Venture in Social Forecasting*. New York: Basic Books

Benhabib, Seyla. (1992). *Models of Public Space: Habermas, and the Public Sphere*. Cambridge Mass.: MIT Press.

Benkler, Y. (2006). *The Wealth of Networks: How Social Production Transforms Markets and Freedom*. New Haven, Conn.: Yale University Press

Benkler, Y., and Nissenbaum, H. (2006). Commons-based peer production and virtue. *Journal of Political Philosophy* 14 (4), 394–419.

Berardi, F. 2003. What is the meaning of autonomy? Republicart. http://republicart.net/disc/realpublicspaces/berardi01_en.htm (accessed August 20, 2011).

Beverungen, Armin, Dunne, S., and Hoedemaekers, C. (2009). The university of finance. *ephemera* 9 (4) 261–270. At http://www.ephemeraweb.org/journal/9-4/9-4ephemera-nov09.pdf.

Blankenburg, Stephanie, and Palma, J-G. (2009). Introduction: The global financial crisis. *Cambridge Journal of Economics* 33 (4), 531–538.

Bohman, James. (2007). *Democracy across Borders, From Dêmos to Dêmoi*. Cambridge, Mass.: MIT Press.

Bohman, James, and Roberts, J. M. (2004). Expanding dialogue: The Internet, the public sphere and prospects for transational democracy. In N. Crossley (Ed.), *After Habermas: New Perspectives on the Public Sphere* (pp. 131–155). Oxford: Blackwell.

Boltanski, L., and Chiapello, E. (2005). *The New Spirit of Capitalism*. (G. Elliott, Trans.). London: Verso.

Boutang, Y. M. (2007). Cognitive Capitalism and Entrepreneurship Decline in Industrial Entrepreneurship and the Rising of Collective Intelligence. Paper presented at the conference Capitalism and Entrepreneurship. Sage Hall, Cornell University, Ithaca, New York, September, 28–29, 2007.

Bria, Francesca. (2009). A crisis of finance: *Financialisation* as a crisis of accumulation of new capitalism. *ephemera*, 9 (4), 388–395.

Brown, Laura, Griffiths, R., and Rascoff, M. (2007). University Publishing in a Digital Age (The Ithaka Report). At http://www.ithaka.org/ithaka-s-r/strategyold/Ithaka%20University%20Publishing%20Report.pdf.

Buroway, Michael. (2010). A New Vision of the Public University. At http://publicsphere.ssrc.org/burawoy-a-new-vision-of-the-public-university/.

Calhoun, Craig. (2001). Civil society/public sphere: History of the concept(s). In *International Encyclopedia of the Social and Behavioral Sciences* (pp. 1897–1903). Amsterdam: Elsevier.

Calhoun, Craig. (2006). The university and the public good. *Thesis Eleven*, 84, 7–43.

Calhoun, Craig, and Rhoten, D. (Eds.). (2011). *Knowledge Matters: The Public Mission of the Research University*. New York: Columbia University/SSRC Books.

Castells, M. (2000). *The Rise of the Network Society*, 2nd ed. Malden, Mass: Blackwell Publishers.

Coleman, D. C. (Ed.). (1969). *Revisions in Mercantilism*. London: Methuen and Co.

Deleuze, Gilles, and Guattari, F. (2004). *A Thousand Plateaus: Capitalism and Schizophrenia II* (Brian Massumi, Trans.). London and New York: Continuum.

Deleuze, Gilles and Guattari, F. (2004). *Anti-Œdipus: Capitalism and Schiziophrenia* (Robert Hurley, Mark Seem, and Helen R. Lane, Trans.). London and New York: Continuum.

Du Gay, P. L. J., and Pryke, M. (Eds.). (2002). *Cultural Economy: Cultural Analysis and Commercial Life*. London: Sage.

Dyer-Witheford, N. (1999). *Cyber-Marx. Cycles and Circuits of Struggle in High-Technology Capitalism*. Urbana: University of Illinois Press.

FED (Federal Reserve Board). (2009). Flow of funds accounts of the United States. At http://www.federalreservebank.gov/datadownload.

Florida, R. (2002). *The Rise of the Creative Class*. New York: Basic Books.

Foray, D. (2000). *The Economics of Knowledge*. Cambridge, Mass.: MIT Press.

Foucault, Michel. (2008). *The Birth of Biopolitics: Lectures at the Collège de France, 1978–1979*. London: Palgrave Macmillan.

Fraser, Nancy. (1990). Rethinking the public sphere: A contribution to the critique of actually existing democracy. *Social Text*, 25 (26), 56–80.

Fuchs, Christian. (2007). Transnational space and the network society. *21st Century Society*, 2 (1), 49–78.

Fuchs, Christian. (2010). Labor in informational capitalism and on the Internet. *Information Society* 26 (3), 179–196.

Ghilarducci, T. (1992). *Labor's Capital: The Economics and Politics of Private Pensions*. Cambridge, Mass.: MIT Press.

Gorz, A. (1980). *Farewell to the Working Class*. London: Pluto.

Granovetter, M. (1973, May). The strength of weak ties. *American Journal of Sociology*, 78 (6), 1360–1380.

Granovetter, M. (1985). Economic action and social structure: The problem of embeddedness. *American Journal of Sociology*, 91(November), 481-510.

Habermas, Jürgen. (1962/1989). *The Structural Transformation of the Public Sphere: An Inquiry into a Category of Bourgeois Society*. (Thomas Burger, Trans.). Cambridge, Mass.: MIT Press.

Hardt, Michael, and Negri, A. (2000) *Empire*. Cambridge, MA: Harvard University Press.

Hardt, Michael, and Negri, A. (2004). *Multitude: War and Democracy in the Age of Empire*. New York: Penguin Press.

Hardt, Michael, and Negri, A. (2009). *Commonwealth*. Cambridge, Mass.: Belknap Press of Harvard University Press.

Hauser, Gerard. (1998). Vernacular dialogue and the rhetoricality of public opinion. *Communication Monographs*, 65 (2), 83–107.

Hearn, G., and Rooney, D. (Eds.). (2008). *Knowledge Policy: Challenges for the 21st Century*. Cheltenham: Edward Elgar.

Howkins, J. (2001). *The Creative Economy: How People Make Money from Ideas*. London: Allen Lane.

Huws, U. (2003). *The Making of a Cybertariat*. New York: Monthly Review Press.

IMF. (2009). Global Financial Stability Report. Responding to the Financial Crisis and

Measuring Systemic Risks. At http://www.imf.org/external/pubs/ft/gfsr/2009/01/pdf/text.pdf.

Jacobs, E. (2009, March 12). Business class. *Financial Times.*

Jameson, Fredric. (1991). *Postmodernism or The Cultural Logic of Late Capitalism.* London: Verso.

Koselleck, Reinhart (2006) *Introduction: Translation of Reinhart Koselleck's "Krise,"* in Geschichtliche Grundbegriffe., by Melvin Richter and Micheala W. Richter. *Journal of the History of Ideas,* 67 (2), 343-356.

Landry, C. (2000). *The Creative City: A Toolkit for Urban Innovators.* UK: Earthscan.

Lorenz, E., and Lundvall, B.-Å. (Eds.). (2006). *How Europe's Economies Learn.* Oxford: Oxford University Press.

Lundvall, B.- Å. (1996). The social dimension of the learning economy. *Druid Working Paper 96–7.* At http://www3.druid.dk/wp/19960001.pdf (accessed September 12, 2010).

Lundvall, B.-Å., and Johnson, B. (1994). The learning economy. *Journal of Industry Studies,* 1 (2), 23–42.

Lyotard, J.-F. (1984). *The Postmodern Condition: A Report on Knowledge* (G. Bennington and B. Massumi, Trans.). Manchester: Manchester University Press.

Machlup. F. (1962). *The Production and Distribution of Knowledge in the United States.* Princeton, N.J.: Princeton University Press.

Marazzi, Christian. (2010). *The Violence of Financial Capitalism* (K. Lebedeva, Trans.). New York: Semiotext(e).

Marginson, S., Murphy, P., and Peters, M. A. (2010). *Global Creation: Space, Connection and Synchrony in the Age of the Knowledge Economy.* New York: Peter Lang.

Margonelli, L. (1999). Inside AOL's 'cyber-sweatshop.' *Wired,* 7(10) Online.

McKinsey & Co. (2008, October). Mapping Global Financial Markets. Fifth Annual Report, Measuring Systemic Risk, April, Washington, DC, IMF. www.mckinsey.com/.../reports/.../*fifth_annual_report/fifth_annual_report* (accessed August 20, 2011).

Miller, J. C. (1988). *Way of Death: Merchant Capitalism and the Angolan Slave Trade.* Madison, WI.: Terrace Books.

Murphy, P., Peters, M.A., and Marginson, S. (2010). *Imagination: Three Models of Imagination in the Age of the Knowledge Economy.* New York: Peter Lang.

Negri, A., and Hardt, M. (2001). *Empire.* Cambridge, Mass., and London, England: Harvard University Press.

Negri, A., and Hardt, M. (2004). *Multitude: War and Democracy in the Age of Empire.* New York: Penguin Press.

OECD. (1996). *The Knowledge-Based Economy.* Paris: OECD.

OECD. (2009). *Policy Responses to the Economic Crisis: Investing in Innovation for Long-Term Growth.* Paris: OECD.

Peters, M. A. (2003). Education policy in the age of knowledge capitalism. *Policy Futures in Education,* 1 (2), 361–380.

Peters, M. A. (2007). *Knowledge Economy, Development and the Future of Higher Education.* Rotterdam: Sense Publishers.

Peters, M. A. (2008). Education and the knowledge economy. In Greg Hearn, David Rooney, and David Wright (Eds.), *Knowledge Policy: Challenges for the 21st Century.* London: Edward Elgar.

Peters, M. A. (2009a). On the philosophy of open science. *International Journal of Science in Society*, 1 (1), 1–27.

Peters, M. A. (2009b). Education, creativity and the economy of passions: New forms of educational capitalism. *Thesis Eleven*, 96, 40–63.

Peters, M. A. (2010a). Three forms of knowledge economy: Learning, creativity, openness. *British Journal of Educational Studies*, 58 (1), 67–88.

Peters, M. A. (2010b). Knowledge economy and scientific communication: Emerging paradigms of 'open knowledge production' and 'open education'. In M, Simons, M. Olssen, & M. A. Peters (Eds.), *Re-Reading Education Policies: A Handbook Studying the Policy Agenda of the Twenty-First Century* (pp. 293–318). Rotterdam: Sense Publishers.

Peters, M. A. (2010c). Open education and the open science economy. In Thomas Popkewitz & Fazal Rizvi (Eds.), *Yearbook of the National Society for the Study of Education* (pp. 203–225) National Society for the Study of Education, Vol. 108. Oxford:Wiley-Blackwell.

Peters, M. A. (2010d). Open works, open cultures, and open learning systems. In T. W. Lukes & Jeremy Hunsinger (Eds.), *Putting Knowledge to Work and Letting Information Play: The Center for Digital Discourse and Culture* (pp. 75–99). Blacksburg: Virginia Tech, Center for Digital Discourse and Culture.

Peters, M. A. (2011a). *Neoliberalism and After? Education, Social Policy and the Crisis of Capitalism.* New York: Peter Lang.

Peters, M. A. (2011b). Manifesto for education in the age of cognitive capitalism: Freedom, creativity and culture. In C. McCarthy et al. (Eds.), *New Times: Making Sense of Critical/Cultural Theory in a Digital Age.* New York: Peter Lang.

Peters, M. A., and Besley, T. (2006). *Building Knowledge Cultures: Education and Development in the Age of Knowledge Capitalism.* Lanham, Md.: Rowman & Littlefield.

Peters, M. A., Besley, T., Olssen, M., Maurer, S., and Weber, S. (Eds.). (2009). *Governmentality Studies in Education.* Rotterdam: Sense Publishers.

Peters, M. A., and Britez, R. (Eds.). (2008). *Open Education and Education for Openness.* Rotterdam & Taipei: Sense Publishers.

Peters, M. A., Britez, R., and Bulut, E. (2010). Cybernetic capitalism, informationalism, and cognitive labor. *Geopolitics, History and International Relations*, 1 (2), 11–40.

Peters, M., Marginson, S., and Murphy, P. (2009). *Creativity and the Global Knowledge Economy.* New York: Peter Lang.

Peters, M. A., and Roberts, P. (1999). *University Futures and the Politics of Reform.* Palmerston North, NZ: Dunmore Press.

Peters, M. A., and Roberts, P. (2011). *The Virtues of Openness: Education, Science and Scholarship in a Digital Age.* Boulder, Colo.: Paradigm Publishers.

Peters, M. A., and Venkatesan, P. (2011a). Biocapitalism and the politics of life. *Geopolitics, History and International Relations*, 2(2), 116-134.

Peters, M.A., and Venkatesan, P. (2011b). Bioeconomy and the third industrial revolution in the age of synthetic life. *Contemporary Readings in Law and Social Justice* 2 (2), 148–162.

Pink, Daniel. (2006). *A Whole New Mind: Why Right-Brainers Will Rule the Future.* New York: Riverhead Trade.

Porat, M. (1977). *The Information Economy.* Washington, D.C: U.S. Department of Commerce.

Porter, M. E. (1992). Capital disadvantage: America's failing capital investment system. *Harvard*

Business Review, September–October, 65–82.

Poulantzas, N. (1973/1982). On social classes. In A. Giddens and D. Held (Eds.), *Classes, Power, and Conflict* (pp. 101–111). Berkeley: University of California Press.

Rajan, K. S. (2003). Genomic capital: Public cultures and market logics of corporate biotechnology. *Science as Culture*, 12, (1), 87–121.

Readings, B. (1996). *The University in Ruins*. Cambridge, Mass.: Harvard University Press.

Resnick, S. A., and Wolff, R. D. (1987). *Knowledge and Class. A Marxian Critique of Political Economy*. Chicago: University of Chicago Press.

Roberts, P., and Peters, M. A. (2008). *Neoliberalism, Scholarship and Intellectual Life*. Rotterdam: Sense Publishers.

Rose, Nikolas. (2007). *The Politics of Life Itself: Biomedicine, Power, and Subjectivity in the Twenty-First Century*. Princeton, N.J.: Princeton University Press.

Samuels, B. (2010, February 24). Student loans: The new big bubble. *Huffington Post*. At http://www.huffingtonpost.com/bob-samuels/student-loans-the-new-big_b_475125.html.

Schuchardt, K., Pancerella, C., Rahn, L., Didier, B., Kodeboyina, D., Leahy, D., Myers, M., Oluwole, O., Pitz, W., Ruscic, B., Song, J., Laszewski, G. von, and Yang, C. (2007). Portal-based knowledge environment for collaborative science. *Concurrency Computation Practice and Experience*, 19 (12), 1703–1716.

Sennett, Richard. (2006). *The Culture of the New Capitalism*. New Haven, Conn.: Yale University Press.

Slevin, James. (2000). *The Internet and Society*. Malden, Mass.: Polity Press.

Susi, T., and Ziemke, T. (2001). Social cognition, artefacts, and stigmergy: A comparative analysis of theoretical frameworks for the understanding of artefact-mediated collaborative activity. *Cognitive Systems Research*, 2 (4), 273–290.

Terranova, T. (2000). Free labour. producing culture for the digital economy. *Social Text*, 18 (2), 33–57.

Tett, G. (2009). *Fool's Gold, How Unrestrained Greed Corrupted a Dream, Shattered Global Markets and Unleashed a Catastrophe*. London: Little, Brown.

Thrift, Nigel. (2005). *Knowing Capitalism (Theory, Culture and Society)*. London: Sage.

Toffler, A. (1980). *The Third Wave*. New York: Bantam Books.

United Nations. (2008). *The Creative Economy Report*. At http://www.unctad.org/en/docs/ditc20082cer_en.pdf.

von Hippel, E., and Krogh, G. von, (2003). Open source software and the "private-collective" innovation model: Issues for organization science. *Organization Science*, 14, (2), 209–223.

Wagner, C. (2008). *The New Invisible College: Science for Development*. Foreword by Francis Fukuyama. Washington, D.C.: Brookings Press.

Wark, M. (2004). A hacker manifesto. Version 4.0. subsol. http://subsol.c3.hu/subsol 2/contributors0/warktext.html (accessed February 6, 2010).

Whalen, C. (2002). Money manager capitalism: Still here, but not quite as expected. *Journal of Economic Issues*, 36 (2), 401–407.

World Bank. (1998). *World Development Report: Knowledge for Development*. Oxford: Oxford University Press.

• CHAPTER THREE •

Education for Resilience and Resistance in the 'Big Society'

Jim Crowther & Mae Shaw

It is clear that, once again, 'community' is positioned as a central policy focus for the new alignment between the state and civil society in the UK. This is already having serious consequences for community-based education and, particularly, for the role of practitioners. Our concerns in the current policy context are primarily informed by our work in undergraduate and postgraduate programmes which are positioned at the intersection between academic and professional rationalities. This requires us to think about what we can do to prepare students for the contingencies of contemporary practice, including developing the capacity to identify the educational options open to them. Whilst there are immediate concerns about the resilience of communities to withstand the consequences of the worst public expenditure cuts since the Second World War, we would argue that there is also a necessity to bring into focus the real causes of the current crisis. We identify two distinctive but interconnected discourses of resilience which are central to transforming the relationship between the state, the market and citizens: a moralising discourse and an entrepreneurial discourse. In contrast, we would argue that resilience is best understood as a collective process with both personal and political dimensions, and that education has an important role in stimulating and resourcing community engagement in these terms as a means of resisting those powerful but disempowering discourses identified above. This chapter focuses, therefore, on the wider implications for educational purposes, processes and practices.

Introduction: The 'Big Society' Imperative

One of the priorities of the UK Coalition government's response to economic crisis has been to reassert the importance of utilitarian measures to reduce the deficit in public finances. Narrow cost-benefit arguments are being systematically used to legitimise massive cuts in public expenditure whilst calling into question the effectiveness of the welfare state itself. The function of 'the big society' advanced so ardently by government is to accommodate both of these concerns in one coherent narrative. It simultaneously justifies the move towards 'the small state' and seeks to remoralise particular individuals, groups and communities away from 'dependency' (based on the right to welfare) and towards an acceptance of the responsibility to provide for themselves and others. This presupposes possession of the necessary resilience to do so.

At one level, the current debate is not new. There are clearly comparisons to be made with Victorian values of self-help and the undeserving poor, but more recent comparisons may be even more instructive. The community solution has been ideologically recycled in British policy since the 1960s as a response to various crises: to address the social consequences of economic restructuring, to give legitimacy to political programmes, and to respond to social unrest and control dissent. For example, a publication from 1977 charts the history of the Community Development Project introduced in 1968 ostensibly to find new ways of overcoming apathy and promoting self-help through poverty programmes—in the context of what was presented as 'the urban crisis'. One newspaper headline of the time—'Britain's cities are rotting at the core'—has more than a hint of the current metaphor of 'Broken Britain'. That publication was titled 'Gilding the Ghetto' (CDP, 1977), the metaphor intended to convey the way that such programmes were, in reality, introduced to cover and disguise the realities of poverty; to regulate, discipline and manage the poor rather than to empower them in any serious way.

The construction of 'the big society' is also predicated on a notion of the state as the enemy of the people, albeit with different ideological roots. Discounting and devaluing the public sector has become the default political language here and elsewhere. The role of the state in civil society has been undergoing a fundamental restructuring for some time, based on the idea that the state is a drain on community life rather than a resource for improving it. It has, in particular, become associated with notions of undesirable dependency (and obstructive and impenetrable managerialism, thanks to the former New Labour government). In a mysterious way, therefore, the public sector has become characterised as self-seeking and expensive, whilst the private sector has become champion of the public good. This has been systematically repeated to justify cutting public expenditure. The strategy of slowly but surely turning public relationships into market ones which has been followed since the 1980s—through successive Conservative, Labour and now Coalition governments—has aided this process, relying, as they do, on the primacy of sturdy competitive individuals who look out *for* and *after* themselves. This political approach is accompanied by what Mooney and Hancock (2010) describe as 'a pervasive media assault on people experiencing poverty': "A 24/7 news media, both print and television, that seizes on any example of 'dysfunctionality' in poor working class communities" (p. 14) which simultaneously works to reinforce negative attitudes towards welfare while at the same time creating fear and distrust of poor people in particular.

The provision of public services through the state has of course always been ambivalent (Williams, 1989). As another publication from 1979 saw it, the state offers us services we need, but it does so in ways which we don't need (LEWRG, 1979). In other words, at its Modernist peak, the welfare state did, arguably, do too many things *to* and *for* people and not enough *with* people (Cochrane, 1996). The universalism it represented was based on roles and relationships which have since been challenged, changed or rejected (Lister, 2010). But this does not necessarily mean that the state should be abandoned. An alternative view would be that this is an argument for making state institutions and processes more democratically open and politically accountable. In this sense, the state is understood as a site of contestation over what it should mean and how its institutions should operate, not merely as an alien force from which we should be liberated. Furthermore, if public services are to be subcontracted or sold off to unaccountable, unrepresentative and fragmented local groups, or worst still, the market, then there are serious questions about how the poorest and most marginalised from power can be protected.

Part of the problem, as Tony Judt (2010) sees it, is a discursive one. Public discourse has been so narrowed and manipulated that there are no opportunities to consider the alternative view. He asks:

> Why are we so sure that...progressive taxation, or the collective ownership of public goods are intolerable restrictions on liberty [and choice], whereas closed-circuit television cameras, state bailouts for investment banks, the breaking up of the NHS, foreign interference and wars are acceptable burdens for a free people to bear? (p. 153)

It is clear that the interests and judgements of the market now hang over everything, setting parameters within which political debate can operate (Massey, 2010, p. 11). Challenging discursive practices has, therefore, been a central strategy of those who are trying to shift the focus away from 'the despised poor' to the concentrations of wealth and privilege which have precipitated 'the crisis' to which all must be sacrificed. In fact the imperative demand of 'crisis' talk in itself rules out other perspectives, in the process camouflaging and legitimising particular ideological positions (Clarke, 2010). As Matt Scott of the Community Sector Coalition sees it, this applies also to 'the Big Society'—'an ideology which pretends it is not one' (p. 133).

So, while it may seem perverse to be undermining the very fabric of what is advocated in 'the big society' by cutting funding to voluntary and community organisations, according to a different logic, may be entirely coherent. It is becoming increasingly obvious that this idea has little to do with encouraging voluntary action and everything to do with creating a legitimating ideology for the withdrawal of the welfare state and the wholesale privatisation of public services. It is also clear that while Margaret Thatcher represented the vanguard of free market ideology, it was deeply consolidated by New Labour and is now embedded to an alarming extent in policy, politics and the public imagination. The question is whether it will be a triumph in terms of articulating and extending the neoliberal settlement, 'an act of wanton provocation', as Clarke (2010) puts it, against the poorest and least powerful groups in society, or is there a means whereby the big society can be exposed for what it is and opposed on its own terms? These questions require us to examine some of its most significant aspects.

First, in what has been described by the Institute of Fiscal Studies as the 'longest, deepest, sustained period of cuts to public services spending at least since the second world war' (Elliott and Wintour, 2010), it is clear that the reforms embodied in the big society will be disastrous for the poorest communities. There is deep concern that in this context, the promise of community empowerment seems a very poor trade-off for the universal rights, benefits and protection which will all but disappear in the dismantling of welfare and its dispersal through the not-for-profit and private sectors. Such a realignment of welfare may, at the same time, create a real challenge to critical and collective educational practice since any meaningful sense of community as an arena for contestation or resistance is virtually 'structured out' of those mechanisms and processes through which 'legitimate' communities are sanctioned (Whitehead, 2007). This will have predictably divisive effects.

It is already becoming clear to many on the ground that the competition culture which pertains will continue to divide community groups, as local organisations try to undercut each other in order simply to keep going. There is a bitter irony in the spectacle of groups whose very roots lie in collective struggles to extend and expand services *for all* in an unedifying battle for their own survival (McCabe, 2010). Such a situation provokes the UK Community Development Exchange (Beddow, 2010, p.3) to ask, 'How can society, let alone a civil one, be built when the very bedrocks of past community activity are being ripped up by the cuts?' In addition, the anger, frustration and disillusionment of community activists both towards state institutions and, increasingly, each other, are hardly going to create a positive context for the voluntary effort required to make any genuine idea of 'the big society' a success.

Second, there are questions to do with representation, given the emphasis on a managerial paradigm which prioritises economic accounting over democratic accountability. Such a culture privileges (and tends to attract) those who are prepared to 'enterprise themselves' (Amin, 2005) and to seek status from their elevated position rather than to challenge or oppose. The incorporation of dissenting community interests can be very effectively achieved in this way (Hodgson, 2004). There is, in other words, a danger that the worthy engaged will be increasingly used to deter the unworthy estranged, fragmenting collective interests and identities and depleting the potential for collective agency.

A third concern is the capacity to deliver the promise of the big society. It is clearly the case that private sector companies are already poised to respond where communities fail—those parasitic communities within the community whose interests do not lie in an articulate and organised community response. Entrepreneurial interests from the local to the global are no doubt anxious to capture those public services which will be floated off, including education. There is a concern that the scattering of services to the voluntary or private sector in this way will lead instead to a small and maybe small-minded society—a fragmented society of neighbourhoods. These ideas are more than redolent of Edmund Burke's notion of attachment to 'the little platoon we belong to in society' as the primary building block of a public consciousness: essentially those who know their place within their place, as it were. This idealised version of a past social order elides questions about how 'the small society' shares responsibility not just for its own concerns and destiny but those of the wider community to which it belongs. Who mediates the competing, perhaps conflicting, claims of different communities? Who protects the interests of the invisible or the shunned? And how does all this relate to a wider context of globalisation when decisions that matter are far removed from locality?

Fourth, the new social morality of community policy has become a means of differentiating 'good' and 'bad' communities. The problem of 'failed communities', where the 'good' community has, despite help, been somehow unsuccessful in eliminating the 'bad' community has serious consequences. Where such policy efforts fail, the implicit assumption will be that communities have only themselves to blame. As Amin (2005, p. 619) puts it, 'They will have chosen to reject community'. Furthermore, the demonization of the poor which is routine fare in the media—what Mooney and Hancock (2010) refer to as 'poverty porn'—has also created divisions within and between communities. According to research, only 25 percent of the population believe that as a society we should be spending money on social security benefits at all (National

Centre for Social Research, 2009). Most of us apparently believe that the reasons for social inequality are that the poor are lazy and feckless and that the affluent are hardworking and responsible. This simplistic caricature erodes trust and creates suspicion, frustration and, increasingly, forms of 'horizontal violence' which are played out in public and private arenas.

Finally, there's a wider question about fairness. As Fudge (2009) succinctly puts it:

> Why should the weakest and poorest in society be expected to carry out the most significant citizenship roles there are whilst public money is used to bail out private financial institutions? (p. 66)

There is legitimate concern among many that the reforms of which the big society is symbolic will bifurcate rights and responsibilities between the citizen and the market, perhaps cutting out the state altogether even as the guarantor of last resort. In their analysis of the current context Taylor-Gooby and Stoker (2011, p. 6) indicate that the proposed reforms involve 'significant transfers of responsibility from the state to the private sector and the citizen'. The emergence of academy schools 'free' from local authority control and open to private competition is a case in point. Whilst a universal system of education is being fragmented the provision of education as a commodity is accelerating. As we shall show, the moralising and entrepreneurial discourses of resilience are systematically deployed to aid this process of undermining and dismantling the universal provision of welfare.

Resilience: What's in a Word?

> *More than education, more than experience, more than training, a person's level of resilience will determine who succeeds and who fails. That's true in the cancer ward, it's true in the Olympics, and it's true in the boardroom.* Dean Becker, Harvard Business Review, May 2002. (online)

As language has a way of shaping what we see—and what we don't see—it is important to be cautious when terms like resilience suddenly become popular and appear to be the solution in all sorts of contexts and for all sorts of problems. The concept of resilience first came to prominence in the United States in relation to disaster management and the ability of communities to respond to cataclysmic events outside their control—the focus was predominantly on how communities could be better organised to reduce their vulnerability and enhance their capacity to 'bounce back' (Morrow, 2008). There are different types of resilience so that it is used to refer to environmental issues (ecological resilience), disasters and cataclysmic events (physical resilience), the capacity of economies to survive economic downturns (economic resilience) and the ability of individuals and communities to deal with change (social resilience). It is also used to refer to the vulnerability of communities to terrorist influences and in this sense implies a type of civic resilience. It is particularly social resilience, and the role it implies for education, that we are concerned with in this chapter.

Meaning is always shaped by the discourse and context in which ideas are placed and applied. We are therefore interested in how the notion of resilience is currently deployed in the management of poor communities. In this respect, two distinct senses of the term are evident but often overlap or are used interchangeably. First, it is commonly used to suggest a stoical attitude of forbearance such as the ability to cope, a gritty determination 'to get by', 'get on with things' and 'make do' whatever the circumstances. Second, resilience is used to describe the capacity of individuals to recover from difficult and trying circumstances and to seize opportunities this might create. In other words, it is more than a capacity to endure because it may enable positive steps forward (Batty and Cole, 2010).

What is evident in the use of this language is that it implicitly reinforces the antistate narrative described earlier by defining the problem psychologically, in terms of character and attitudes. However, resilience is only partly seen as an individual disposition because it is also characterised as a process of interaction between individuals and their communities (Batty and Cole, 2010). In the following sections, we show how the vocabulary of policy is strewn with particular ways of constructing the 'problem of community', which education is then deployed to resolve.

Problem Social Capital

> Community resilience requires more than just resilient individuals. It also depends on the right kinds of social networks and structures. (http://www.youngfoundation.org/research/tips/community-resilience)

One of the dominant explanations current in policy is the idea that poor communities lack the social capital to benefit from opportunities that arise; therefore educational interventions need to foster it so that vulnerable communities can empower themselves. The usual interpretation of social capital refers to the norms of reciprocity and trust that are undermined by the breakdown in human relationships. Robert Putnam's (2000) metaphor of Americans 'bowling alone' captured the sense of the loss of trust, cooperation and shared activities that bind people together. Putnam's research (see also Coleman, 1994) spurred the growth of a social capital industry amongst academics. Distinctions have been made between 'bridging' social capital (making ties between different groups), 'bonding' social capital (developing contacts between like-minded people) and 'linking' social capital (connecting different levels of power or social status in networks) (Kay, 2005).

The framing of the problem of poor communities in terms of their social capital networks has led to the growth of community initiatives focussing on the importance of trust, reciprocity and participation in civic affairs in order to create, enhance and consolidate social capital in communities. In the UK, the Centre for the Wider Benefits of Learning has documented various positive social, political and health outcomes related to the impact of adult education on social capital (Schuller et al., 2004). Participation in post-compulsory education—including adult literacy—is identified as one way of developing trust and building civic responsibility (Field, 2005; Tett et al., 2006). Social capital, it is argued, may also contribute towards civic involvement through volunteering and people becoming more active members of their community (Schuller et al., 2004). Furthermore, some research suggests it can increase the likelihood of enhanced economic activity as confidence levels increase and networks of connections ease the path into work (Falk and Kilpatrick, 2000). However, the notion that social capital is a remedy to particular community ills has proven to be an oversimplification in that too much 'bonding social capital' amongst groups with negative dispositions towards education has also been given as an explanation for nonparticipation in adult education (McGivney, 2001).

The contradictions between different types of social capital is exemplified in Francis Fukuyama's (2002) work, influential in IMF and World Bank circles, which stresses the importance of incorporating a cultural analysis into models of economic development. He argues that the failures associated with neoliberal economic policies in Latin America in the 1990s (e.g., privatization, deregulation, etc.) were not because these policies were wrong but because they did not take into account social capital and its functional role in cooperation. The dominance of small numbers of powerful family cliques in Latin America, with strong bonds, limited the scope for multinational investment from outside these countries. Fukuyama endorses the view that the type of social capital that has to be fostered is that which reinforces dominant values and practices—in other words, social capital has to be understood as a hegemonic project which simultaneously reinforces dominant practices and obscures the need for critical analysis. This one-dimensional focus on social networks allows inequalities in social structure and resources to be ignored. Separating the experience of communities from the structure of the economy leads away from politically controversial issues such as the distribution of wealth and power. According to this view, the solution to Britain's 'broken society' involves enhancing a distinctive type of social capital—that which develops entrepreneurial values and relationships.

Entrepreneurial Resilience

The growth of entrepreneurial resilience as a response to economic crisis goes hand-in-hand with the rise of neoliberalism. Davidson and colleagues (2010) make the distinction between two distinctive periods of neoliberalism; the first period involves a 'rolling back' of the welfare state through policies and discursive practices which involve dismantling state provision, privatising state assets, undermining trade unionism and cutting back on welfare benefits. The second period of 'rolling out' involves consolidation, where principles and values are extended over a range of public sector activity and the fusion of economic and social priorities are closely aligned. In discursive terms, neoliberal values are asserted with little public discussion of alternatives so that in official discourse the range of policy options is narrowed down. The current UK government is, for example, committed to an extensive level of cuts in public expenditure whereas the main opposition parties argue about the depth of cuts, their timing, scope and implementation. None question the necessity or rationale behind them. The need for a diminished welfare state, the priority of global competition, the importance of individuals taking responsibility for their own future are ingrained in mainstream policy and politics.

Eric Fromm's notion of 'social character' is instructive. Defined as 'an ideological formation through which people learn habits and dispositions that support the existing system' (see Brookfield, 2005, p. 159), it is highly relevant to the sustaining of neoliberal politics. In this instance, the development of 'social character' could be said to involve acquiring the ambition to be wealthy, developing creativity and enterprise, learning the skills of leadership and teamwork, independence and determination and so on—above all, taking responsibility for oneself rather than expecting to be supported. To this end, entrepreneurial attitudes are to be fostered in schools, communities and society through a range of institutions and media that 'educate' people into accepting that it is their own qualities that will make the difference and that, consequently, those who fail in this respect lack the desirable and necessary attributes for success. The agenda for community intervention is therefore framed in terms of fostering such attitudes and beliefs, and it is this ideological project which has to be exposed and resisted at the level of community.

One of the difficulties in responding to the latest government initiatives, as the above, is that the language of a radical social justice agenda has been co-opted for neoliberal purposes. For example, *Locality*, the name of the national organisation awarded a £15 million contract to deliver the UK government's community organiser's training programme which will facilitate 'the big society', draws extensively on the rhetoric of radical educators such as Paulo Freire and Saul Alinsky. On the front cover of their tender document are quotes from Freire on dialogue, Alinsky on citizenship, Barack Obama on community organising and David Cameron, the coalition prime minister, on communities helping themselves. In this way, diametrically opposed perspectives are blended together and throughout the document the radical language of Freire and Alinsky is used to serve the ideological purpose of welfare cuts. The Cabinet Office of the government underlines the fact that the community projects of 'the big society' will have the right to 'bid for public services', that is, they are to become agencies for the further privatization of public services. Of course if communities fail to help themselves, then they have only themselves to blame. Inequalities of power and resources—issues central to Freire's (1972) analysis of the need for a pedagogy of the oppressed—are notably ignored. In fact, instead of a transformation of structures of oppression, the transformation of attitudes which foster resilience are proposed. Freire and Alinsky join hands with Samuel Smiles in a neoliberal appropriation of radical ideas for conservative purposes. What the above developments entail is not only a political blunting of radical messages but also the incorporation of the language of radicalism within an entirely different tradition and for an entirely different purpose. This appropriation of ideas and language can be beguiling, so we need to turn to a radical understanding of resilience to steer clear of this quagmire.

Resilience for Social Justice

Historically, working-class communities developed collective values and principles of organisation to buffer themselves from the vagaries of capitalism. The emergence of the trade union and cooperative movement are examples of these values developed in the spheres of production and consumption. Underpinning such activity have been commitments to democracy, equality and social justice—values that have informed radical work in community-based education and development (Lovett, 1988).

In the current context, leading opposition to the neoliberal policy agenda is a coalition from below of trade union groups, community groups, academics and civil society organisations which are arguing that 'there is a better way' (http://www.thereisabetterway.org/), through developing a counter discourse to the dominant one. Mobilisation of resistance has developed in a number of different sectors. Perhaps the most prominent is the growth of student- and trade-union protest against cuts in higher education. New organisations drawing on critical and creative forms of protest have been formed. For example, UK Uncut emerged rapidly after the Coalition government's austerity budget and has developed a distinctive campaigning presence through the use of social media and mobile technology to organise 'flash mobs' against particular capitalist enterprises and individuals who are benefitting from tax avoidance or current government policies (http://www.ukuncut.org.uk/about/ukuncut). The vision informing this protest is the need for grassroots opposition to struggle for alternatives to neoliberal policies. In addition to the potential that such organisations create for building alliances of resistance in communities, it is also essential that educational work in communities seeks to highlight and respond to the deeper material and social divisions which undermine resilience in communities. We identify three highly significant issues that are missing, silenced or appropriated in the debate on resilience in the UK context: poverty, inequality and insecurity.

Poverty

There is a degree of complacency in the policy literature on resilience that issues, such as poverty, have been solved in rich societies. This does not square with the facts. Taking the median measure of poverty as earning 60 percent or less of household disposable income the UK had, in 1979, around 7.9 million people living in poverty. By 1996 this increased to 14.5 million, and although this trend was slightly arrested by New Labour in 2008–2009, it was still at 13.4 million or around 22.3 percent of the population (Sinfield, 2010).

In terms of policy and the big society the absence of serious discussion of poverty as a causal mechanism in undermining communities speaks volumes about the ideological nature of the project. But poverty is an issue that practitioners can and should address as a collective concern. We were recently involved in an in-service training programme for adult educators which was to address combatting poverty. In designing the curriculum, the programme organisers agreed it would be important to provide good examples from practice and relevant literature to help participants make the link between poverty and their practice. Needless to say we struggled on both counts to find contemporary texts and examples of practice in Scotland. This experience suggests that poverty as an issue has slipped off the agenda of community educators at a time when its reality as an issue in communities is growing.

Inequality

Another fact that is missing from the resilience agenda is growing inequality. A key text in this respect is Wilkinson and Pickett's book (2010), *The Spirit Level.* Its subtitle indicates the book's central theme: 'why equality is better for everyone'. In this account the authors, provide exhaustive and detailed statistical international comparisons, which highlight the level of inequality as the critical factor in subjective well-being, that is, a state of readiness to take on challenges implied by the notion of resilience. By examining comparable data sets on a range of social problems (levels of trust, mental illness, life expectancy, obesity, educational performance, teenage births, homicides, imprisonment rates and social mobility) from twenty-three countries, they provide conclusive evidence that levels of inequality matter in terms of developing resilience.

Wilkinson and Pickett accept the argument that, after a certain standard of living is achieved, affluence does not result in improved levels of well-being. As people acquire more, diminishing returns sets in. But attention to this fact, in isolation, may miss the important point. As they state:

> The problems in rich countries are not caused by the society not being rich enough (or even by being too rich) but by the scale of material differences between people being too big. What matters is where we stand in relation to others in our own society. (2010, p. 25)

Income differences, or where people are placed in the social 'pecking order' has significant nonmaterial outcomes. More unequal societies (e.g., the United States, the UK, Portugal) do significantly worse on all measures than the more equal ones (e.g., Japan and various Scandinavian countries). This differential experience suggests that whilst rampant capitalism results in greater inequality, this outcome can be checked and its pernicious effects reduced. Those societies with stronger commitments to social welfare come out better. In other words, capitalism may be the primary cause of inequality, but how we manage and ameliorate it is also important.

Insecurity

Another important structural cause underlying the ability of communities to be resilient can be explained by a significant change in the nature of advanced capitalism. Sennett (1998) argues that the development of flexible capitalism has a deep impact on our relationships, particularly at work, which in turn has a corrosive effect on how people relate to each other. In particular, it undermines established and stable patterns of relationships between workers because it introduces uncertainty and instability into the equation. The growth of 'short-termism' in relationship to work is matched in the organization of welfare and service provision. Increasingly, community level interventions are organized as flexible projects which have a limited timeframe rather than being supported as a long-term commitment (see Crowther, 2004). Those employed in project work have to build a portfolio of experience rather than develop a linear career trajectory. Those lucky enough to have more secure, long-term contracts have to spend their time creating new ways to obtain short-term funding in order for projects to exist.

Insecurity creates fear which, in turn, undermines people's abilities to react to events constructively and collectively. If our relationships with others are constantly short term, then we are less likely to give time and commitment to their maintenance. The networks that are developed through contacts with others are constantly threatened or need to be replaced. Separation from the opportunity to develop deep and authentic relationships with others can create a process of estrangement and isolation or, at worst, despair.

These missing issues in the narrative of resilience—poverty, inequality and insecurity—are concerns that community educators have an interest in and need to develop educational responses towards. Some of the possible educational responses are taken up in the conclusion below.

Conclusion

Educators have an important role in developing counterarguments which address the reality of life for people in poor communities. Counterinformation may also help those who live there develop the resilience to withstand hostile policy discourses and market forces that undermine services and resources which they may ultimately depend on.

One determined omission in the resilience agenda is that what constitutes a good and fair society will always be contested. Making that contestation explicit may be the only rational response to the magnitude of the current political project.

There are no easily available shortcuts to equality and social justice because there are different and competing interests in defining what they mean. The struggle to define and pursue the kind of politics which addresses social need before private profit will always be necessary. Standing up to the realities of brute power can be one very significant way of sustaining a spirit of defiance and resistance—an aspect of resilience which is grossly underestimated, as is the necessity of hope. Reminding ourselves of what has been achieved through collective action over time can be one very effective way of reconnecting with the past and remotivating ourselves for the future. A local project has recently spent two years, with community work support, piecing together a history of activism that has seen both victory and defeat. They are aware that collective action guarantees nothing in terms of the outcomes, but they are convinced that the process itself is what is ultimately of most importance. In the words of one of their number: 'When people stop speaking out, democracy dies'. To reduce resilience to a technique or, worse, a therapy ignores this simple fact. An alternative definition to the sanitised version of resilience in policy is perhaps best summed up in the words of the title of the publication arising from the work just mentioned: *Never Give Up* (North Edinburgh Social History Project, 2011). A more optimistic direction for educational work in communities is to find ways to resource this very different kind of resilience.

References

Amin, A. (2005). Local community on trial. *Economy and Society, 34*, 4, 612–633.

Batty, E., & Cole, I. (2010). *Resilience and recession in six deprived communities: Preparing for worse to come*. York: Joseph Rowntree Foundation.

Becker, D. (2002). Resilience. Retrieved August 9, 2011. from www.centreforconfidence.co.uk/pp/overview.php?p=c2lkPTU

Beddow, N. (2010). 'Sewing seeds on scorched earth', *CDX Magazine*, Issue 63, 3-5.

Brookfield, S. (2005). *The power of critical theory*. San Francisco: Jossey Bass.

CDP. (1977). *Gilding the ghetto: The state and the poverty experiments*. London: CDP Inter-project Editorial Team.

Clarke, J. (2010). What crisis is this? *Soundings* http://www/lwbooks.co.uk/ReadingRoom/public/Clarke

Cochrane, A. (1996). From theories to practices: Looking for local democracy in Britain. In D. King & G. Stoker (Eds.), *Rethinking local democracy* (pp. 193-214). Basingstoke, England: Macmillan.

Coleman, J. S. (1994). *Foundations of social theory*. Cambridge, MA: Belknap Press.

Crowther, J. (2004). In and against lifelong learning: Flexibility and the corrosion of character. *International Journal of Lifelong Education, 23*, 2, 125–136.

Davidson, N., McCafferty, P., & Miller, D. (2010). (Eds.). *Neoliberal Scotland: Class and society in a stateless nation*. London: Cambridge Scholars.

Elliott, L., & Wintour, P. (2010, June). Budget will hit poor harder than rich, according to IFS report. *Guardian*, 23, p. 4.

Falk, I., & Kilpatrick, S. (2000). What is social capital? A study of a rural community. *Sociologia Ruralis, 1*, 40, 87–110.

Field, J. (2005). *Social capital and lifelong learning*. Bristol, UK: Policy Press.

Freire, P. (1972). *Pedagogy of the oppressed*. London: Penguin.

Fudge, S. (2009). Reconciling agency with structure: The contradictions and paradoxes of capacity building in Wales, 2000–2006 Objective 1 Programme. *Critical Social Policy, 29*, 1, 53–57.

Fukuyama, F. (2002). Social capital and development: The coming agenda. *SAIS Review, 22,* 1.

Hodgson, L. (2004). Manufactured civil society: Counting the cost. *Critical Social Policy, 24,* 139–164.

Judt, T. (2010). *Ill fares the land.* London: Allen Lane.

Kay, A. (2005). Social capital, the social economy and community development. *Community Development Journal, 41,* 2, 160–173.

LEWRG. (1979). *In and against the state.* London: Pluto Press.

Lister, R. (2010). *Understanding theories and concepts in social policy.* Bristol, UK: Policy Press.

Lovett, T. (1988). *Radical approaches to adult education.* London: Routledge.

Massey, D. (2010). The political struggle ahead. *Soundings, 45,* http://www/lwbooks.co.uk/Reading Room/public/Massey

McCabe, L. (2010). Capacity building for activism: Learning from the past for the future. In A. Emejulu, & M. Shaw (Eds.), *Community empowerment: Critical perspectives from Scotland, the Glasgow Papers.* Edinburgh: Community Development Journal.

McGivney, V. (2001). *Fixing or changing the pattern?* Leicester: National Institute of Adult Continuing Education.

Mooney, G., & Hancock, L. (2010, Winter). Poverty porn and the broken society. *Variant, 39/40 www.variant.org.uk/*

Morrow, B. H. (2008). *Community resilience: A social justice perspective, CARRI Research Report 4.* Retrieved April 13, 2011, from www.resilientus.org/publications/reports.htm1

National Centre for Social Research. (2009). *British Social Attitudes Survey.* London: NCSR.

North Edinburgh Social History Group. (2011). *Never give up: A community's fight for social justice.* Community Development Journal Ltd & North Edinburgh Social History Group, Oxford.

Putnam, R. (2000). *Bowling alone: The collapse and revival of American community.* New York: Simon & Schuster.

Schuller, T., Brasset-Grundy, A., Green, A., Hammond, C., & Preston, J. (2004). *Wider benefits of learning.* London: Routledge Falmer.

Scott, M. (2010). Reflections on 'The Big Society.' *Community Development Journal, 46,* 1, 132–138.

Sennett, R. (1998). *The corrosion of character.* New York: W. W. Norton.

Sinfield, A. (2010). *Poverty: Perceptions and deceptions.* Unpublished presentation, University of Edinburgh.

Taylor-Gooby, P., & Stoker, G. (2011). The Coalition programme: A new vision for Britain or politics as usual? *Political Quarterly, 82,* 1, 4–15.

Tett, L., Hall, S., Maclachlan, K., Thorpe, G., Edwards, V., & Garside, L. (2006). *Evaluation of the Scottish Adult Literacy and Numeracy [ALN] Strategy.* Edinburgh: Scottish Executive Social Research.

Whitehead, M. (2007). The architecture of partnerships: Urban communities in the shadow of hierarchy. *Policy & Politics, 35,* 1, 3–23.

Wilkinson, R., and Pickett, K. (2010). *The spirit level: Why equality is better for everyone.* London: Penguin Books.

Williams, F. (1989). *Social policy: A critical introduction.* Cambridge, UK: Polity Press.

• CHAPTER FOUR •

Capitalist Crisis and Fascism: Issues for Educational Practice

Mike Cole

Introduction

In times of capitalist crisis, given certain additional political, economic or social circumstances, the barometer of racism rises, both within mainstream political parties and at the fringes. In June 2009, two members of the fascist British National Party (BNP)[1] were elected to the European parliament. The following years also witnessed the appearance on the streets of various Islamophobic 'Defence Leagues'. These developments need to be seen in the context of a lurch to the right in British politics, unprecedented since the Thatcher years. In this chapter, I begin by considering the concept of a capitalist crisis per se, before moving on to a detailed examination of the rise and fall of the BNP. Throughout the chapter, I address issues for Marxist educational practice, anticapitalist and antifascist education and education for socialism.

The 2008 crisis in capitalism and the further lurch to the right in Britain[2] are interconnected events that will be analysed as such in this chapter. We are in the midst of a continuing major world crisis in capitalism. In the UK, the year 2010 witnessed the collapse of New Labour, and the rise of an ideological formation that has continued the Thatcherite revolution with a vengeance. This collapse was not, however, because workers seized the opportunity of a counterhegemonic challenge to capitalism, and not because workers have embraced socialism as capitalism's major alternative. On the contrary, workers have moved even more to the right. Whether workers or capitalists support one or other of the mainstream parties will depend on specific historical conjunctures. At the present juncture, the drift has been to the Conservative Party—at least in England; in Scotland and Wales, the Conservatives do not get general support.

Voting for capitalism, or not voting at all, means that workers see no point in even considering alternative ways of running the world, such as democratic socialism. The 2010 general election resulted in a hung parliament, that is, no political party gained an overall majority. A little over 36 percent of voters voted for the Conservatives, 29 percent for New Labour, just over 23 percent for the Liberal Democrats, and about 12 percent for others. This last figure included nearly 2 percent for the BNP and over 3 percent for the very right-wing anti-European Union UK Independence Party (UKIP). Even though, as we shall see later in the chapter, this was a disastrous vote for the BNP, theirs and the BNP's share of the vote (next in percentage terms to the three main parties) was higher than the combined vote for a number of small socialist parties, whose support was totally insignificant.

The emerging coalition was between the Conservative Party and the Liberal Democrats (in line with the other mainstream parties, its leader and current Deputy Prime Minister Nick Clegg promised "bold and even 'savage' cuts in government spending" prior to the election). In the months following the formation of the new government, politicians stated, "Cuts are the only way" and (in a cabinet where 80 percent are millionaires) "We're all in this together." This was interspersed with "it's all the previous (New Labour) government's fault."

The Socialist Equality Party (2010) describes the ConDem coalition as a "right-wing cabal, dedicated to waging economic and social warfare against the working class." The firmly established hegemony of this ruling bloc, boosted by the highly successful pre- and postelectioneering by the media, militates against the working class seeing the ending of world capitalism and imperialism as a solution to the economic crisis. In the aftermath of the election, prior to the formation of the coalition government, the various organs of the media bombarded the public with the urgent need for the formation of such a government in order to "stabilize the markets" – in other words, in order to "satisfy UK and international capital" that its needs will be accommodated sooner rather than later, and thus attempting to subordinate workers' real needs and to merge their priorities with those of capitalism.

That the cuts are *permanent* and the welfare state in danger of destruction is signalled by the fact that Prime Minister David Cameron is on record as stating that, even after the crisis is over, he will not restore the familiar provisions of public service (Hasan, 2010)—a clear attempt to hasten the end of the welfare state. When asked on BBC television whether the welfare state was under threat, Thatcherite Lord Michael Forsyth, who has described Margaret Thatcher as one of the most compassionate people he ever met in his life

(Rhodes, 2009), replied with scarcely believable audacity: "No, no, this is economics, not ideology" (Hasan, 2010).

Judith Orr (2010, p. 12) argues that, following the interventions of Thatcher and Blair, we are witnessing a qualitative shift: "The government is attempting to do something even Thatcher didn't try, a generalised offensive against the whole of the working class and the poor." Gary Day (2011, p. 48) talks of "crushing poverty and crumbling public services," and of "a country trafficked by its political class to feed the diseased appetites of multinational corporations."

Just before the 2010 annual Trades Union Congress, Rupert Murdoch's right-wing tabloid, *News of the World*, formerly Britain's most popular Sunday newspaper, attempted to deal with challenges to this massive assault on the working class, to counter threats to ruling class hegemony by the trade union movement in the form of strikes, with a headline on September 12, 2010, screaming, "Halt the Union suicide squad." It interpellated its readers: "Britain demands better, and will not forgive industrial thuggery."[3] In a similar fashion, using Gramscian "common sense," the associate editor of the UK's most popular daily newspaper, the *Sun* (another very right-wing tabloid owned by Rupert Murdoch), Trevor Kavanagh, declared on page 9 of its October 21 edition, "Sensible Sun readers know there is no alternative" to the loss of half a million public sector jobs.[4]

All the while, the rich continue to amass huge profits. It was reported in 2010 that six "fat cat bankers" were to share £23 million in bonuses. This was a result of U.S. investment bank Citigroup making £4.4 billion in profits in the first half of 2010 (the bank suffered £4.8 billion in losses during the "credit crunch" of 2008 and has received two U.S. government bailouts totalling £27 billion) (Hayward, 2010, p. 2).

Issues for Educational Practice: The Exploitative Nature of Capitalism and Economic Crises

Educators need to explain that, from a Marxist perspective, capitalism is an inherently exploitative system. An understanding of the source of this inherent exploitation can be facilitated by Marx's labour theory of value (LTV). The LTV explains most concisely why capitalism is objectively a system of exploitation where capitalists systematically, consistently and constantly exploit the working class. This is the case whether the exploited realize it or not or, indeed, whether they believe it to be an issue of importance for them or not. The LTV also provides a *solution* to this exploitation. It thus provides praxis—the union of theory and practice. According to the LTV, the interests of capitalists and workers are diametrically opposed, since a benefit to the former (profits) is a cost to the latter (Hickey, 2006, p. 168). Marx (1887/1965) argued that workers' labour is embodied in the goods they produce. The finished products are appropriated (taken away) by the capitalists and eventually sold at a profit. However, the worker is paid only a fraction of the value created in labour; the wage does not represent the *total* value created. We *appear* to be paid for every single second we work. However, underneath this appearance, the working day (like under serfdom) is split in two: into socially necessary labour (and the wage represents this), and surplus labour, labour that is not reflected in the wage and which is appropriated by the capitalist, eventually to be turned into profits, which in reality was generated by the workers (for a more detailed explanation, including numerical examples, see Marx (1887/1965), pp. 177–98; for a much briefer summary, also including numerical examples, see Cole, 2011, pp. 42–44).

The plus side of this for the working class is that capitalism is always open to challenge. As Tom Hickey (2006) has explained, capitalism has an inbuilt tendency to generate conflict, and is thus *permanently* vulnerable to challenge from the working class. As he puts it:

> The objective interests of [capitalists and workers] are incompatible, and therefore generate not a tendency to permanent hostility and open warfare but a permanent tendency toward them. The system is thus prone to economic class conflict, and, given the cyclical instability of its economy, subject to periodic political and economic crises. It is at these moments that the possibility exists for social revolution. (ibid., p. 192)

Social revolution, the overthrow of capitalism, and the creation of socialism is the solution to the exploitation inherent in capitalist society (the socialist alternative to capitalism is discussed at the end of this chapter).

Capitalist Boom and Slump

Former prime minister Gordon Brown's mantra during his prior ten years at the Treasury was that there would be no return to the economic cycle of boom and bust (Summers, 2008). Marxist educators need to explain that, in reality ever since its origins, the boom and slump cycle has, like its exploitative nature, been another inherent feature of the capitalist system. As Rob Sewell (2009) argues, "It is equivalent to the normal inhaling and exhaling of a human being." As he explains, capitalism piles up contradiction upon contradiction. The cause of the current crisis, he goes on, was the artificially pumping into the capitalist system over a sustained period of "astronomic amounts of fictitious capital and credit" (p. 2). "Fictitious capital" is a term used by Marx to explain the seeking of profits in the world of finance as opposed to production. It does not mean capital that does not exist but rather investment in "paper claims" over a share of value to be produced in the future (Choonara, 2009a). As Joseph Choonara (2009a, online) explains, "The fact that fictitious capital entitles the owner to a stream of income makes it appear like real capital that a capitalist might throw into production to generate surplus value or loan out at the going rate of interest." This has led to the mighty crash that the whole world is experiencing:

The booming housing market—a classic speculative bubble—allowed extensive borrowing on the increased paper value of property. This created the biggest credit bubble in history. Credit, which allows capitalism to go beyond its limits by temporarily expanding the market, exploded. Nevertheless, even cheap credit has its limits. Debts have to be repaid with interest sooner or later. House prices can fall. The "credit crunch" was an expression of this limit as borrowers began to default on a massive scale (Sewell, 2009). As long as capitalism exists, so will "boom and slump."

ISAs, RSAs and Interpellation

Marxists need to point out that the driving force of capitalism is the accumulation of more and more profits. Given this fact, capitalism's objective in the current crisis is to restore, maintain and, indeed, increase its profit base. It is thus determined to make workers pay for the crisis in capitalism by slashing public spending and freezing wages.

Capitalism needs a way of justifying this and does so by invoking the ideological apparatuses of the state (ISAs) (e.g., politics, law and communications) and the repressive apparatuses of the state (RSAs) (e.g., army and police) (Althusser, 1971). It should be pointed out that, for Marxists, *the state* is considered to be far more than "government." In addition, the capitalist state is not neutral and acts directly or indirectly in the interests of the capitalist class. As we have seen, the politicians and the pro-capitalist media interpellate individuals on the lines of "we're all in this together." If the *ISAs* are the source of ruling-class hegemony, interpellation is the *process* by which the legitimation, values, and attitudes required by capitalism are instilled in the populace. Interpellation is the concept Althusser (1971, p. 174) used to describe the way in which ruling-class ideology is upheld and the class consciousness of the working class—that class's awareness of its structural location in capitalist society—undermined. Interpellation makes us think that ruling-class capitalist values are actually congruent with our values as *individuals*. Althusser stressed that it is individuals rather than classes or groups that are interpellated or hailed.

This is important in order to bypass counterhegemonic voices. When confronted with the "inevitability" of workers paying for the cuts to save the nation, the response is, "That's obvious! That's right! That's true!" (ibid., p. 172). Given that the current crisis in capitalism is clearly *caused* by capitalism—a fact that workers recognized, at least at the time of the onset of "the credit crunch" in August 2007—an interesting question for Marxist educators to pose is, "Why are a number of workers not only not questioning capitalism, but are solidly in support of it?" In the crisis, workers are responding to procapitalist solutions as required: "Yes, that's how it is; that's really true!" (Althusser, 1971, p. 140). Their subjection is thus freely accepted (ibid., p. 183). Thus in the conventional parliamentary political game, when confronted with the notion that New Labour has failed and the only solution is to give other procapitalist parties a chance, the response is: "That's obvious! That's right! That's true!" (ibid., p. 173).

Marxists should make the case that such is the power of interpellation that, amazingly, in the wake of the bailing out of the banks which drastically affects workers' living standards and quality of life, a *Guardian*/ICM poll in July 2009 suggested that some workers were opting for greater sacrifices for their own class. Even the poorest UK workers were in favour of cuts in public spending (Glover, 2009). Moreover, one hundred days into the new ConDem government, a *Guardian*/ICM poll (August 18, 2010) revealed continuing support for the draconian cuts being implemented and proposed by the government (Elliott and Clark, 2010).

Interpellation, however, can be contested especially when the assault on the working class intensifies. Orr (2010, p. 12) notes that the ConDem project is a "high-stakes" strategy like that which eventually brought down the Thatcher government after her attempt to introduce the poll tax (a tax on individuals irrespective of means). There are already some signs of resistance to the current attacks on the working class. Autumn 2010 witnessed a number of counterhegemonic responses to the government's assault on the working class, particularly from students (incensed at increases in student fees and at the abolition of the Education Maintenance Allowance [EMA]—introduced by New Labour to encourage young people from poor backgrounds to stay in education and training after the age of sixteen), but also from trade unions. The extent of further counterhegemonic resistance remains to be seen. If and when it happens, the RSAs will be on hand to attempt to crush the resistance.

The Rise and Fall of the BNP: The Rise[5]

In June 2009, two candidates of the BNP were elected to the European Parliament. This minority support of fascism by the electorate can be seen partly as a result of racist interpellation by the communication ISA, particularly, the right-wing tabloids. It should be pointed out that, while this embrace of fascism is not in the general interests of capitalism at this juncture, the traditional procapitalist parties do gain by being given the opportunity to claim not to be "racist" when compared to the BNP, whereas, in reality, their policies *are* racist. The typical reaction to the BNP of the mainstream political parties is to adopt more and more stringent racist legislation particularly that aimed at migrant workers and asylum seekers. As Alex Callinicos (2009, p. 4) argues, political leaders probably believe quite sincerely that this is the best means of stopping alienated workers voting for fascism. The mainstream parties also tend to adopt the language of the overt racists, as with Gordon Brown's adoption in 2007 of "British jobs for British workers." More recently Prime Minister David Cameron proclaimed in 2011, a "sea-change" in the fight against "home-grown" terrorism in Britain, arguing that the root cause was neither social deprivation nor hostility to "western foreign policy," but the product of "state multiculturalism" that had "encouraged different cultures to live separate lives, apart from each other and apart from the mainstream" (Hyland, 2011). Cameron demanded that there be "stronger identities at home. . . . Frankly, we need a lot less of the passive tolerance of recent years and much more active, muscular liberalism" (ibid.). As Julie Hyland argues, it is "not mere coincidence that Cameron's speech coincided with the first-ever national march by the English Defence League (EDL), which attracted 3,000" (see Gillborn, 2008; and Cole, 2011, for extended analyses of the racism of mainstream parties in the UK).

Nick Lowles, a leading campaigner for "HOPE not hate," has argued against the widely held and promulgated assumption that the election to the European Parliament amounted to a "protest vote." On the contrary, that fascist vote was based on "political and economic insecurities" that were moulded by deep-rooted racism (Lowles, 2009). Lowles cites a YouGov poll that demonstrated that:

> ...the racism of many BNP voters goes well beyond simple opposition to current immigration and eastern European migrant workers which one might expect if their support for the BNP was prompted simply by economic insecurity. Belief in the intellectual superiority of white people over non-whites, the view of nearly half of BNP voters that black and Asian people can never be British, the almost universal dislike of even moderate Islam and the contempt and suspicion many of their voters

have towards a liberal and multicultural society show how hardline much of the BNP support is.[6] (online)

Lowles summarizes the poll that shows that BNP voters are mainly working class and drawn from former Labour-voting households. Underlining the significance of the interpellation process, Lowles points out that one-third of BNP voters read the *Sun* or the *Daily Star* (like the *Sun* but more pornographic and with less news). YouGov points out that 44 percent (compared to 12 percent of all voters) disagreed with the statement: "Non-white British citizens who were born in this country are just as 'British' as white citizens born in this country" (cited in Lowles, 2009, online), while 31 percent of BNP voters believed there was a difference in intelligence between the average black Briton and the average white Briton (ibid.). Although only 2 percent of BNP voters deny that six million Jews, Gypsies, and others died in the Holocaust, a further 18 percent accept that the Holocaust occurred but believe it has been exaggerated (ibid.). One of the most startling results, Lowles goes on, was the response to the statement that "there is a major international conspiracy led by Jews and Communists to undermine traditional Christian values in Britain and other western countries." One-third of BNP voters "completely" or "partially" agreed (ibid.).

The Rise and Fall of the BNP: The Fall

Recent fascist gains were reversed in the 2010 UK general election when the BNP suffered massive losses, which included the failure of party leader Nick Griffin's bid for a seat in Parliament in Barking, and the loss of all twelve of its seats on Barking and Dagenham Council in the council elections of the same year. On this council, it was feared that it might have taken overall control.

Part of the reason for the demise of the BNP might have been the racist collusion of New Labour. For example, the 2010 Labour manifesto carried a section titled "Crime and Immigration," as if the connection was obvious (Trilling, 2010a). Another contributory factor was the reputation of the victorious Labour MP for Barking, Margaret Hodge. Although she gave a stirring antifascist speech at the declaration of results, she had previously proposed that migrants must earn the rights people born in this country take for granted, such as social housing and benefits, in a new points-based system determined by length of residence or national insurance contributions. Moreover, in 2006, shortly before that year's local elections, Hodge told the right-wing broadsheet, the *Daily Telegraph*, that eight out of ten of her constituents were considering voting for the BNP, noting, "They see black and ethnic-minority communities moving in and they are angry. They can't get a home for their children." When the BNP went on to win the twelve seats on the council, the GMB trade union called for Hodge's resignation.

A year later, she said that British families had "a legitimate sense of entitlement" to housing. This prompted the then education secretary Alan Johnson to suggest that her words were "grist to the mill" for the BNP. Finally, in February 2010, Hodge argued that migrants should be made to wait up to twelve months before they could get access to the benefits system. Hodge conceded that "the left don't like what I've been saying, but I think you can puncture racism by dealing with the feeling of unfairness that people have." "Politicians always shy away," she concluded, "from talking about immigration and the difficult issues that are associated with it. If we don't address those issues, we allow that territory to be captured by the extreme right" (Trilling, 2010a, ibid.). Hodge claimed that Barking had experienced "the most rapid transformation of a community we have ever witnessed" (ibid.). In reality, as pointed out by social statistician Ludi Simpson, between the 1991 census and the 2001 census, Barking and Dagenham's boundaries were redrawn to include 9,200 people, mainly from nearby Redbridge. So the "rapid" change is partly a statistical anomaly (cited in ibid.). Simpson further points out that the most recent evidence, the 2008 School Census, indicates that Barking and Dagenham still have a lower proportion of minority ethnic pupils than most other London boroughs. "Hodge is wrong," Simpson explains, "if she suggests that her constituents' local services, community spirit and jobs will be raised by restricting immigration or by diminishing immigrants' rights as citizens" (ibid).

Perhaps the biggest reason for the demise of the BNP, however, was a concerted and unremitting campaign by antifascists, such as Unite Against Fascism and HOPE Not Hate. In the run up to the national and council elections, for example, those on the HOPE Not Hate mailing list, including myself, were tirelessly urged, sometimes several times a day, to take action to prevent further victories by the BNP. Lowles commented on the BNP's defeat as follows:

> We mobilised in a way our country had never seen before. In fact, in just the past few weeks, almost a thousand volunteers have joined us in Barking & Dagenham to deliver over 350,000 pieces of literature and nearly 300 volunteers came to Stoke-on-Trent, to distribute leaflets and knock on doors to turn out the anti-BNP vote. Last year's BNP victory was not in our name—but last night's BNP defeat certainly was. We made the world a better place. (cited in Trilling, 2010b [online])

The final body blow to the BNP came in the local elections of May 2011. They were wiped out in one of their strongholds, Stoke-on-Trent, lost all but one of the 268 seats they were contesting in English council elections, and saw their vote collapse in the Welsh Assembly elections. As Nick Lowles (e-mail correspondence to his supporters, May 6, 2011) puts it:

> The BNP is now in disarray and huge credit must go to you. For the past few years HOPE not hate has campaigned in the areas where BNP support was strongest. We've exposed their racism, lies and incompetence and we've offered people a more positive alternative. This year's campaign has been no exception. In Stoke-on-Trent alone hundreds of people have delivered almost 150,000 pieces of literature since the beginning of the year. Fifteen months ago the BNP had nine councillors in Stoke-on-Trent—now they have none. The same is true in Thurrock, Burnley, Charnwood, Calderdale and a host of other areas we have campaigned in.

Lowles (ibid.) explains that the "BNP is on the verge of collapse. They have debts of over £600,000 and members and supporters are leaving in droves. They are rats leaving a sinking ship."[7]

Issues for Educational Practice: Antifascist Education

Antifascist education needs to be part of a more general multicultural antiracist education, which I have discussed in detail elsewhere (see Cole, 2011, pp. 177–80). Now is not the time for complacency. As Lowles (May 13, 2011, e-mail correspondence to his supporters) explains, while the

> BNP might be on its knees...the far-right threat will re-emerge, be it as a renewed BNP, the English Defence League or as a new party. We have to be ready to meet that threat when it emerges but in the meantime we should continue to push HOPE in our communities. The BNP might have been defeated but the despair, myths and racism which gave rise to it remain.[8]

What then are the dimensions of antifascist education? What issues should be part of educational practice in the various educational institutions and, indeed, as part of educative processes in the wider society? For Marxists, these should include, I would argue, a conceptual awareness of fascism as political practice; an analysis of the relationship between fascism and capitalism; key moments in the history of fascism and fascism today; the differences between fascism and racism; and arguments in favour of "no platform for fascists."

What Is Fascism?

Fascism is a political philosophy based on racism and a strong patriotic belief in the nation. Fascists believe that life is about the struggle for survival, based on Nietzsche's concept of the "will to power." Fascism is against internationalism in all its forms. Once in power fascists centralise authority under a dictatorship and promote belligerent nationalism. Only one party is allowed and all other parties are crushed. Workers and their organizations are smashed through terror and censorship. Fascists believe firmly in the malleability of human personality, thus fascism is not just essentially authoritarian: its aims are, in essence, totalitarian. Fascism is against all forms of democracy, and fascists hold in contempt not just Marxists but also the holders of all other political views. Accordingly, no forms of opposition are tolerated. Fascism is male supremacist, tending to celebrate a "cult of masculinity," and favours military options which entail glorifying warriorhood through a fictitious racist and nationalist "bloodline." It insists on "racial breeding" for "blood purity." Fascism entails the worship of and unbroken rule of a "superman."[9]

Fascism and Capitalism

Marxist educators need to explain that fascism tends to arise when capitalist democracy becomes unable to sustain capitalism. As Leon Trotsky put it, "The historic function of fascism is to smash the working class, destroy its organizations, and stifle political liberties when the capitalists find themselves unable to govern and dominate with the help of democratic machinery" (1944, online). Anindya Bhattacharyya (2009) succinctly explains the relationship between capitalism and fascism. As he puts it, "Fascist organisations offer themselves to the ruling class as a deadly weapon to use against the left. But the use of this weapon comes at a price–stripping away any pretence that capitalism is a fair or progressive system" [online]. This is because the ruling class has to use the full force of the repressive state apparatuses (RSAs) rather than just rely on the ISAs. Thus fascism is "a weapon of last resort for our rulers, one that they turn to in periods of acute crisis but keep their distance from at other times" (ibid.). In other words, as we have seen, while the ruling class is quite happy to up the barometer of racism, it tries hard not to admit to doing that. As Bhattacharyya (2009) explains:

> The contradictory political relationship between the ruling class and fascism manifests itself as a contradictory ideological attitude and contradictory action. So the Daily Mail attacks Muslims, but also attacks the BNP for attacking Muslims. The mainstream parties denounce the BNP, but play to its agenda on issues like immigration.[10] (online)

While the BNP concentrates on "respectable" party politics, the English Defence League (EDL), like the Scottish Defence League (SDL) and the Welsh Defence League (WDL), is a street-fighting organization. As Hyland (2011) puts it, the EDL:

> styles itself as a "grassroots" upsurge against the threat of Islamic extremism and its consequences for Britain's "democratic values". In truth, it consists for the most part of football hooligans and fascists with links to the far-right across Europe that have helped spearhead anti-Muslim propaganda. (online)

Street-fighting organisations are typical of fascist complementarity (Mussolini had the "Squadre d'Azione"; Hitler, the "Brownshirts" [Smith, 2010, p. 13]). As noted above, the EDL was prominent in the wake of the BNP's electoral successes and gained street prominence in 2010. While the BNP and the EDL deny links with each other, from the latter's beginnings in March 2009, the BNP has played a major role in building and directing the EDL (ibid., p. 12). For example, the person behind the EDL Web site, Chris Renton, is a BNP member, as are other key EDL personnel (ibid.). Many EDL activists are also in violent soccer-related gangs—"firms"—forced away from soccer terraces in the light of increased policing and surveillance at stadiums (ibid.).

Martin Smith (2010, p. 13) cautions, "From his prison cell in Mussolini's fascist Italy, the revolutionary socialist Antonio Gramsci wrote, 'One of our biggest mistakes was not understanding the sudden rise of the squadre d'azione, and in turn our failure to combat it." While the situation in Britain is not, of course, "as serious as Italy in 1920," Smith concludes, "The danger signals are there and we mustn't underestimate the threat from the new fascists" (ibid.).

Key Moments in the History of Fascism and Fascism Today

Educative processes here should include an investigation of developments in fascist Italy, in fascist Spain, and, of course, in Nazi Germany. Holocaust education must figure prominently in any discussion of Nazi Germany. It is my view that everyone should be made aware of the obscenities of concentration camps, either by visiting one in person or by linking up to one virtually. It must also be stressed that Nazi fascism was not only virulently anti-Semitic but also included the attempted genocide of groups of people other than Jews, based on "racial," ethnic or national origin; on religion; on sexual orientation; and on disability. People were also annihilated because their politics was in opposition to fascism. Key moments in the history of fascism should also include the rise of neofascist groups worldwide in the post–World War II period and into the twenty-first century. An exploration of current fascist groups throughout the world must be central to antifascist education. There should also be a comprehensive analysis of contemporary anti-Semitism.[11]

The Differences between Fascism and Racism

It is important for Marxists to distinguish between fascism and racism, and not to use "fascism" or "fascist" lightly. This is because racism is an everyday occurrence that saturates all societies in the world, a fact that Critical Race Theorists (e.g., Gillborn, 2008) are particularly adept at pointing out.[12] Large numbers of states worldwide routinely practice racism in their day-to-day policies and practices. Fascism, on the other hand, is rarer and encompasses the characteristics outlined earlier in this section of the chapter.

There is a need to oppose both fascism and racism while understanding the distinctions and relationships between them (Gillborn, 2008). As Bhattacharyya argues:

> That means understanding that the "right wing anti-fascism" of [sections of the media] isn't simply a matter of hypocrisy. There are material political motives for why the ruling class is ordinarily opposed to fascism...[but we] cannot ever rely on this right wing anti-fascism that can rapidly reverse into support for the Nazis. (2009, online)

The left thus has a responsibility to take on both fascism and the racism that feeds it (Bhattacharyya, 2009) (for an in-depth discussion of racism in the UK, see Cole, 2011, chapter 2).

No Platform for Fascists

It is my view that antiracists, including Marxists, should make the case for "no platform" for fascists (not allowing fascist groups a joint platform with other political parties or interest groups; no access to the media; against fascists' right to participate in mainstream political debate; and against fascists' right to work in the public sector). These are my reasons:

- giving a platform to fascists makes them appear acceptable and respectable;
- far from being "respectable," fascists operate by instilling fear and claiming "no right to be here" for specific groups (e.g., Jews; Muslims; Gypsy Roma and Traveller communities; lesbian, gay, bisexual, transgender people; disabled people; etc.);
- "no right to be here" can only be brought about by terror, internment, deportation, and murder (Rosen, 2009);
- the right for fascists to have free speech is less important than the right of those on the receiving end not to be intimidated and abused

verbally and physically, and (as pointed out earlier in this chapter) physical attack tends to follow fascist victories);

- giving a platform to fascists should not be seen as part of the "democratic process" because, if in power, fascists' aim is to smash any form of democracy; and
- whereas Marxists want to destroy an economic and political *system* and replace it with democratic socialism, fascists want to destroy *literally*—if considered necessary or expedient—specific constituencies of humankind.[13]

If I am right that it is totally inappropriate for the BNP to be given the "respectability" of mainstream politics, it is even more inappropriate for BNP members to be teachers. However, in March 2010, after fifteen teachers were identified as BNP members in the aforementioned leaked list, a review commissioned by the British government recommended that teachers should be allowed to be members of the BNP or other racist organizations. Its author, Maurice Smith, a former chief inspector of schools, said barring school staff from joining such organisations would be a "disproportionate response" and a "profound political act." The views of the report were accepted by government ministers.

It is my view that BNP members should be banned from working in the public sector per se, since, as Janice Godrich, cited in Sally Kincaid (2009, p. 9), has argued, the "BNP's message of hate and fear" stands in stark contrast to the values of equality and access for all on which public services are based." As Godrich puts it, when considering schools, "What would a fascist teacher's response be if there was a racist attack in their school? What if there was a homophobic attack?" (ibid.).

Issues for Educational Practice: Marxist Educators and the Socialist Alternative

In this chapter, I began by discussing the current lurch to the right in British politics which has its origins in the legacy of Thatcherism and New Labour. I then concentrated on the rise and fall of the fascist British National Party. Throughout the chapter, I have made suggestions for educational practice for Marxist educators, including an agenda for antifascist education. However, simply defeating fascism (and racism), while crucial, is not enough. Marxists must provide a credible socialist alternative to the capitalist system itself. To this end I advocate the teaching of democratic socialism in educational institutions, which I have called "the last taboo" (e.g., Cole, 2011, pp. 180–82).

Space constraints prevent a consideration here of a full discussion of the democratic socialist alternative to racism and fascism (for a comprehensive analysis, see Cole, 2011). Suffice it to say that Marxist educators need to explain that there is a viable alternative to capitalism and that the alternative is democratic socialism. They also need to address common objections to Marxism and to respond to these (for extended examples, see Cole, 2008, chapter 10, and Cole, 2009, chapter 7).

Exciting developments with respect to twenty-first-century socialism are taking place in Latin America (e.g., Raby, 2006; Motta and Cole, 2012), in particular in Venezuela (e.g., Martinez, Fox and Farrell, 2010; see also Cole, 2011, chapter 5). In that country, a massive radical social democratic transformation of the society has been undertaken since President Hugo Chávez assumed office in 1999. These developments are extremely worrying for world capitalism, which is precisely why Chávez is constantly, totally inaccurately and unfairly vilified by both the UK and the U.S. media (see Salter, 2009; and Navarette, 2010; see also Cole, 2011, pp. 146–47).

This chapter has presented a depressing but, in my view, accurate representation of the current UK political scenario. Let us conclude on a note of optimism. Women of color (to use U.S. terminology) are prominent leaders of the Bolivarian revolution. I will leave the last word to one resident in the Caracas barrio of Baruta, who joined the hundreds of thousands of people, maybe a million, descending from the barrios around Caracas, successfully demanding the reinstatement of Chávez after a very brief military coup in 2002 (Blough, 2010):

> We love our president, but this is not his revolution. This is our revolution and it will always be the revolution of the people. If President Chávez goes, we will miss him dearly but we will still be here. We are revolutionaries and we will always be here. We will never go back! (cited in Blough, 2010, [online])

Jean-Paul Sartre (1960) described Marxism as a "living philosophy" continually being adapted and adapting itself "by means of thousands of new efforts." To Sartre's observation, Crystal Bartolovich (2002, p. 20) added, Marxism is not "simply a discourse nor a body of (academic) knowledge" but a living project. In the barrios of Caracas and elsewhere in Venezuela, where "the people have awoken" (Martinez, Fox and Farrell, 2010, p. 24), and in other spaces where the poor live and the spark of socialism has been lit, people are engaging with the possibility of a *practical* democratic socialism. Part of the contribution of Marxists to these movements for socialist transformation is an unremitting struggle against fascism whenever and wherever it occurs.

Acknowledgments

I would like to thank David R. Cole, Dave Hill, Glenn Rikowski and Richard Woolley for their helpful comments on various versions of this chapter. As always any inadequacies remain mine and mine alone.

Notes

1. The BNP do not self-describe as "fascist," but there is considerable evidence (e.g., Copsey, 1994; Richardson and Wodak, 2009; Goodwin, 2010) that their core beliefs are such. A wide spectrum of political opinion concurs, including right-wing Conservative prime minister David Cameron (*Telegraph*, May 27, 2009).
2. This section of the chapter draws heavily on Cole, 2011, pp. 31–33.
3. Interpellation, the hailing of individuals to believe what capitalists want them to believe, is discussed in the next section of this chapter.
4. As Diana Coben (2002, p. 285) has noted, Gramsci's distinction between common sense and good sense "has been revealed as multifaceted and complex." For common sense "is not a single unique conception, identical in time and space. It is the 'folklore' of philosophy, and, like folklore, it takes countless different forms. Its most fundamental characteristic is that it is . . . fragmentary, incoherent and inconsequential" (Gramsci, 1978, p. 419). Good sense, on the other hand, for Gramsci, is exemplified by Marxism. As Coben (1999, p. 206) has argued, good sense, for Gramsci, "may be created out of common sense through an educative Marxist politics."
5. This section of the chapter draws heavily on Cole, 2011, pp. 34–36.
6. In the UK, racist attacks tend to increase when the BNP gains seats in local elections (e.g., Booth, 2010) or in European elections. Thus, following the election of BNP leader Nick Griffin to the European Parliament in June 2009, a string of racist attacks took place in the northwest of England, the area from which Griffin was elected (Choonara, 2009b).
7. As Richard Woolley (his comments on this chapter) has pointed out, the anonymous publication of the BNP's membership list in 2009 might also have contributed to the BNP's decline in membership.
8. For example, there have been rumours for some time that the Yorkshire & Humber BNP MEP (Member of the European Parliament), Andrew Brons, is considering launching a new far-right party. In May 2011, Brons publicly broke ranks with Nick Griffin in a sign that could eventually lead to a split in the party (Lowles, 2011).
9. I would like to thank Dave Hill and Glenn Rikowski for their help in the formulation of these defining characteristics of fascism.
10. Whereas the *Sun*'s target readership is, in sociological terms, "working class" (in a Marxist framework, all those who have to sell their labour power are workers), the *Daily Mail* interpellates in similar ways to the *Sun*, but is aimed at the "middle class."
11. I have omitted the usual hyphen and the capital 'S' on the grounds that Jewish communal organizations in the UK–such as the Community Security Trust–use the unhyphenated "antisemitism." This more closely reflects Wilhelm Marr's use of the word that he and others advocate to describe a policy toward Jews based on "racism". Not using a hyphen or a capital "S" denotes that antisemitism is a form of racism directed at Jewish people per se,

and not at those who speak a Semitic language per se. Semitic languages are spoken by nearly five hundred million people across large parts of the Middle East, North Africa, and Northeast Africa. The most widely spoken Semitic language is Arabic.

12. For a Marxist response to CRT's weaknesses and strengths, see Cole, 2009.
13. In October 2009, BNP leader Griffin appeared on the BBC current affairs "Question Time," a program in which a panel with a "cross section" of views answers questions from the audience. Griffin stated that Islam was incompatible with life in Britain; admitted sharing a platform with the Ku Klux Klan; and described gay men kissing in public as "really creepy." He said that "legal reasons" prevented him from explaining why he had previously sought to downplay the Holocaust and that he had now changed his mind. He was challenged by Jack Straw, the then justice secretary and a fellow panellist, who said there was no law preventing him from giving an explanation.

References

Althusser, L. (1971). Ideology and ideological state apparatuses. In L. Althusser, *Lenin and Philosophy and Other Essays*. London: New Left Books. Retrieved May 31, 2011, from http://www.marx2mao.com/Other/LPOE70NB.html

Bartolovich, C. (2002). Introduction. In C. Bartolovich and N. Lazarus (Eds.), *Marxism, Modernity and Postcolonial Studies*. Cambridge: Cambridge University Press.

Bhattacharyya, A. (2009). The Daily Mail vs. the Nazis? *Socialist Worker*. Retrieved May 31, 2011, from http://www.socialistworker.co.uk/art.php?id=19454

Blough, L. (2010, April 14). Bolivarian Republic of Venezuela: It is not Chavez. It is the people. *Axis of Logic*. Retrieved May 31, 2011, from http://axisoflogic.com/artman/publish/Article_59344.shtml

Booth, R. (2010, January 15). Rise in hate crime follows BNP council election victories. *Guardian*. Retrieved May 31, 2011, from http://www.guardian.co.uk/politics/2010/jan/15/hate-crime-bnp-local-council-elections

Callinicos, A. (2009, November 21). Labour's policies boost the racists. *Socialist Worker*, p. 4.

Choonara, J. (2009a). Marxist accounts of the current crisis. *International Socialism, 123*. Retrieved May 29, 2011, from http://www.isj.org.uk/index.php4?id=557&issue=123

Choonara, E. (2009b). BNP gains led to this racist attack. *Socialist Worker*, July 4. Retrieved May 29, 2011, from http://socialistworker.co.uk/art.php?id=18366

Coben, D. (1999). Common sense or good sense: Ethnomathematics and the prospects for a Gramscian politics of adults' mathematics education. In M. van Groenestijn & D. Coben (Eds.), *Mathematics as Part of Lifelong Learning. The Fifth International Conference of Adults Learning Maths–A Research Forum, ALM–5* (pp. 204–209). London: Goldsmiths College, University of London, in Association with ALM. Retrieved May 29, 2011, from http://www.nottingham.ac.uk/csme/meas/papers/coben.html

Coben, D. (2002). Metaphors for an educative politics: "Common sense", "good sense" and educating adults. In C. Borg, J. Buttigieg, & P. Mayo (Eds.), *Gramsci and Education*. Lanham, MD: Rowman & Littlefield.

Cole, M. (2008). *Marxism and educational theory: Origins and issues*. London and New York: Routledge.

Cole, M. (2009). *Critical race theory and education: A Marxist response*. New York and London:

Palgrave Macmillan.

Cole, M. (2011). *Racism and education in the UK and the US: The Socialist alternative.* New York and London: Palgrave Macmillan.

Copsey, N. (1994). Fascism: The ideology of the British National Party. *Politics, 14,* 101–108.

Day, G. (2011, May 19–25). Love Hurts. *Times Higher Education,* 48.

Elliott, L., & T. Clark. (2010, August 18). Public backs Coalition on Economy—Poll. *Guardian,* pp. 1–2.

Gillborn, D. (2008). *Racism and education: Coincidence or conspiracy?* London and New York: Routledge.

Glover, J. (2009, July 13). Voters want Tory spending axe to fall, poll shows. *Guardian,* pp. 3-6.

Goodwin, Matthew J. (2010). *The new British Fascism: Rise of the British National Party.* Abingdon, England: Routledge.

Gramsci, A. (1978). *Selections from prison notebooks.* London: Lawrence and Wishart.

Hasan, M. (2010, August 18). Thatcherism gilded with piety. *New Statesman.* Retrieved May 31, 2011, from http://www.newstatesman.com/blogs/mehdi-hasan/2010/08/david-hare-cameronism-crisis

Hayward, S. (2010, September 26). 6 Bankers Share £23M. *Sunday Mirror,* p. 8.

Hickey, T. (2006). "Multitude" or "class": Constituencies of resistance, sources of hope. In M. Cole (Ed.), *Education, Equality and Human Rights* (2nd ed.). London: Routledge.

Hyland, J. (2011, February 9). Britain's prime minister whips up anti-Muslim sentiment. *World Socialist* Web site (WSWS). Retrieved May 31, 2011, from http://wsws.org/articles/2011/feb2011/pers-f09.shtml

Kincaid, S. (2009, September 26). Fighting the Nazis in the workplace. *Socialist Worker,* pp. 23-26.

Lowles, N. (2009, July). The way forward. *Searchlight.* Retrieved May 31, 2011, from http://www.searchlightmagazine.com/index.php?link=template&story=284

Lowles, N. (2011). Andrew Brons breaks ranks. Retrieved May 31, 2011, from http://www.hopenothate.org.uk/blog/article/1265/andrew-brons-breaks-ranks

Martinez, C., Fox, M., & Farrell, J. (2010). *Venezuela speaks: Voices from the grassroots.* Oakland, CA: PM Press.

Marx, K. (1887/1965). *Capital, Vol. 1.* Moscow: Progress.

Motta, S. C., & M. Cole. (2012). *Constructing twenty-first century Socialism in Latin America: The role of radical education.* New York and London: Palgrave Macmillan.

Navarrete, P. (2010). Venezuela deserves a fair hearing. *Guardian.* Retrieved May 31, 2011, from http://www.guardian.co.uk/commentisfree/cifamerica/2010/apr/09/venezuela-hugo-chavez

Orr, J. (2010, September). Tories declare war. *Socialist Review,* 10–14. Retrieved May 31, 2011, from http://www.socialistreview.org.uk/article.php?articlenumber=11369

Raby, D. L. (2006). *Democracy and revolution: Latin America and Socialism today.* London: Pluto Press.

Rhodes, M. (2009, September). The Forsyth saga. *Holyrood Magazine.* Retrieved May 31, 2011, from http://www.holyrood.com/index.php?option=com_holyrood&func=article&artid=2872&edition=219&brick=3

Richardson, J. E., & R. Wodak. (2009). Recontextualising fascist ideologies of the past: Right-wing discourses on employment and nativism in Austria and the United Kingdom. *Critical Discourse Studies*, 6(4), 251–267.

Rosen, M. (2009, September 22). Why Nick Griffin shouldn't be on question time: No platform for Nazis. *Socialist Worker*. Retrieved May 31, 2011, from http://www.socialistworker.co.uk/art.php?id=19072

Salter, L. (2009). A decade of propaganda? The BBC's reporting of Venezuela. Retrieved May 31, 2011, from http://venezuelanalysis.com/analysis/5003

Sartre, J.-P. (1960). *The Search for Method (1st Part). Introduction to critique of dialectical reason*. Retrieved June 2, 2011, from http://www.marxists.org/reference/archive/sartre/works/critic/sartre1.htm

Sewell, R. (2009, September 4). The unfolding capitalist crisis—A nightmare for workers everywhere. *Socialist Appeal*. Retrieved May 29, 2011, from http://www.socialist.net/unfolding-capitalist-crisis.htm

Smith, M. (2010, March). Nazis in the election, racists on the streets...the BNP and EDL. *Socialist Review*, pp. 11-15.

Socialist Equality Party. (2010, May 6). After the general election: Where is Britain going? *World Socialist* Web site (WSWS). Retrieved May 31, 2011, from http://www.wsws.org/articles/2010/may2010/pers-m06.shtml

Summers, D. (2008, September 11). No return to boom and bust: What Brown said when he was chancellor. *Guardian*. Retrieved May 29, 2011, from http://www.guardian.co.uk/politics/2008/sep/11/gordonbrown.economy

Telegraph. (2009, May 27). David Cameron attacks "fascist" BNP. Retrieved May 31, 2011, from http://www.telegraph.co.uk/news/newstopics/mps-expenses/5395358/David-Cameron-attacks-fascist-BNP.html

Trilling, D. (2010a, April 16). Gone to the dogs. *New Statesman*. Retrieved May 31, 2011, from http://www.newstatesman.com/uk-politics/2010/04/bnp-party-barking-hodge

Trilling, D. (2010b, May 7). BNP suffers a crushing defeat at the ballot box. *New Statesman*. Retrieved May 31, 2011, from http://www.newstatesman.com/blogs/the-staggers/2010/05/bnp-party-councillors-losses

Trotsky, L. (1944). *Fascism: What it is and how to fight it*. Retrieved May 31, 2011, from http://www.marxists.org/archive/trotsky/works/1944/1944-fas.htm

• CHAPTER FIVE •

Teach for *What* America? Beginning Teachers' Reflections about Their Professional Choices and the Economic Crisis

Gustavo E. Fischman & Victor H. Diaz

> Our country has long prided itself on being a meritocracy, and I too believe that all children should be afforded the opportunity to choose the future they desire.—Martha, in her post-summer reflection.

The above quote comes from a member of the 2010 corps of Teach For America, a program that for more than the past twenty years has become perhaps the most well-known and reputable alternative certification and education reform program in the United States. Although any contemporary discussion about teaching and teacher education in the United States seems unavoidably tied to polarized perspectives about the influence of alternative certification and education reform programs such as Teach For America, this debate has more than a decade in the making.

In 1998, Thomas Popkewitz published *Struggling for the Soul: The Politics of Schooling and the Construction of the Teacher*, a book exploring the original corps of Teach For America. The ethnographic exploration of corps members' experiences resulted in Popkewitz casting of teaching within the program as "struggling for the soul," both in terms of saving the souls of low-income urban and rural students, as well as restoring the souls of corps members who feel anguish about the privileges they hold that are denied to their students. He concluded that teaching in Teach For America results in corps members saving both their own souls, as well as the souls of their students. Martha's statement gives initial evidence of the incredible continuity with our findings two decades later.

At first glance the redemptive logic does not seem to be very challenging: One of the key "problems" that schooling attempts to solve is the transfer of knowledge between generations. To solve the "problem," schools offer students access to new forms of knowledge and the students need to accept that the new knowledge is somehow better or more useful than what they have previously held to be true. The difficulty arises when the "problem" of transferring knowledge is localized in the identity of the students. In these cases, the solution to the problem of transferring of knowledge requires students to exercise a sense of agency that denies their own agency.

Subscribers to the neoliberal discourses in education are among the most active and consistent promoters of the narrative of the redemptive function of schools (Hursh & Martina, 2003; Torres, 2005; Weiner, 2005). The many advocates of the neoliberal reforms in education articulate their discourses around the core belief in the self-correcting qualities of the free market, but they take pains in depicting their positions as part of a self-proclaimed ideologically neutral discourse of efficiency and accountability (Fischman, Ball & Gvirtz, 2003).

Within the neoliberal discourses, institutions associated with the market and loosely defined notions such as the taken-for-granted efficiency of the private sector, the supremacy of "individual choice," and the transformative power of business-like, entrepreneurial actions are sanitized and romanticized. Market failings such as the 2008 crisis as well as corrupt operations (such as Bernie Maddoff, Enron and WorldCom) and potentially disastrous policies (such as ignoring global warming or neglecting to implement adequate "public policies" as demonstrated during the Hurricane Katrina evacuation) are minimized or erased while the "perfections" of markets and rational choice economic actors are set over and against the "inefficiencies" of state bureaucracies.

The role of the state and of public agencies in regulating the corporate sector and in implementing policies aimed at promoting basic social fairness or even timidly redistributing forms of social capital (such as education, health, and retirement benefits) are glossed over as the "nanny state" in the enthusiasm for neoliberal politics (Cato, 2005; Huntington, 2005). In the field of education, we are facing what the late Pierre Bourdieu brilliantly termed the "'gospel' of neo-liberalism, a conservative ideology which thinks itself opposed to all ideology" (1998, p. 126). This gospel is one that serves as a clarion call to combat "by every means, including the destruction of the environment and human sacrifice, against any obstacle to the maximization of profit" (1998, p. 126).

The neoliberal paradigm seeks to have maximum control and predictability in systems and has taken hold of the United States' education system over the past four decades. These policies include high-stakes testing, school and teacher accountability, value added models, pay for performance, charter schools, and, in particular, alternative teacher certification models. We loosely define this paradigm and the resulting policies in education as the redemptive narrative of the neoliberal model (Haas & Fischman, 2010), and we believe it has become the modus operandi of public schools in the United States (Hursh, 2001; Bartlett, Frederick, Gulbrandsen & Murrillo, 2002; Kovacks & Boyles, 2005; Weiner, 2007; Kumashiro, 2007).

Martha's words also connect to the redemptive neoliberal education model well. It recognizes the pretense of meritocracy in the United States and in particular in its education systems (Gabbard & Atkinson, 2007; Kovacks & Boyles, 2005). Martha is a teacher, who is also a member of the program that is perhaps the most emblematic of the redemptive neoliberal education model, Teach For America.[1] Additionally, this statement was written in the midst of the Obama administration's promise to break from the various policies from the past, a promise that has not necessarily been kept. Finally, the United States was in the middle of experiencing its worst financial crisis since the Great Depression.

Although the 2008 economic downturn in the United States has highlighted several of the flaws and contradictions in neoliberal economic policies, the responses within teacher education institutions to the constraints of the economic crisis appear to still be framed within a managerial, neoliberal model (Cochran-Smith, 2005; Imig & Imig, 2006). One would imagine that in the throes of financial crisis, when very well-educated and highly credentialed people experience high levels of unemployment in spite of their education level, the redemptive power of schools would at least be brought into question. Yet, in our study of beginning teachers' reflections on their decision to become teachers through Teach For America, we found the opposite. After surveying 46 beginning teachers in Teach For America (known in the program as corps members) and reading through their application materials for the program, the vast majority of these teachers do not seem to believe that the financial crisis should create education responses, in the form of accommodations or modifications, that differ from the policies of the past.

In this finding, we were left to wonder why these teachers appear to be consciously or unconsciously ignoring the impact of the economic downturn on public education in the United States. One could imagine that perhaps these teachers come from a status of such privilege that they were not personally influenced by the economic crisis. Yet, several of the teachers in our study pointed to a slim job market as one of the reasons, though certainly not the most important, that they decided to apply to the program. Also, the downturn's impact on all sectors of the economy and social hierarchy of the country has been well documented. Another hypothesis could be that the teachers are perhaps simply unaware that such a crisis exists. Yet, these teachers' levels of social awareness and consciousness seem to be incredibly deep and an important part of their desire to join the program. A final hypothesis could be that at the beginning of their careers, they are simply naïve about the connections between the economy and education systems. While we do not have the data to investigate this claim yet, as all of these teachers are in their first year, we have collected data that spans anywhere between 12 and 16 months, from the teachers' application to Teach For America, to reflections gathered in the spring semester of their first year, and in that time, we do not see any significant shift in these teachers' avoidance of discussion of breaks in current education policies due to the economic downturn.

The best explanation of our finding, we believe, is that the redemptive narrative of the neoliberal model in education is so strong that not even a level 5 hurricane of a financial crisis is wavering this narrative's hold over the imagination of these teachers. We will use our data to substantiate three inferences about the teachers in our sample that explain their adoption of the redemptive narrative: they have been redeemed themselves, they seek to redeem other people, and they believe they have the power to be a redeemer.

The Redemptive Narrative in Teach For America First-Year Teachers

For this project, we collected and analyzed narratives produced by 37 first-year, alternative-certified teachers in Teach For America. Each teacher provided three narratives for our analysis. First, with the help of Teach For America, we collected these teachers' application essays to the program. We will refer to this as the participants' *application essay*. These essays serve as one of many parts of the application process and are intended to offer the applicants a chance to explain why they seek to join Teach For America and why they think they would make effective teachers. Second, we collected another narrative from the teachers at the end of their summer training in Teach For America, revisiting the questions of why they joined Teach For America and why they believe they would be effective teachers. We will refer to this set of data as teachers' *post-summer narrative*. Third, in the spring semester of their first year, we sent a short survey that asked them to reflect on the most important events that led to their decision to join Teach For America. This data set will be referred to as teachers' *spring survey*. Without exception, all the narratives were organized following redemptive notions, but for this project we want to highlight the narratives of six teachers who illustrate well the general tendency of the group. We have found a redemptive sequence to be strongest in three inferences we have made from the data: these teachers have been redeemed themselves, these teachers want to redeem others, and these teachers believe they have the qualities of a great redeemer.

Teach For America Corps Members Redeemed by Education

One of the most salient aspects of the redemptive narrative is that its power is derived from the fact that these first-year teachers pointed to their own schooling experiences as redeeming without question. Redemption could be pedagogical, social, or economic and often involves a sequence of events where families suffer hardships and one of the members follows the path of schooling. This path will be rewarded in the future.

Martha (age 22 when she applied to Teach For America, White, B.A. Mathematics, College of Wooster) explains in her spring survey:

> Having worked in low-income communities, I have seen how a lack of education can hinder a person's life prospects. I feel that this violates the American Dream—that we are all supposed to have an equal shot at choosing the life we want to lead. I attended an amazing college, and want all students to have the opportunity to have their horizons broadened. I hope that all students have as many options upon graduation as I had. My parents come from modest homes, and have shown how hard work can lead to a very comfortable lifestyle. I know that this scenario is made possible because of their [her parents'] educational status.

This statement shows continuity with the ideas presented before she began teaching in her placement school. In Martha's post-summer narrative, she wrote,

> I seek to join Teach For America because I want to share my passion for education. Having been fortunate to receive a thorough education, I often marvel at the ways in which my own worldview and problem solving skills have been refined in direct proportion to the academic rigor of my course load. I want to share this experience with others—I want to challenge students to think critically, to push back the limits they have come to believe they have, and to succeed when they thought they could not. Idealistic goals? Yes, but I know they are possible.

Martha has seen firsthand the redemptive power of education in her own life. The "amazing" college education gave her more options than her parents' "modest" lifestyle, and through hard work within education institutions, her options can expand even more. Furthermore, she sees other benefits of her rigorous college education that have shaped her worldview. Martha and her parents endured hardships and very likely learned and accepted that they needed to change ways to "fit" into the culture of the "amazing" college. Martha's admittedly idealistic belief that she can be a redeemer for others is a concept that will be discussed later.

Another corps member, Helen (White, age 23 when she applied to Teach For America, B.S. Biology, Colorado State University) simply states in her spring survey, "I was very fortunate to have great teachers throughout my life and wanted to give back by being a great teacher!" In her post-summer narrative, she offers more detail, writing,

> Having no direct experience teaching, but understanding the impact that my teachers and my education have had on me, made me want to join an organization that would give people the same opportunities that I have had to become well educated. I realized that my education is what has cultivated my environmental and social consciousness, and that the lack of quality education for many in our country is negatively affecting our society as a whole.

Like Martha, Helen points to the imagined power of schooling to influence her "environmental and social consciousness," indicating that education is not doing enough to do the same for other people. In her application essay, Helen explained that she wanted to join Teach For America, after working for an environmental advocacy organization for two years, because she saw a lack of education as the source of poor social and environmental choices made by people that had negative consequences on the environment. Education enabled Helen to make more informed decisions in her life that influence the environment and has redeemed her from making unconscious, poor choices that have significant environmental consequences.

Robert's (White, age 21 when he applied to Teach For America, B.A. Psychology, Northwestern University) narrative is different from that of Martha and Helen, because he connects the redemptive power of education with "luck." In his application essay, Robert writes:

> The question I am faced with is, who am I to have had the esteemed educational history that I have had? How am I so lucky and what is it that I can do to assist children who are not so lucky?

Later, in his spring survey, he adds:

> I had experiences with some underprivileged students that showed me the real achievement gap. Realizing that I had been extremely lucky in my schooling and wanting to make this a reality for my potential students made me want to join Teach For America.

Robert sees that the coupling of education and redemption needs a stroke of luck. It is not uncommon to hear people use such language as "being one of the lucky ones" or "drawing the right cards" when they describe their education experiences and, therefore, situate their understanding of their redemption in what Freire (1973, p. 39) describes as "magic consciousness." Freire explains that this consciousness is a state of attributing facts and reality to a higher power over which people have no control and must, thus, submit to. This level of consciousness only furthers the use of redemptive narratives, as people see this narrative as something that exists naturally and resign themselves to fatalism in accepting the higher power of the narrative.

While Martha, Helen, and Robert all reflect as adults on the redemption they experienced in their youth, Leslie (age 21 when she first applied to Teach For America, White, B.A. in Economics, minor in Psychology from Scripps College) offers an example of a person who is able to identify that the redemptive narrative is not homogenous and linear. In her application essay, she writes,

> I was sitting in my fourth grade classroom, excited by my mammal research project, looking forward to stickers for participation, and thrilled by the older students who were teaching us French. In that moment, I realized I wanted to be a teacher. Education is my passion. I love to learn and to share my love of learning with anyone and everyone. The number of ways to discover, explain, and teach the multitude of phenomena in the world thrills me.

Leslie offers a much nuanced depiction of schools as redemptive institutions, as she recognizes that she was put at advantage and disadvantage at different times in her educational experiences. In her spring survey, she explains,

> I am really disturbed by the achievement gap that I saw in my high school and in my college experience. I saw that my high school experience was dramatically different from those students who looked different than I did and lived in different places. In my college experience, I was the one at a disadvantage because of the quality of my writing and experience at a public school versus an elite, private, prep school. Educational success is the key to living a comfortable life in the United States. It's hard to get jobs that will keep a family above the poverty line without a BA. I want everyone to have the opportunity to have a life that isn't constantly a battle of finances.

Despite her mixed experiences in schools, Leslie believes that academic success in school will lead to the redeemed state of "comfortable life." Additionally, her experience of having educational success, earning a degree, and getting a job that will keep her above the poverty level, in spite of her disadvantage in college, reinforces the redemptive narrative as truthful for those who have benefitted from it. It only stands to reason that people who are aware of their own process of being the beneficiaries of the narrative of schools as redemptive institutions and who feel a commitment to others would seek to pay that redemption forward by becoming teachers in a program like Teach For America.

Becoming Redeemers through Teach For America

While Martha, Helen, Robert, and Leslie all exemplify being redeemed and now seeking to redeem, we highlight two other teachers who seek to become redeemers while not explicitly recognizing their own redemption. We do this in order to tease out the dual ideas of being redeemed and becoming a redeemer for analytic convenience, although we recognize the mutual constitution of these two ideas.

In her spring survey, Amelia (age 21 when she first applied to Teach For America, White, B.A. Public Relations, Pennsylvania State University) could not point to specific events that led her to joining Teach For America. Rather, she described a general feeling she had that becoming a teacher was the right thing for her to do. She writes,

> I wanted to be a teacher because I wanted to make a difference. There is no one "event" that influenced it, but rather the beliefs that I have towards education and the survival of this country. Our education system is extremely flawed and I wanted to be part of Teach for America because I believe in their mission. If it was not for TFA, I would not be a teacher today. I believe the education is the single most important factor in a child's or teenager's life. Their education determines what their future will be. The kids in school today are the future of America and to be honest, I am terrified of what that future will hold if the education system is not improved and worked upon. I want to be a teacher because I will work my life away to make sure my students leave my class being able to succeed in future classes and seriously thinking about attending college. No matter what background someone is from or how much money they have, education allows everyone to make something of themselves if they realize the importance of it.

In this statement, Amelia notes her desire to be a redeemer and her understanding that being a part of Teach For America will offer her this opportunity. It is important to pay particular attention to her idea that she would not have become a teacher today if not for her participation in Teach For America. This can be understood as a demonstration that it is not teaching per se that offers the opportunity to be a redeemer but rather teaching in Teach For America. Additionally, Amelia's strong language highlights the power of redemptive narratives, describing her terror about the future of the nation given its education systems, as well as her desire to work her life away to ensure the redemption of not only her students but the nation as well.

Russell (White and American Indian,[2] age 27 when he applied to Teach For America, B.A. Classical Studies and M.A. Comparative Literature and Classical Studies, University of Arkansas) is another teacher who demonstrates the desire to become a redeemer. He sees his participation in Teach For America as a continuance of his commitment to others, and enhances his work as a redeemer in other institutions and systems. In his spring survey, he writes,

> Since graduating high school, I have consistently fought for better protection for our nation's youth, especially foster children and orphans. Civil rights has [*sic*] always been close to my heart, and it has always troubled me that the pervading mentality is that equal rights exist in America. The simple fact is that poor education has been a tool for oppression in this country. The continued lack of focused, rigorous educational opportunities in low-income communities perpetuates a 200-year long stratification of our nation's people. Teach for America does more than allow me to teach; it provides an opportunity to fight this cycle from the inside out.

Like Amelia, Russell seeks to be a redeemer not only for his students as individuals, but for the future of the United States as well. He displays a strong social consciousness and awareness in this statement, as well as in a statement he made in his spring survey. He wrote,

> I have long believed that education directly correlates to one's place in society, and too many children are denied a good education either because poor school districts cannot pay their teachers well or because teachers prefer to teach with a wealth of resources at their fingertips. This pushed me to seek a teaching position in a low-income neighborhood, as I wanted to give these students the same opportunity for quality education as their more affluent peers.

His social consciousness and his belief that schools and education systems perform a redemptive function for low-income youth drive his desire to be a redeemer. In combining both his statements in his post-summer narrative and spring survey, we can see a clear demonstration of a person who sees Teach For America as offering the best possible opportunity to act on redemptive beliefs and to embody a redeemer over other professional opportunities. This makes sense, given the incredible amount of people who apply to the program each year (in 2010, 46,000 people applied for only 8,200 positions). Yet, in order to gain acceptance into the program and act on their redemptive sensibilities, these teachers must demonstrate that they are capable of being redeemers, which is the third instance of performativity of the narrative of redemption that we found in our data.

Teach For America Corps Members: Having the Qualities of a Redeemer

In its application essay, Teach For America asks applicants to respond to the question, "Why do you believe you would make an effective corps member?" This question offers candidates the opportunity to demonstrate that they possess the qualities needed to be a great teacher within Teach For America's model of effective teaching. Given the redemptive qualities of the program, which is based on the idea that social and personal transformation can take place through closing the achievement gap in schools, the model of effective teaching employed by the program surely carries traces of the qualities needed to be a great redeemer. In answering this question, and through other data points, all of the teachers in our study wrote about their possession of redemptive qualities.

Martha highlights one of the most important qualities of redeemers: being passionate about what they do. She explains,

> When I think through all the teachers I have had, the excellent teachers were those that were not only passionate about their area of study, but they were enthusiastic outside of the classroom as well. They held me to my highest potential inside the classroom and willing assisted me after class was over. They took the time to not only learn my name and my spot on the seating chart, but who I was and what life was like for me beyond the school walls. I know that life for the students I would teach would be far different than my own upbringing, and I know that I cannot fix all of the circumstances that they face, but I do know that I can care, and I can listen, if nothing else.

In this statement, she also highlights other important qualities of being redeemers. They must hold others to high standards, they must make human connections to those that they work with, and they must care about the people they work with.

Helen offers other qualities of redeemers that are very important, as well as a brief analysis of those qualities that are less important. She sees experience as a quality that is not needed in redeemers, as long as other, more important, qualities exist. In her post-summer narrative she explains,

> Having no direct experience teaching, but understanding the impact that my teachers and my education have had on me…I will be an effective Corps Member because I have a positive attitude, a very strong work ethic, and am very organized. I also believe very strongly in what we are working towards with Teach For America and the impact that we will have on youth in the United States.

Her lack of experience is not a problem for her due to her cultivated consciousness, her positive attitude, her strong work ethic, and her strong sense of purpose. She also offers a more pragmatic, managerial quality of redeemers—that of being well organized.

It is important to note that Helen is not saying that she has no experience in being a redeemer, but rather she has little teaching experience. This is an important distinction in the minds of the teachers in our sample, who see that their experience as redeemers in other contexts positions them well to be strong redeemers as teachers. Robert exemplifies this point well in his application essay, when he writes,

> I feel I would be an ideal member of the TFA corps because of my leadership experience, my dedication to my pursuits and my people skills. As a corps member, I would hope to impact my students by being able to connect with them as a mentor and a crutch. Having been a motivator within my Fraternity as the President and through my service experiences with Habitat for Humanity and Special Olympics, I know that I can help motivate students to be the best that they can be. I would aspire to create a classroom atmosphere where my students can be confident with themselves. I feel that by building confidence and motivation within students a teacher can really make a difference. I would like to impart in students, who may not have felt engaged in their education, a love of and a desire to learn. I would consider my time as a corps member a success if I were able to instill these principles within my students.

Later in his post-summer narrative, he explains,

> I believe that I will be an effective Corps Member because I have had success in almost all endeavors I have undertaken thus far in my life. Along with that, the training that I have gone through during the past few weeks has shown me that I have the skills and ability to be an effective teacher. The combination of the intensive training that I received and my previous leadership positions will drive me to success during my time as a Corps Member. In terms of my personal qualities, I think that my determination to do well, my ability to get along with many people and my resourcefulness will all contribute to the skills I learned at Institute. This combination will help me to really achieve as a TFA Corps Member. As a Corps Member I hope to become a truly great teacher and to get my students on a winning life path. I hope to invest my students in their education and to empower them with the ability to direct their own education.

Thus, Robert offers other qualities of a great redeemer. They must be dedicated leaders, with strong people skills. They must be motivators and confidence builders, and they must be successful in other areas in their lives when they have played the role of a redeemer. Robert offers his work prior to joining Teach For America as evidence of this. Amelia does something very similar in explaining her qualities that position her well to be a strong redeemer. In her application essay, she writes,

> Throughout my life, I have overcome obstacles with the combination of my confidence and hard work, along with the help of others that believe in me. If it were not for these heroes [teachers] that have touched me through the years that I have been pursuing my education and working to achieve my goals, I would not be where I am today. I want to participate in Teach for America because the country needs strong leadership in education. I have always been a leader to my friends, peers and co-workers. I have held a job in addition to attending school and involving myself in extracurricular activities since the age of 16 and that has helped me develop excellent organization and time management skills. I know that I can succeed in all that I put my mind to because I don't give up or let obstructions set me back in my ability to achieve my goals. My current goal is to become a corps member because I know that I can make a difference.

In Amelia's conception of a strong redeemer, self-confidence seems very important in addition to the other qualities discussed by the other teachers. Russell demonstrates the same idea in his post-summer narrative when he writes,

> I'm confident that I will be successful in the program because I am passionate about providing my students with the absolute best education possible and presenting them with the opportunities necessary to achieve whatever goals they might have. While it's true that I have a lot in common with the community I'll be teaching in, I don't pretend to know the struggles that my students face. What my own upbringing does equip me with is the ability to empathize, which will drive me to do everything possible to help students overcome their personal struggles.

Confidence, simplicity, personal agency, commitment, fairness, transformation, and similar are qualities presented not only in Russell's words but also in the narratives of all the teachers in this study. These qualities give evidence about the strength of redemptive themes and motives in these teachers' decisions to join Teach For America and become teachers. Redemptive narratives are powerful because they are simple, have the appearance of being effective, and seem to resolve difficult situations, by allowing students who are usually labeled as "problematic" to be part of the solution. Very often the solution requires students to abandon whatever felt identity they perform (ethnic, sexual, class, linguistic, etc.) in exchange for being allowed to access the academic knowledge valued by the institution. It is well known that this type of bargain is easier for some performed identities than others, and to what extent the redemptive narrative is more successful with certain individuals and groups and not others is beyond the scope of this paper. What our study shows is that for this group of Teach For America teachers, the narrative of redemption provides a legitimizing way of allocating "access to education" by imagining a "fair and just" meritocratic system concerning the power of schools to change a person's social situation and moral compass for the better.

Conclusion

> We never found the promises our teachers gave//If we worked hard, if we behaved//The graduations hang on the wall//But they never really helped us at all. ("Allentown", Billy Joel)

The economic crisis of 2008 signaled a period of high anxiety and disruptions globally, but it also provoked debates, reflections, introspections, and the possibility for imagining that there were other alternatives, other models. As with other recent critical events in the United States like the September 11 terrorist attacks and the destruction caused by Hurricane Katrina, the economic downturn has led many in the United States to ask important, introspective questions about our nation and society, presenting a powerful opportunity to investigate the common sense assumption that educational success and academic credentials create a seamless transition up the social and economic ladder.

In the mid-1980s, a similar economic downturn led American songwriter Billy Joel to write the lyrics opening this section. In "Allentown", the lament of a steelworker who has lost his job because the mill has closed goes straight to the limitations of the redemptive narrative: "We never found the promises our teachers gave//If we worked hard, if we behaved//The graduations hang on the wall//But they never really helped us at all." Are words like those in "Allentown" falling on deaf ears with the Teach For America corps members in our study? What makes these Teach For America corps members immune to the enormous social and individual pressures and constraints associated with the 2008 economic crisis? What compels these teachers to believe in and act on the redemptive promise of schools?

We don't have comprehensive answers to all these questions, but we explore these issues with the firm conviction that these Teach For America corps members are NOT THE PROBLEM, and indeed, they are part of the solution. Their faith in the redemptive promise of schools runs so deep historically, socially, culturally, and personally that little good will come from just criticizing their redemptive belief systems, without taking the responsibility of working together with them in imagining alternatives, exploring solutions, and staying with them through conflicting times.

We are aware of the difficult task of building new narratives about public schools, not as sites of redemption but rather as sites of possibility and agency. As we pointed out before, the creation of new narratives needs questioning common sense and deeply engrained redemptive pedagogical imagination, but it also needs to keep alive the sense of commitment and transformation that the Teach For America teachers in our study bring to their schools. It is in their commitment that we see the kernel of Gramscian good sense and the possibility of becoming "committed intellectuals" (Fischman & McLaren, 2005). For a committed intellectual, political-pedagogical actions are not an exclusively rational decision, a matter of having the right knowledge, but also of commitment to the situation, of understanding that before being something you need to "be there." We believe that Milan Kundera is correct when he notes that:

> *I think therefore I am* is the statement of an intellectual who underrates toothaches. *I feel therefore I am* is a truth much more universally valid, and it applies to everything that's alive. My self does not differ substantially from yours in terms of its thought. Many people, few ideas: we all think more or less the same, and we exchange, borrow, steal thoughts from one another. However, when someone steps on my foot, only I feel the pain. (Italics in the original, 1990, p. 200)

We are also aware of the great gap and sense of mistrust that dominates the field of education. The traditional distinction between practitioners and scholars, teachers and researchers, and teachers and intellectuals is that those who are working also examine rules and institutions in order to foster agency against the organization and acts of power (Foucault, 1988). Rather than bankrupting narratives of redemption in teachers such as the ones in this study, teacher educators, scholars, and researchers need to engage with those narratives, abandoning simplistic notions of intellectualism and redemptive narratives. Our work needs to focus on equipping all teachers with the space and tools to engage in the development of new narratives and possibilities. Those new narratives cannot but have their starting point in the current reality of our schools and public education.

We are also convinced that these Teach For America teachers need to have opportunities to reflect on their own narratives and explore alternatives, remembering as in the old fable that the emperor does not need to simply be told he wears no clothes; we must remember that in the end the emperor continues the procession although he is aware of his nudity. We must also keep in mind the keen reflections of the band Arcade Fire: "All the kids have always known that the emperor has no clothes//But they bow down to him anyway, 'cause it's better than being alone." We firmly believe that many Teach For America teachers can be committed intellectuals, and we shouldn't let them be alone.

Notes

1. Teach For America is a program for recent college graduates to commit two years to teaching in a low-income rural and urban community in an effort to close the achievement

gap that exists between youth in low-income communities and their more affluent peers. Through their participation in Teach For America, corps members not only embark on an alternative path to teacher certification through partner universities, they also receive the full salary and benefits of a new teacher in their assigned school district, as well as educational grants and a student loan deference via their affiliation with AmeriCorps. Since its inception in 1990, the program has sparked controversy and heated debate over its role in education reform and teacher preparation, a full discussion of which lies outside the scope of this chapter. For additional discussion, see Labaree (2010) and Koerner, Lynch, & Martin (2008).

2. Observant readers may notice that Russell is the only one of seven corps members in this study who racially identifies as something other than White. While 32 percent of the 2010 corps in Teach For America racially identifies as other than White (http://www.teachforamerica.org/admissions/diversity-in-the-corps/) our study utilized convenience sampling that, unfortunately, did not capture such racial diversity.

References

Bartlett, L., Frederick, M., Gulbrandsen, T., & Murrillo, E. (2002). The marketization of education: Public schools for private means. *Anthropology and Education Quarterly, 33*(1), 5-29.

Bourdieu, P. (1998). *Acts of resistance: Against the tyranny of the market.* New York: New Press.

Cato, I. (2005). *Handbook on policy* (6th ed.). Washington, D.C: Cato Institute.

Cochran-Smith, M. (2005). The politics of teacher education and the curse of complexity. *Journal of Teacher Education, 56*(3), 181–185.

Fischman, G. E., Ball, S., & Gvirtz, S. (2003). Towards a neo-liberal education? Tension and change in Latin America. In G. E. Fischman, S. Ball & S. Gvirtz (Eds.), *Education, Crisis and Hope: Tension and Change in Latin-America* (pp. 1–19). New York: Routledge-Falmer.

Fischman, G. E., & McLaren, P. (2005) "Rethinking Critical Pedagogy and The Gramscian Legacy: From Organic to Committed Intellectuals" *Cultural Studies ↔ Critical Methodologies,* 5(4) 425-447.

Foucault, M. (1988). The political technology of individuals. In L. Martin, H. Gutman & P. Huttan (Eds.), *Techonologies of the Self* (pp. 145–162). Amherst: University of Massachusetts Press.

Freire, P. (1973). *Education for critical consciousness.* New York: Continuum.

Gabbard, D., & Atkinson, T. (2007). Stossel in America: A case study of the neoliberal/ neoconservative assault on public schools and teachers. *Teacher Education Quarterly, 34*(2), 85–109.

Haas, E., & Fischman, G. E. (2010). Nostalgia, entrepreneurship, and redemption: Understanding prototypes in higher education. *American Educational Research Journal-SIA,* 47(3), 532–562.

Huntington, R. (2005). *The nanny state: How new labor stealthed us.* London: Artnik.

Hursh, D. (2001). Neoliberalism and the control of teachers, students and learning: The rise of standards, standardization and accountability. *Cultural Logic,* 4(1), Retrieved May 20, 2011, from http://clogic.eserver.org/4-1/hursh.html

Hursh, D., & Martina, C. A. (2003). Neoliberalism and schooling in the U.S.: How state and federal education policies perpetuate inequality. *Journal for Critical Education Policy Studies, 1*(2), Retrieved May 20, 2011 from http://www.jceps.com/?pageID=article&articleID=12

Imig, D. G., & Imig, S. R. (2006). The teacher effectiveness movement: How 80 years of essentialist control have shaped the teacher education profession. *Journal of Teacher Education, 57*(2), 167–180.

Koerner, M., Lynch, D., & Martin, S. (2008). Why we partner with Teach For America: Changing the conversation. *Phi Delta Kappan, 89*(10), 726–729.

Kovacks, P., & Boyles, D. (2005). Institutes, foundations and think tanks: Neoconservative influences on U.S. public schools. *Public Resistance, 1*(1), 1–40.

Kumashiro, K. K. (2007). *The seduction of common sense: How the right has framed the debate on America's schools*. New York: Teacher's College Press.

Kundera, M. (1990). *Immortality*. New York: Harper Perennial.

Labaree, D. (2010). Teach For America and teacher ed: Heads they win, tails we lose. *Journal of Teacher Education, 61*(1–2), 48–55.

Popkewitz, T. S. (1998). *Struggling for the soul: The politics of schooling and the construction of the teacher*. New York: Teachers College Press.

Torres, C. (2005). NCLB: A brainchild of neoliberalism and American politics. *New Politics, 10*, 94–100.

Weiner, L. (2005). Neoliberalism, teacher unionism, and the future of public education. *New Politics, 10*. Retrieved December 20, 2005, from http://www.wpunj.edu/~newpol/issue38/Weiner38.htm

Weiner, L. (2007). A lethal threat to U.S. teacher education. *Journal of Teacher Education, 58*(4), 274–286.

• CHAPTER SIX •

Transversality and Innovation: Prospects for Technology-Enhanced Learning in Times of Crisis

Patrick Carmichael & Kate Litherland

> If the three ages of the concept are the encyclopedia, pedagogy and commercial professional training, only the second can prevent us from the heights of the first into the disaster of the third: an absolute disaster for thought whatever its benefits might be, from the viewpoint of universal capitalism. (Deleuze and Guattari, 1994)

Introduction

Over the past decade, the higher education sector in the UK has been marked not only by expansion in terms of the number of institutions, staff and students but also, more recently, by financial strictures and a controversial move to predominantly fees-based funding of teaching. Debate about funding and governance of universities has inevitably spilled over into broader ideological questions about the desirability of a 'mass' higher education system and what students-as-consumers can expect of higher education. Our particular interest in this chapter is the role played by technology-enhanced learning,[1] an area that has been particularly affected by these changes and in relation to which many broader debates about the future of higher education have been enacted and highlighted.

As universities seek to reduce costs or to insulate themselves from an uncertain financial future in which they are more dependent on student fees rather than central funding, many of the units responsible for development, support and evaluation of learning technologies have been incorporated into library and information services, devolved to faculties or departments, or dissolved entirely. And yet, at the same time, learning technologies are seen as part of the solution to the crisis in university funding. The 'positive rhetorics' around 'cyberlearning' identified by Suoranta, Tomperi, and Fitzsimmons (2005, p. 193) of 'freedom, flexibility, autonomy, self-direction, openness, effectivity, productivity' are now part of the 'offer' being made to prospective students as universities seek to attract their custom in a shrinking but consumer-led higher education market, without any recognition of Suoranta and colleagues' 'gloomier vision' of pedagogical limitations, learner isolation and a curriculum controlled by commercial imperatives, or Conole and Dyke's (2004) observation that any 'affordance' of learning technologies can be considered to have both positive and negative connotations. The risk, then, is that against this background, learning technologies are mobilized primarily in support of a pedagogically impoverished, delivery-oriented model of the curriculum, contributing to the 'disaster' envisaged by Deleuze and Guattari. But at the same time, the current uncertainties open a space for alternative envisioning of how learning technologies might come to be, how they come to be understood, and what role they might play in pedagogical practices and the discourses that accompany them.

Transversality and Innovation in Technology-Enhanced Learning

Deleuze and Guattari's own writings provide a pointer as to how technology-enhanced learning might be reconceptualized and reorganized, with the clearest articulation of this in Guattari's work on transversality. This was informed both by his professional practice in psychiatric hospitals and as a political activist, and it avoids the tendency to see everywhere the smooth and striated, or the arboreal and the rhizomic. Central to his analysis is the idea of transversality as a set of practices and discourses that characterize what he terms the 'subject group...that endeavours to control its own behaviour and elucidate its object, and...produce its own tools of elucidation' (Guattari, 1984, p. 14). Transversality in such groups:

> is a dimension opposite and complementary to the structures that generate pyramidal hierarchisation...this dimension can only be seen clearly in certain groups which, intentionally or otherwise, try to explore the meaning of their praxis and establish themselves as subject groups. (Guattari, 1984, p. 23)

The transversality of groups is not reducible to its membership or purpose, nor is it a mechanism by which some form of social capital is concentrated; but, rather, it is an expression of the 'extractions' from the heterogeneous levels at which it operates and the interchanges and inquiries that it enables: the transverse group both "hears and is heard" (Guattari, 1984, p. 14). Guattari describes how such groups often form in institutional lacunae and interstices, often in response to uncertainties or ambiguities in policy or practice. Unlike working parties, consultation panels, or other organizational forms with circumscribed remits, limited timeframes and predetermined roles and responsibilities, the transverse subject group is self-directing and reflexive: transversality involves continued inquiry into one's own role and those of others, as well as that of the directions being taken by the subject group. In contrast to other kinds of collectivities which do not question their own existence, the transverse group 'keeps asking whether it is right, whether it should be totally transforming itself, correcting its aim, and so on' (Guattari, 1984, p. 39). Guattari cautions against the tendency to create new hierarchies and elites to replace established 'group phantasies', but also warns of the dangers of falling back into lateral associations in which the main purpose of the group is the mutual reinforcement of 'togetherness' or some kind of faux collegiality.

In educational contexts, the transverse group, therefore, is more than a mechanism by which existing practices are directed in order to address a predetermined task or policy imperative; and while they may bring together a heterogeneous group of individuals (teachers and students, researchers, archivists and technologists, for example), this must be with more than (for example) 'student consultation' in mind. In the particular case of technology-enhanced learning, the notion of transversality becomes particularly valuable as a means of developing both mutual understandings and a programme of action which itself is then open to scrutiny and redirection. This aligns well with models of participatory design that are sometimes (but not always) employed in computer software development. In a research and development study into the potential of 'Web 2.0' tools and approaches for postgraduate research students, for example, the establishment of a project team which included teachers, researchers, students at different stages in their academic careers and software developers allowed the development both of better understandings of the practices, discourses and challenges with which researchers were engaged *and* the most useful kinds of technologies that could be developed to support them (Carmichael and Burchmore, 2010). Key to the success of this activity was that it was not presented as training for participants in the use of technologies over which they had little control, or gathering of 'user requirements' to aid the software developers in building something new. Instead, it was couched in terms of extractions, innovations and new combinations: one activity being a 'paper-prototyping' activity in which participants drew on their prior use of different technologies in order to develop proposals of the online environments and applications they would most value in their learning and research. These designs, and the discourses that accompanied them, informed the development of 'rapid prototypes' of learning technologies, which were then reintroduced to subsequent meetings of the group, where they were, in turn, scrutinized, evaluated and in some cases 'redirected'.

Such fluid and contingent relationships can be achieved within relatively small, self-directed groups in the context of learning technology *design*. But is it possible to enact such transversality in the learning environments of the university? And, how might the role of learning technologies be affected by doing so? The argument we will advance here is that the current crises and lacunae in higher education present opportunities to enact the Deleuzo-Guattarian interpretations of learning technologies and their role in higher education (offered by, for example, Bayne, 2004; Dyer-Witheford, 2005) through the formation of, and work within 'transverse groupings', composed of students, staff and researchers, which Guattari suggests can 'overcome both the impasse of pure verticality and that of mere horizontality' (Guattari, 1984, p. 18). We draw on writers and activists in the autonomist tradition to present an alternate view of how technological and pedagogical innovation might be initiated; where expertise lies; and how technology relates to pedagogical environments, activities and outcomes. And in the latter part of this chapter we present a brief account drawn from a recent research and development project in which these ideas framed and were enacted in the development of new Web technologies—in the course of which teachers and students creatively appropriated elements of existing technologies in pursuit of pedagogical ends. Can this kind of rethinking of the place of learning technologies reinforce the central role of pedagogy in higher education in times of economic and educational crisis?

Learning Technologies and the Post-Historical University

Peters (2005, 2007) discusses the prospects for what he terms the 'post-historical' university: that is, one where the dominant rhetorics of Kantian criticality, Humboldtian sensitivity to different cultures, or the Leavisite literary canon are incorporated into new kinds of institutions, without the kind of collapse towards the provision of corporate, on-demand training against which Deleuze and Guattari caution. Peters is, at the same time, cautiously optimistic about the shift from educational elitism to 'massification', the commitment to which, in his view, underpins 'the greatest institutional transformation of the university' (2005, p. 81).

Currently, discussions of the role of technology-enhanced learning in such post-historical, mass universities are underpinned by a number of premises, although these are contested. The first of these is the notion that the modern mass university is dependent on learning technologies, and online collaboration environments in particular, that represent spaces that have to transcend the limitations and striations of physical learning environments. Certainly Virtual Learning Environments (VLEs) offer teachers and students opportunities to communicate using different modalities (audio, video, synchronous and asynchronous discussion, collaborative authoring and sharing of work in progress and completed), but, at the same time, for all of the rhetoric of free association of individuals and ideas, the reality is that university learning is increasingly defined in terms of predetermined learning outcomes and careful circumscription of demands, expectations and support. The typical VLE is therefore 'a space of pure striation...of closure, of regulation—a formal structured domain of control where hierarchies are reasserted and Internet functionality is appropriated by a regime of productivity and efficiency' (Bayne, 2004, pp. 312–14). Rather than experiencing a smooth space that they are free to explore as self-directing nomads, learners are therefore likely to experience the environments of technology-enhanced learning as a normative and constraining (and often frustrating) space in which to work and learn.

The second premise is, in part, a response to the assertion that emergent technologies such as 'Web 2.0' platforms (such as Facebook and YouTube), social software applications (blogs, wikis, citation managers) and mobile devices represent the learning media, of choice amongst what Prensky (2001) describes as 'digital natives': naturally competent and confident users of such technologies. Older generations, on the other hand, are condemned to the status of 'digital immigrant', who will always have a less assured relationship with technology. Prensky's contentions and the binary oppositions they encapsulate have been widely challenged (Jones, 2011; Margaryan, Littlejohn and Vojt, 2011), and it has been suggested that, far from being a 'generation', the 'digital native' is rather the current representative of an elite group, whilst those with historically limited access to education are liable to see their marginality reinforced by practices which assume them to have constant access to, and mastery of, connective technologies (Brown and Czierniewicz, 2010; Selwyn, 2009).

Although there is evidence to the effect that even superficially experienced student users of technology 'lack the intellectual tools to think critically about much of their experience' (Anderson, 2008, p. 200), and despite the fact that the technology-enhanced practice that accompanies conceptualizations such as the 'digital native' can be profoundly disempowering to both learners and teachers (Bayne and Ross 2007), and regardless of what Selwyn (2009) describes as "the obvious shortcomings of the transformatory and empowering rhetoric of the digital native literature" in informing and guiding the actions of policymakers and practitioners (p. 374); versions of the 'digital natives' idea have found their way into much thinking about teaching and learning in higher education. In higher education contexts in which there is less of a historically grounded conception of learners (or, indeed, a claim that they are part of a wholly 'new generation') conceptions of the learner as digital native, customer, or 'user' of online services become very powerful. What may have begun as a set of analytic categories have progressively come to define normative conceptions of the '21st century learner' and shape institutional responses to their perceived preferences, aptitudes and needs (see, e.g., Currant, Currant and Hartley, 2010, for a typology of 'Generation Y' learners). What is most problematic about such developments is that they are grounded in the perceived or reported relationships between learners and technologies, many of which (like 'social software') were not initially developed with pedagogical applications in mind, and for which, while there are 'enablers' for their adoption, there are far fewer pedagogical 'drivers' (Armstrong and Franklin, 2008; CLEX, 2009).

A third premise relates to research into learning technologies, which is similarly disempowered and circumscribed by a view of research itself as being primarily concerned with the assessment of the potential of externally generated technologies to be seamlessly embedded into learner experience, and of how this is to be achieved. Sharpe and Beetham (2010) talk about 'creative appropriation' of learning technologies but use the term to mean mastery, subsumption and embedding, the aim being to aid learners in developing 'strategies [that] have been adopted and practised to the extent that the choices involved become unconscious'; and Ellis and Goodyear's 'ecological model' (2009), although presenting examples of how technologies can indeed enhance and transform learner experience, still emphasizes stabilization and 'embedding' of technologies within 'resilient' infrastructures where the role of research is to monitor effectiveness and inform decision making. While the aims of dialogue, informed decision making and resilience are laudable, the current situation in higher education systems is anything but 'stable', and what might have seemed only recently to have been successfully embedded and sustainable may now be much more precarious.

Learning Technologies in Times of Crisis

Regardless of the debates around these premises, the image of the technology-enhanced university offering flexible support for digitally adept learners has, in the current climate of students-as-customers and 'efficiency savings' by institutions, gone from being part of a phenomenon driven by changing user expectations to being part of the 'solution' to crisis which brings with it both economic and educational advantages. John Stone (2010, online) articulates this position:

> The delivery of technology-enabled distance learning instead of, or alongside traditional face-to-face tuition potentially brings many benefits, both educationally, and in terms of cost-efficiency. For the learner, it can foster development of a wide-range of skills, such as independent enquiry, self-management as well as technological awareness and media literacy. For the institution, it delivers well-reported cost-efficiencies.

Accompanying this image of learner 'self-management' is the 'packetization' of work described by Berardi (2005) as characteristic of many technology-rich environments in which the fundamental unit of capital is no longer the 'person' or the 'job' but the 'packet' of time or content that is 'separated from their interchangeable and occasional bearers'. This is very much the reality in higher education systems in which hourly-paid posts are replacing full-time and tenured ones and temporary 'online tutors' are recruited to mediate and support student interactions in virtual environments. But alongside this packetization of labour is a broader tendency by which the deepening integration of higher education into cognitive capital depends on and reinforces an image of 'knowledge-as-product' (Dyer-Witheford, 2005). Learning technologies, including those characterized as 'Web 2.0' applications are seen as playing a critical role in this: their content, the processes by which they are produced, and the nature of the learner interactions they encourage and enable all represent varieties of packetization.

This is not to say that online learning content cannot be of high quality, or that trends towards 'openness', such as MIT's 'Open Courseware' initiative (Carson, 2009) or recent interest in 'Open Educational Resources' more generally, are not encouraging developments: their potential role in informal education, in encouraging access to higher education, and in lifelong learning settings has been well documented (see, e.g., Hylén, 2006). But against a background in which the curriculum is being reduced to knowledge-as-product and pedagogy to the provision of those products for self-directed access by learners, even those resources originally envisaged as elements of rich, discursive learning environments may be repurposed as low-cost alternatives to providing space and time for interaction with teacher and other learners.

In a recent interview with the BBC, Jim Knight, Minister of State for Schools and Learners under the UK Labour Administration and a commentator on learning technologies, presented a vision of higher education in which technologies provide the 'peer-to-peer' learning enabled by VLEs and Web 2.0 environments:

> We should be looking at perhaps more of an American model, where you do the first year or two of your degree from home at a community college...and you only go to finish off when you really need access to the research, your senior lecturer, your

> director of studies face to face. Until that point you can do it at distance, having peer-to-peer learning and using some of the things we are used to, like social networking, for exchanges of ideas and papers.

And at the same time, online content provides access to expertise and excellence:

> Why would you go along to a university and hear someone who may or may not be the best in their field when you can go on to iTunes-U and hear a lecture by the very best? (Knight, cited in BBC, 2011)

Again we see a powerful rhetoric of self-direction and 'just-in-time' learning, now conflated with the quality of knowledge-as-objects as measurable (the 'very best' academics delivering superior content via iTunes); and with technological infrastructures providing low-cost ways of transmitting this high quality but 'pedagogically-neutral' learning content, enlivened by the perceived tools of choice of the current generation of 'digital natives'. For all of the '21st century' rhetoric, what remains of pedagogy has Gradgrindian resonances, with a technologically enabled 'monitor system' alongside the online delivery of 'gallons of facts' into waiting vessels.[2]

It seems reasonable to suggest (both on the grounds of the quotation that opened this chapter and on the basis of their writing relating to education more generally) that Deleuze and Guattari would, indeed, regard this situation as 'a disaster'. Given that their ideas have themselves been selectively appropriated both to analyze online technologies and the social formations that accompany them, and to justify new conceptualizations of learners, we should perhaps explore further what they offer as a basis for alternative envisionings of technology-enhanced learning in higher education. In doing so, we need to go beyond ideas that learning technologies, hypertexts and the Internet as a whole are essentially rhizomic: rather, the emphasis needs to be on the lacunae and interstices in their structures which are formed as previously stable and striated formations are disrupted by systemic changes.

Knight's comments, reported above, are typical of responses to the current crisis education in that they present appealing images of technologically enabled *laterality* (sharing, peer-learning, and social networking) but that at the same time reinforce *hierarchy* (elitism, representation, and transmission). But do Guattari's notions of subjectivity and transversality, by contrast, offer another way of thinking about learning technologies and the role that they might play in pedagogical practice? What might the work of a 'subject group' involve, what might happen in the holey spaces where room for transverse practices can be carved out?

Transversality and Innovation: Dance and Semantic Technologies

We offer here an illustrative example of transverse practices from a recent research and development project in which new Web technologies were being developed and deployed but so too were new pedagogical practices and discourses. And while this is about what is ostensibly 'classroom practice', what emerged involved a heterogeneous group of teachers, students and technologists creating a space that transcended the classroom, a view of the curriculum as more than representation and reproduction, and allowed the initiation of new kinds of reflection on practice.

We are conscious that we do not wish to present these approaches as panacea or as 'best practice' to be slavishly followed, and it is worth pointing up several important challenges. The first relates to the status of this account itself and the extent to which anything that is as sensitive to local conditions as a transverse, self-directing subject group can be generalized. This is a general issue for approaches informed by Deleuzo-Guattarian positions (not just in education but in political and social projects more generally): namely, the 'incommunicability' of the microhistories and microsociologies that emerge in smooth, nomad and holey spaces, as any kind of generalization or reproduction would therefore constitute a striating force, molarizing the molecular and overcoding local subjectivities (Bonta and Protevi, 2004, p. 145; see also Hardt and Negri, 2001, p. 54).

The other important issue is that pedagogical practice informed by transversality encourages critical interrogation of subject matter, intended learning outcomes and the material practices of the learning environment, including, of course, the nature and role of the technologies within them. Following Burbules (2000), *aporias* and moments of confusion are tolerated, recognized, and seen as opportunities to take stock, review, decide future direction and critique pedagogical practice. And this is characteristic, according to Guattari's account, of the transverse subject group at work: transversality engenders 'risk-taking' and in higher education may demand that both teachers and learners surrender any special claims to power and knowledge, while demanding that they remain engaged with the group's activities.

In the course of a large research and development project, 'Ensemble',[3] a group of university teachers, students, researchers and technologists have worked together for 18 months to explore the potential of emerging 'semantic web' technologies to support and enhance teaching, learning and performance in undergraduate Contemporary Dance. Semantic Web technologies enable 'linking' of heterogeneous data from around the Internet (as well as from local sources); these data are then typically presented to users using a range of visualizations such as maps, timelines, galleries and 'faceted search' tools (Bizer,

Heath, and Berners-Lee, 2010). The potential for these technologies to be used in support of teaching and learning has been recognized; part of the role of the 'Ensemble' project is to explore enablers, drivers, barriers and applications of these in different educational settings. Contemporary Dance is one of six research settings across three universities that have been involved with the project (others include undergraduate and postgraduate settings in Pure and Applied Sciences; Maritime Operations and Management; and Education Studies). There have been aspects of 'transverse working' in each of these settings, with, for example, students and teachers working alongside software designers; students being employed by the project as researchers; and teachers learning to use new Web technologies; but our experiences in Contemporary Dance have been particularly interesting in terms of the pedagogical practices and discourses of transversality that already existed and have emerged in the course of learning technology developments, so this is presented here as an illustration of more broadly applicable approaches and findings.

Teachers and students in undergraduate Contemporary Dance already had experience and expertise in the use of network technologies to support teaching, learning and performance, most notably through the development of a final year course in 'telematic performance' (Brooks and Kahlich, 2009), in which students used webcams to collaborate across sites, not only for tutorial purposes but also as a critical element in their performances. What emerged from initial discussions with staff and students was a picture of expansive and rapidly developing learning environments devoted to the production of a 'telematic performance' over a period of several months, and within which not only the video link but also a range of other learning and generic technologies played a role, including a 'site' within the institutional VLE; video editing and hosting services; instant messaging; social software and personal Web sites developed by the students themselves.

Two particular episodes give a flavour of the processes of learning, research and development that took place. The first was a weekly review session in which a group of students took part in a participatory design 'workshop' which included 'paper prototyping' of Web applications and other activities in order to explore how semantic Web technologies might be integrated into their practice. In the course of these, the students drew on their experiences: in the telematic dance course, in other learning environments, and in the informal and 'social' use of technologies. In some cases, they referred directly to the sources (and benefits and drawbacks) of these (e.g., annotation tools like the picture 'tagging' from social software applications, or the management of access and privacy settings familiar from the VLE), but they also suggested more ambitious innovations: 'Is there a way it could do this? Could you combine these features?' And, most tellingly, 'If the technology could do this, we would be able to...'. What was happening even at this stage was a rethinking of what technologies might offer in the context of a specialized, situated kind of learning: adoption, design and development clearly in the pursuit of, but also contributing to, emergent pedagogical and professional discourses.

What was also notable was that this session was not understood by teachers or students to be about something in any way separate from their *learning*: for these students, assessing the potential of technologies and envisioning how they might contribute to their current project and their future professional practice were legitimate and highly valued learning activities. Both they and the teachers also saw these activities as contributing to their individual learning and to a collective capacity to use technologies in learning that would have implications and effects more widely across the institution and in future teaching, learning and performances.

The second episode came a few months later, by which time a series of prototypes had been built in the light of some of the suggestions from the earlier design activities. Students had participated in the development processes and had also contributed content, in one example, to an interactive photo gallery application, which allowed them to sort images from different parts of their performances and to relate these to key concepts in Contemporary Dance. This application had been well received by the teaching staff and had been demonstrated to learning technologists outside the project team, where it had been received with some enthusiasm. Now it was introduced into a small-class meeting including several new dance students who were about to embark on the telematic dance course. While these students were interested and impressed by the gallery viewer, having discovered that this was a prototype and could be developed in different directions, they were quick to offer constructive critique. 'That's all right', said one, 'but what we *really* want is something that lets us link *those tags* [and she indicated the existing prototype] to bits of the videos we watch in class. Like this...' and she began to sketch a differently configured Web application, the central element of which was the kind of video controller familiar from video sharing Web sites such as YouTube. Through further discussion involving students, teachers and a software developer, the group's priorities shifted; a new direction was identified; a different technological assemblage was defined; and its pedagogical affordances began to unfold.

This is more than the selective appropriation of emergent technologies for incorporation and stabilization within an established technological environment, in the way that some 'Web 2.0' features have appeared in institutional VLE platforms, although often without a clear pedagogical rationale

(McLoughlin and Lee, 2007; Hemmi, Bayne, and Land, 2009). Transverse working encourages the kind of innovation that Virno, drawing on Schumpeter, describes as 'entrepreneurship': disruptive of existing ways of thinking and practicing, potentially risky, directed yet unpredictable, but also grounded in critical reflection on experience.[4] Rather than simply 'problem solving' within given parameters:

> the entrepreneur stakes all her/his chips on the polysemy of the available elements. S/he breaks with the 'state of equilibrium' and differently combines elements that have been available all along...at stake here is not the quantity or quality of productive factors, but the modification of their form. (Virno, 2008, p. 147)

Our experiences on Ensemble also suggest that, while the focus of the discussions of the transverse group might be the development and use of learning technologies, it is not just technologies that are being 'extracted' and combined in new ways. The entrepreneurial, counterfactual 'what if' reasoning of teacher and students in Contemporary Dance, for example, ranged across pedagogical practices, choreographic techniques, patterns of discourse and material resources (images, music, texts) from many sources. So one of the outcomes of the shift in emphasis in thinking about the learning technologies (from collection management to rich annotation of video content) was the subsequent impact it had on teacher and student thinking about the content, scope and audience for the 'electronic portfolios' that the students produced as part of another course, and with which they not only demonstrated their competences but also positioned themselves as newly qualified professionals.

In this kind of technology-enhanced learning environment, everything is open to scrutiny, including existing ways of working and what have previously been the hegemonic discourses of the institution, the discipline and the learning environment. Roles and responsibilities, as much as the subject matter, are debated, and following Guattari, the group constantly questions its direction. Design, development, evaluation and agreement of future directions are all part of a broader learning process driven by pedagogical commitments and concerns that are in turn open to debate and critique.

As in later characterizations of the rhizome, Guattari (1984) recognizes the interconnectedness of every element in a heterarchic network: so individual transformation or group formation has the potential to change the organization as a whole. The heterogeneity of the networks across which these debates range also extends to a social aspect which draws in the existing connections, past associations and 'weak ties' of the personal networks of participants: so what emerges is not just as an isolated technological construction with a 'user group' but a new social-material-methodological assemblage with the potential for uptake across other transverse groupings. This is not about the molarizing 'embedding' or adoption of 'best practice' but rather the transverse appropriation, territorialization and remaking of elements of the work of one transverse group by another. And how this happens is unpredictable and 'entrepreneurial': within the Ensemble project, sometimes what is recognized as promising and worthy of the attention of a new group is the technological artifact (the Web site, the visualization tool, the interface, the online resource), but just as often it is the pedagogical practice or the design activity that we have seen adopted and taking on a new form in a different setting.

Concluding Remarks: Shifting the Locus of Innovation

What we have presented in our account relocates learning technologies not as a mechanism for collaboration or curriculum delivery but as part of the object of educational inquiry, a change that demands a central role for pedagogy and the discourses that accompany this kind of critical inquiry. This is a different strategy from deployments of technologies that (by design or in practice) restrict, constrain and striate, and within which teachers and students then struggle to engage in flexible and generative learning activities. This is not to say that it is impossible to critically examine these systems or for interesting 'repurposings' of institutional technology systems to take place, of course, but a combination of technological, organizational and pedagogical factors may militate against this happening.

In the same way, it goes beyond encouraging appropriation of social software or other recent developments in order to engage with students, either on the part of individual teachers or by the providers of institutional systems, but to leave other aspects (curriculum content, assessment, and the power relations of the classroom) untouched. The point here is not that appropriation is limited to working with the scraps from the technological table, but rather a qualitative shift in the locus of innovation. This cannot be achieved solely by a change of focus in the curriculum but demands the restoration of the centrality of pedagogical discourses that extend to the nature, use and non-use and potential of technologies. As Virno suggests, the notion of innovation itself needs to be 're-appropriated' so that it means more than 'willingness to adopt' and instead is understood as a principled entrepreneurship in pursuit of discursively constructed pedagogical aims.

As the role of learning technologies is reconsidered in the face of institutional and sectorwide constraints, there are opportunities for this to occur, whether through research and development projects (as in our case), as part of the redesign of curricula, courses and assessment systems, or through other mechanisms by which subject groups can be established. Key to this is a willingness to engage in the 'long conversations' that Guattari identifies as critical to transversality; initially restrictive organizational forms themselves can be appropriated and become self-directing and expansive, and we have been heartened, in the example of the contemporary dance teachers and students introduced above, by the enthusiasm to 'continue the work' and advance both the technological developments and their applications in new performances and pedagogical activities, and to apply them beyond the university to community projects.

This positions the role of learning technologies and the design and development processes by which they come into being not as something that either replicates the habitual and assists in the delivery of a curriculum founded in representation and reproduction, but instead that allows and encourages the envisioning of divergent trajectories and poses challenging and existential questions. In our example of Contemporary Dance, these are not limited to 'How might this technology support our practice as teachers or performers?' but extend to 'What might it mean to be a teacher or performer in an uncertain future, and how might these technological developments and accompanying discourses shape that?' The emphasis here is not upon effecting change with the intention of achieving the stability or equilibrium as suggested by Ellis and Goodyear (2009). Instead, as Pelljero (2009) suggests, the object is not the fulfillment of some utopian possibility, but a commitment to pedagogical and social practices that encourage continuing divergence and 'multiplication of perspectives' (p. 106). The role of small-scale innovations (such as the example we have presented, or initiated by other kinds of transverse subject groupings) is not then to produce something with an eye to 'scaling up' to institutional or sector level, but rather to make the case for the location of participatory design, development and evaluation of technologies as ongoing processes within situated, locally remade and relational pedagogical practice.

At the risk of slipping the language of self-improvement coaching and suggesting that 'where others see problems we see opportunities', we would argue that organizational upheavals do provide spaces where transversality can emerge and this multiplication of perspectives can occur. Even in straitened circumstances, universities and the capitalist system that supports them necessarily tolerates academic innovation and divergence as long as its inevitable troublesomeness is outweighed by its apparent or potential usefulness (Ticktin, 2009). Dyer-Witheford suggests that, as new stabilizations and striations emerge, so do new lacunae and interstices in their structures which allow for the formation of transverse groupings, which ultimately have the potential to act as divergent counter forces to the same hierarchical processes which fostered them (2005, p. 77). Significantly, the problematic and still-emergent role of learning technologies, when combined with the uncertainties that persist as to their 'usefulness', means that more expansive, cross-curricular and democratic groups are probably easier to form around technological themes than around other issues. One is more likely, for example, to find student voices represented in advisory groups (within which may reside the germs of transverse activity) on technologies than on those concerned with assessment, quality assurance or university governance. But at the same time, such openings need to be fully exploited: in the absence of radical, innovative, transverse thinking, we may be left with a technologically rich but pedagogically impoverished 'lowest-common denominator' version of higher education for the majority of students.

In the UK, at the time of writing, we are experiencing not simply an institutional but a sectorwide *aporia:* we are facing reductions in funding across the board and we do not know the effects of changes in the funding of teacher education and other vocational courses, still less the impact of increased student fees on recruitment or the expectations of the students who will enter UK higher education after 2012. And the role of technologies in learning is, as we have seen, central to the debates about the priorities, shape and patterns of participation in higher education. In such circumstances, the notion of transversality extends beyond individual classrooms and research projects of the kind we have described here, and it can be used to reframe Peters' question about the aspects of the historical university and the possibilities of future universities we might wish to extract and combine. Positioning learning technologies not just as part of the infrastructure of universities but as the focus of transverse working and discussions *about* pedagogy provides a means of initiating more wide-ranging discussions: about how elements of the Kantian, Humboldtian and Leavisite visions of the university identified by Peters can be extracted and incorporated in a way that is responsive to 'massification'; where learning environments promote critical engagement with new technologies; and which contribute to multiple, generative and excitingly unpredictable models of learning in higher education that have pedagogy firmly at their core.

Acknowledgments

The empirical work reported in this paper was funded under ESRC/EPSRC Research Grant RES-139-25-0403 ('Ensemble: Semantic Technologies for the Enhancement of Case Based Learning'). We are grateful for the participation of the teachers and students who participated and to our colleagues, in particular, Pauline Brooks, Augustina Martinez-Garcia, Simon Morris and Fran Tracy.

Notes

1. We are using here the term 'Technology Enhanced Learning' (TEL) rather than the more common 'e-Learning' as the former, more expansive term includes not only 'distance learning' applications of technologies but also their use within learning environments, including libraries, classrooms, laboratories, studios, fieldwork settings and workplaces. The term is also preferred as it suggests a more complex relationship between the technology and learning (although the notion of 'enhancement' remains subjective, situated and often problematic).
2. Mr. Gradgrind is featured in Charles Dickens's *Hard Times* (1854). A parodic representation of the utilitarianism, he is a businessman who sees the primary purpose of education as being the acquisition of "facts, not fancy" and learners as empty pitchers to be filled with knowledge.
3. Ensemble: Semantic Technologies for the Enhancement of Case Based Learning: (http://www.ensemble.ac.uk), funded under the Technology-Enhanced Learning Programme of the UK Economic and Social Research Council and Engineering and Physical Sciences Research Council.
4. Virno is clear that his understanding of entrepreneurship is distinct from what he sees as a capitalist appropriation and bowdlerization of the term. Think here of Trevor Baylis and his development of the 'clockwork radio' to disseminate health information in Africa, rather than Donald Trump or Alan Sugar.

References

Anderson, B. (2008). Social Networking in Higher Education. In R. N. Katz (Ed.), *The Tower and the Cloud: Higher Education in the Age of Cloud Computing*. Boulder, CO: Educause.

Armstrong, J., & Franklin, T. (2008). *A Review of Current and Developing International Practice in the Use of Social Networking (Web 2.0) in Higher Education*. Manchester: Franklin Consulting.

Bayne, S. (2004). Smoothness and Striation in Digital Learning Spaces. *E-learning*, 1(2), 302–16.

Bayne, S., and Ross, J. (2007). *The "digital native" and "digital immigrant": A dangerous opposition*. Paper presented at Society for Research in Higher Education Conference, Newport, UK, December 2009.

BBC. (2011). Going to Harvard from your own bedroom. BBC News—Business, 21 March 2011. Retrieved Aug 25, 2011, from http://www.bbc.co.uk/news/business-12766562.

Berardi, F. (2005). *Info-Labour and Precarisation* Translate—Beyond Culture: The Politics of Translation. Retrieved May 1, 2011, from http://eipcp.net/transversal/0704/bifo/en.

Bizer, C., Heath, T., and Berners-Lee, T. (2009). Linked Data—The Story So Far. *International Journal on Semantic Web and Information Systems*, 5(3), 1–22.

Bonta, M., and Protevi, J. (2004). *Deleuze and Geophilosophy: A Guide and Glossary*. Edinburgh: Edinburgh University Press.

Brooks, P., and Kahlich, L. (2009). Reflections on a Two-Year Joint International Project Using

Web-Cam Technology to Create New Opportunities for Student Choreographic Collaborations. *Innovations in Practice*, 2(1), 41–48.

Brown, C., and Czierniewicz, L. (2010). Debunking the "Digital Native": Beyond Digital Apartheid, towards Digital Democracy. *Journal of Computer Assisted Learning*, 26(5), 357–69.

Burbules, N. (2000). Aporias, Webs, and Passages: Doubt as an Opportunity to Learn. *Curriculum Inquiry*, 30(2), 171–87.

Carmichael, P., and Burchmore, H. (2010). Social Software and Academic Practice: Postgraduate Students as Co-Designers of Web 2.0 Tools. *The Internet and Higher Education*, 14(3), 233–41.

Carson, S. (2009). The Unwalled Garden: Growth of the OpenCourseware Consortium, 2001–2008. *Open Learning: The Journal of Open, Distance and e-Learning*, 24(1), 23–29.

Committee of Inquiry into the Changing Learner Experience. (2009). Higher Education in a Web 2.0 World: Report of an Independent Committee of Inquiry into the Impact on Higher Education of Students' Widespread Use of Web 2.0 Technologies. Bristol, England: Committee of Inquiry into the Changing Learner Experience.

Conole, G., and Dyke, M. (2004). What are the Affordances of Information and Communication Technologies? *Research in Learning Technology*, 12(2), 113–24.

Currant, N., Currant, B. and Hartley, P. (2010). Defining and Supporting the New Digital Student. In P. Hartley, J. Hilsdon, S. Sinfield, C. Keenan, and M. Verity (Eds.), *Learning Development in Higher Education* (pp. 212-224). Basingstoke, England: Palgrave.

Deleuze, G., and Guattari, F. (1994). *What Is Philosophy?* London: Verso.

Dyer-Witheford, N. (2005). Cognitive Capitalism and the Contested Campus. In G. Cox and J. Krysa (Eds.), *Engineering Culture: On the Author as (Digital) Producer* (pp. 71–93). Brooklyn, NY: Autonomedia.

Ellis, R., and Goodyear, P. (2009). *Students' Experiences of E-Learning in Higher Education: The Ecology of Sustainable Innovation.* London: Routledge.

Guattari, F. (1984). *Molecular Revolution: Psychiatry and Politics.* Harmondsworth: Penguin Books.

Hardt, M., and Negri, A. (2001). *Empire.* Cambridge, MA: Harvard University Press.

Hemmi, A., Bayne, S., and Land, R. (2009). The Appropriation and Repurposing of Social Technologies in Higher Education. *Journal of Computer Assisted Learning*, 25, 19–30.

Hylén, J. (2006). *Open Educational Resources: Opportunities and Challenges.* Paris: OECD Center for Educational Research and Innovation.

Jones, C. (2011). First Year University Students and New Technologies: A Complex Picture with no Evidence of a Net Generation of Digital Natives. Paper presented at Computer Assisted Learning Conference, CAL 2011, Manchester, UK, April 2011.

Margaryan, A., Littlejohn, A., and Vojt, G. (2011). Are Digital Natives a Myth or Reality? University Students' Use of Digital Technologies. *Computers and Education*, 56, 429-440.

McLoughlin, C., and Lee, M. J. W. (2007). Social Software and Participatory Learning: Pedagogical Choices with Technology Affordances in the Web 2.0 Era. Paper presented at ASCILITE 2007, Singapore, December 2007.

Pelljero, E. (2009) Minor Marxism: An Approach to a New Political Praxis. *Deleuze Studies*, 3 (Supplement: 'Deleuze and Marx'), 102–18.

Peters, M. (2005). The Posthistorical University? Prospects for Alternative Globalisations. In G. Fischman, P. McLaren, H. Sünker, and C. Lankshear (Eds.), *Critical Theories, Radical*

Pedagogies and Global Conflicts (pp. 69–86). Lanham, MD: Rowman & Littlefield.

Peters, M. (2007). *Knowledge Economy, Development and the Future of Higher Education*. Rotterdam: Sense Publishers.

Prensky, M. (2001). Digital Natives, Digital Immigrants. *On the Horizon 9 (5)*, 1-6.

Selwyn, N. (2009). The Digital Native–Myth and Reality. ASLIB Proceedings: New Information Perspectives, 61(4), 364–79.

Sharpe, R., and Beetham, H. (2010). Understanding Students' Uses of Technology for Learning: Towards Creative Appropriation. In R. Sharpe, H. Beetham, and S. deFreitas (Eds.), *Rethinking Learning for the Digital Age: How Learners Shape Their Experiences*. London: Routledge Falmer.

Stone, J. (2010). Technology Revolution Is the Way for Education to Deliver through the Cuts. ALT-N, 21, Retrieved Aug 25, 2011, from http://archive.alt.ac.uk/newsletter.alt.ac.uk/ervn69imqm5.html.

Ticktin, H. (2009). A Marxist Theory of Freedom of Expression. *Critique* 37(4), 513-530.

Suoranta, J., Tomperi, T., and Fitzsimmons, R. (2005). Revolutionary Pedagogy in Media Culture. In G. Fischman, P. McLaren, H. Sünker, and C. Lankshear (Eds.), *Critical Theories, Radical Pedagogies and Global Conflicts* (pp. 185–206). Lanham, MD: Rowman & Littlefield.

Virno, P. (2008). *Multitude: Between Innovation and Negation*. Cambridge, MA: Semiotext(e) and MIT Press.

• PART TWO •

Case Studies of Argentina

• CHAPTER SEVEN •

When the Sun Does not Shine after the Rain: The Effects of the 2001 Crisis on the Educational System of Argentina

Silvina Gvirtz & Ana Laura Barudi

Introduction

Towards the end of 2001 Argentina experienced a crisis that would come to be known as one of the worst in its history. The dire economic and financial situation which affected the entire political and social system had been building up for at least four years. This unfavorable context also affected variables in education. We propose to describe and analyze the effects of the crisis on education by simultaneously reviewing the three dimensions described above. First, internal efficiency of the system is discussed based on changes in enrolment, repetition and dropout rates at primary and secondary school levels. Second, academic performance is analyzed based on student achievement tests in reading, mathematics and science through OECD's Program for International Student Assessment (PISA). Finally, we will examine variations in material conditions such as government investment in education (in relation to public spending) and instructional time (based on the number of school hours and days a year) which allow the education process to develop.

The study aims at a description of changes in the country's education system before and after the economic and financial debacle of 2001–2002, as a first step to future research on the topic to generate more advanced conclusions. The central hypothesis is that system performance measured through evaluation of internal efficiency, academic performance and teaching and learning material conditions significantly worsened after the crisis. And that although Argentina's economy showed signs of significant reactivation beginning in 2003, the education system recovered much more slowly, with noticeable signs of improvement observed only after 2005. Economic recovery would seem to require less time to bounce back than the time needed for the educational system to recover.

The Crisis: End of 2001, Beginning of 2002

During most of the 1990s, Argentina was widely considered by the international community as a successful model of neoliberal reform in a developing country. Although unemployment rates were high and many social problems remained unresolved, significant economic development was achieved, with growth surpassing regional Latin American averages between 1991 and 1998, resulting in large scale foreign investment and the elimination of years of endemic inflation (Chudnovsky, López and Pupato, 2003).

Nevertheless, in 1998, the country hit a recession which, after a series of misguided government policies, quickly became an economic depression lasting four years, during which time the general economy shrank by 28% (Saxton, 2003). As a result of these events, and further compounded by another set of poor political decision making, at the end of 2001, Argentina suffered a severe economic and financial crisis which affected the entire social and political system. Unfortunately, "throughout 2002, it became evident that the significant economic reforms introduced in the nineties, although generating a brief period of growth, had not resulted in the country's much awaited development" (PNUD, 2003, p. 10).

According to Saxton (2003) several external factors triggered the recession. Between 1997 and 1998, two separate crises hit, one in Southeast Asia and one in Russia, both decidedly affecting the stagnation and ultimate collapse of Argentine trade and commerce, particularly with Brazil. The author also described how a budding economic recovery in late 1999 and 2000 was killed by heavy government tax increases in 2000 and 2001. Later that year, government authorities announced a preferential exchange rate for exports which backfired, evaporating any remaining confidence in Argentine government finances. Interest rates in dollars skyrocketed, causing many investors to fear default on foreign public debt. Saxton concludes: "The government was in a 'debt trap': at the interest rates it faced, its debt would quickly grow beyond the capacity of the Argentine economy for repayment" (Saxton, 2003, p. 34).

Gradual capital flight accelerated towards the end of the crisis, explaining how better-informed international and local investors were not entirely taken by surprise by the crisis (Chudnovsky, López and Pupato, 2003). To counter the savings drain already in motion, the government imposed bank withdrawal restrictions on citizens early in December 2001, which in turn triggered massive civilian demonstrations and riots, ultimately leading to the resignation of then president of Argentina Fernando de la Rúa late in December 2001. In just over two weeks, and after successive provisional presidencies, the government defaulted on its foreign debt with private-sector investors, access to frozen deposits was reestablished, putting an end to the convertibility model and the peso's longstanding link to the dollar, based on a fixed 1:1 exchange rate. Local investors paid the price of forced conversion of dollar deposits and loans into Argentine pesos at unfavorable rates and voiding of contracts. The measures, however, had a strong calming effect on certain sectors of the population. Notwithstanding, problems persisted, generating strong negative impact on the general well-being of most citizens.

During 2002, economic activity in Argentina fell to an all-time low. GDP, for example, fell to just under 11% and private spending 15% (National Census and Statistics Institute [INDEC], 2003), resulting in a serious fall in social indicators. The National Ministry of Economy issued a statement indicating: "Unemployment rates reached 21.5% in May 2002 for all urban conglomerates, and population levels under the poverty line surpassed even hyperinflation records from the early nineties" (2003, p. 1). Chudnovsky, López and Pupato (2003) actually believe that "between May 2001 and May 2002, six million new members joined the ranks of the poor in Argentina, causing the proportion of Argentines below the officially defined poverty line to reach 53%, 24% of whom were living under indigent conditions." In light of the current analysis, it is also important to point out that, according to United Nations Development Program estimations, on average 15,000 people a day fell below the poverty line between October 2001 and June 2002, and one in three were children under 18 (PNUD, 2003, p. 33).

By the end of 2002, the economic decline had begun to slow down, and progressive recovery was observed, in spite of unstable financial and monetary conditions. However, even as the crisis was overcome and strong and steady economic growth began, social indicators still did not show signs of improvement, and poverty and indigence levels, for example, fell only slightly in 2004 and 2005. One of the policies contributing to this gradual rebound, the effects of which were witnessed years after its implementation in early 2002, was the government's Social Aid Program for Unemployed Heads of Households, *Plan Jefes y Jefas de Hogar Desocupados*, with unprecedented coverage from the beginning, helping around two million beneficiaries.

In spite of these measures, Sosa Escudero and Petralia (2010) claim income distribution in Argentina never recovered its pre-crisis patterns. They believe that even after clear signs of economic improvement, in terms of inequality and of median income, poverty did not return back to pre-crisis levels mainly because the poor became a larger, more homogeneous and more stable group than in the 1990s. By the end of 2002, the economy had turned, and employment and salaries showed strong recovery during 2005; however, damage resulting from the 2001–2002 crisis on living conditions would continue to prevail, at least in part, until 2006 (Cosse, 2006).

Crisis Effects on the Education System

One of the social policy areas most affected by the crisis was education. We propose therefore to analyze crisis effects on the Argentine educational system by reviewing three dimensions: internal efficiency, academic performance, and material conditions. In order to establish whether an educational system improves or worsens, these dimensions need to be taken into consideration simultaneously. As an example, if in any given education system, the rate of repeaters decreases, but academic performance tests show students fare more poorly, it cannot be established that this system has improved. There is no doubt that it is important for students to pass on to the next grade level in a timely manner, but this cannot happen at the expense of students not learning content bearing significance, which is what they will require for adequate insertion into society. Similarly, an educational system can hardly be categorized as good, if the results of academic performance testing decline, but the rate of leavers does not, or worse, actually the rate increases.[1] These reasons justify a multidimensional evaluation of the education system for years before, during and after the crisis.

a. Education System Internal Efficiency

Internal efficiency in education systems refers to resource allocation management in the pursuit of results. Several variables exist to measure educational internal efficiency: enrolment, attendance, promotion, repetition, dropout, overage, and so forth. In this analysis we consider three variables of educational internal efficiency par excellence: enrolment, repetition rate and dropout rate.

For decades now, the Argentine educational system has shown signs of considerable expansion, in other words, every year more and more children and adolescents go to school. For example, gross enrolment ratio[2] increased at primary and secondary school levels until recent years. For primary schools the gross enrolment ratio was 106.3% in 1990, 114% in 1999, and 116% in 2007, and for secondary schools the figures were 71.1% in 1990, 85% in 1999, and 85% in 2007 (UNESCO, 2002, 2011). This more extended coverage of the system is usually signaled out as a major achievement of contemporary education policies; however, the stagnation in the gross enrolment ratio in secondary school is an issue that deserves attention:

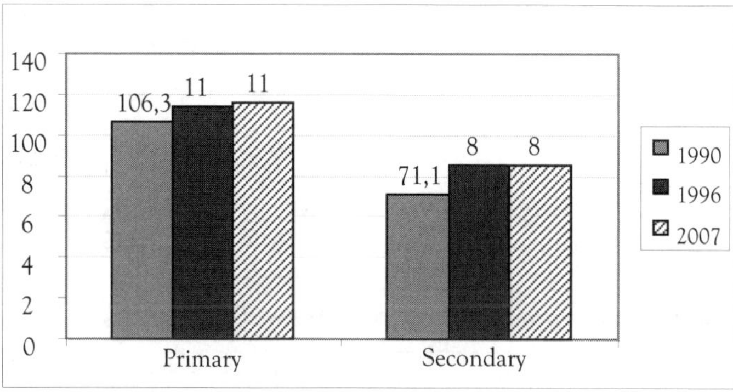

Figure 7.1: Gross enrolment ratio, 1990, 1996 and 2007

This increase in scholarization rates did not translate into equal or quality educational services. Although the system starts to incorporate greater numbers of students, it begins to generate a different type of discrimination: the system is not able to retain students, with problems in the quality of education it provides and unfair distribution of educational goods to different population sectors (Tedesco, 1987). This discrimination continues to occur even today, and it becomes particularly evident through the specific analysis of repetition and dropout rates.

We will now study repetition[3] and inter annual dropout[4] levels observed in the Argentine education system between 1996[5] and 2008, linking their behavior to the 2001–2002 crisis. First let us review primary and secondary school grade repeaters. In general terms, the repetition rate remained more or less constant between 1996 and 2008 at the primary school level (5.52% to 5.18%), and increased considerably for both secondary school cycles and for middle school in particular (from 8.96% to 12.18% in middle school and 5.68% to 7.73% in subject-oriented senior high).

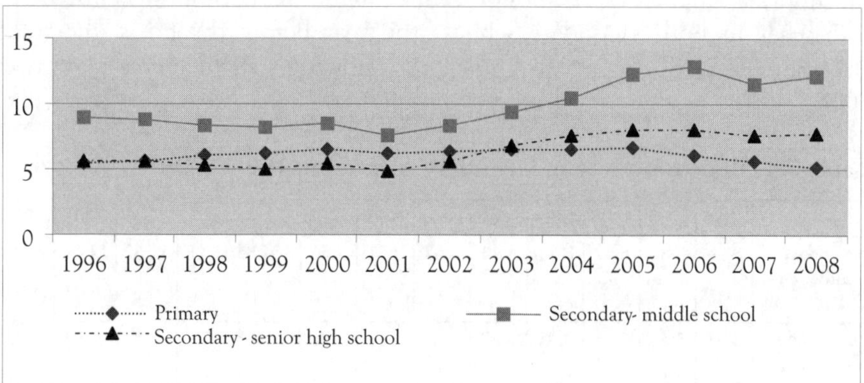

Figure 7.2: Evolution of repetition rate in primary and secondary education, 1996–2008

For primary schools, the repetition rate was, on average, 6.06%, with a minimum of 5.52% in 1996 and a maximum of 6.6% in 2005. Rates increased considerably, 17.57% between 1996 and 2000, dropped 5.08% in 2001, increased once again 5.52% between 2001 and 2003, fell slightly in 2004, increased 2.01% in 2005, and fell 21.51% between 2005 and 2008. Repetition varied in numbers through the years increasing before and after the crisis, showing relatively constant improvement only after 2005.

Table 7.1: Repetition rate in primary education, 1996–2008

	1996	1997	1998	1999	2000	2001	2002	2003	2004	2005	2006	2007	2008
Primary	5.52	5.61	6.02	6.25	6.49	6.16	6.31	6.50	6.47	6.60	6.13	5.57	5.18

Repetition rates at secondary school level present similar and considerable variations for both cycles. On average, repetition rates were 9.79% for middle school, with a minimum of 7.61% in 2001 and a maximum of 12.82% in 2006. This rate dropped 8.37% between 1996 and 1999, increased 2.68% between 1999 and 2000, dropped 9.73% in 2001, increased 68.4% between 2001 and 2006 (it increased 9.20% in 2002, 12.64% in 2003, 10.91% in 2004, 18.3% in 2005, and 4.4% in 2006), fell 9.91% in 2007, and increased 5.45% in 2008. The repetition rates for senior high school were on average 6.42% with a minimum of 4.83% in 2001 and a maximum of 8.09% in 2006. The rate fell 13.20% between 1996 and 1999, increased 2.24% between 1998 and 2000, fell 11.70% in 2001, increased 67.49% between 2001 and 2006 (rising 16.56% in 2002, 21.85% in 2003, 10.49% in 2004, 6.46% in 2005, and 0.25% in 2006), fell 6.67% in 2007, and increased 2.38% in 2008. The largest rises in rates corresponded to those observed during 2005 for middle school and 2003 for senior high. Repetition rates increased somewhat in both secondary schools the year before the crisis, increased again almost 70% after it, up until 2006, showing a slight increase again in 2008.

Table 7.2: Repetition rate in secondary education, 1996–2008

	1996	1997	1998	1999	2000	2001	2002	2003	2004	2005	2006	2007	2008
Secondary–middle school	8.96	8.86	8.32	8.21	8.43	7.61	8.31	9.36	10.38	12.28	12.82	11.55	12.18
Secondary–senior high school	5.68	5.64	5.35	4.93	5.47	4.83	5.63	6.86	7.58	8.07	8.09	7.55	7.73

Second, we shall review inter annual dropout rates at primary and secondary school levels of the Argentine education system between 1996 and 2008. In general terms, inter annual dropout rates fell by a little under 1.5 points between 1996 and 2008 at the primary school level (from 2.59% to 1.16%), a little under 4.5 points for middle school (from 12.77% to 8.43%), and increased just over 2.5 points in senior high (from 15.13% to 17.79%).

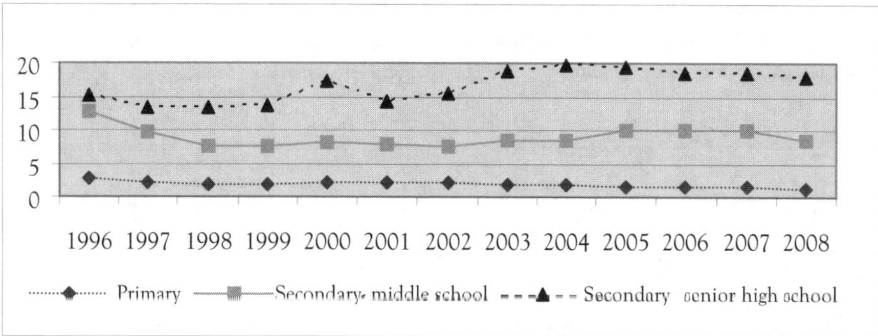

Figure 7.3: Evolution of inter annual dropout rate in primary and secondary education, 1996–2008

In primary schools, the inter annual dropout rate was 1.89% on average, with a maximum percentage of 2.59% in 1996 and a minimum of 1.16% in 2008. The rate fell 26.25% between 1996 and 1998, increased 17.80% between 1998 and 2000, dropped 33.33% between 2000 and 2005, increased slightly in 2006, and dropped 27.5% between 2006 and 2008. Rates of yearly leavers in primary school were slightly less alarming than rates for repeaters but showed wider variation over the years. During the period following the crisis, this rate dropped constantly until it reached 1.5% in 2005, and increased slightly in 2006. The largest variation observed for inter annual dropout rate in primary school was the fall it experienced until reaching its lowest level, 1.16% in 2008.

Table 7.3: Inter-annual dropout rate in primary education, 1996–2008

	1996	1997	1998	1999	2000	2001	2002	2003	2004	2005	2006	2007	2008
Primary	2.59	2.14	1.91	1.96	2.25	2.19	2.18	1.81	1.80	1.50	1.60	1.48	1.16

Inter annual dropout rates in secondary school were more significant and showed greater variation than in primary. The average inter annual dropout rate was 8.94% for middle school, with peak values at 12.77% in 1996 and lowest values of 7.51% observed in 2002. This rate dropped 40.17% between

1996 and 1998, increased 7.85% between 1998 and 2000, dropped 8.86% between 2000 and 2002, and increased again by 32.09% between 2002 and 2006 (8.1% increase in 2003, 1.55% in 2004, 15.57% in 2005, 0.51% in 2006), and fell 15.02% between 2006 and 2008. The average inter annual dropout rate was 16.58% for senior high school, with a minimum value of 13.36% in 1997 and a maximum value of 19.79% in 2004. It fell 10.75% between 1996 and 1997, increased 29.27% between 1997 and 2000, fell 18.18% in 2001, and surged 40.06% between 2001 and 2004 (up 9.98% in 2002, 21.56% in 2003, and 4.76% in 2004), then falling 10.11% between 2004 and 2008. The greatest increase in dropout rates was observed in 2005 for middle school and in 2000 for senior high. The rate for both cycles increased more after the crisis than before: 30% for middle school between 2003 and 2006 and a little more than 40% for the senior high between 2001 and 2004. Also, the rate takes several years to recover and a longer time for middle school.

Table 7.4: Inter annual dropout rate in secondary education, 1996–2008

	1996	1997	1998	1999	2000	2001	2002	2003	2004	2005	2006	2007	2008
Secondary–middle school	12.77	9.64	7.64	7.65	8.24	7.78	7.51	8.41	8.54	9.87	9.92	9.85	8.43
Secondary–senior high school	15.13	13.36	13.41	13.62	17.27	14.13	15.54	18.89	19.79	19.44	18.63	18.55	17.79

To conclude, although every year a larger number of students start school, the internal efficiency of the Argentine education system measured through repetition and inter annual dropout rates was clearly affected after the 2001–2002 crisis, more in the secondary education than in the primary level. Even when these rates had already shown an increase prior to the crisis, especially in yearly dropout rates, these increases were greater during and after the crisis. In other words, larger numbers of students had difficulty passing on to the next grade, and this figure was even higher for secondary students. Repetition rates increased after 2001 in a constant fashion and for several years, both in primary and in secondary school, although the highest rates and increase were observed for middle school. Primary school dropout rates fell in the years immediately following the crisis. Nevertheless, this rate increased in secondary level: after 2002 in the senior and after 2003 in middle school years. The highest dropout rates were seen in senior high, although these begin to decrease slightly in 2005. In this regard, it is interesting to note what Cosse (2006) has to say about secondary schools: education conditions appear to be worse between 2003 and 2004, the crisis exit years, compared to 2001 and 2002, actual years during which the crisis took place. Repetition and dropout rates only begin to improve in 2007: although employment has improved in recent years, poverty levels remain high.

b. Academic Performance in the Educational System

In this section, we will analyze the effects of the 2001–2002 crisis on academic performance by evaluating results of student achievement through the Organization for Economic Cooperation and Development Program (OECD) tests between 1998 and 2009. We will consider student achievement in reading, mathematics and science using the Program for International Student Assessment (PISA) implemented by this organization. We think PISA is the most appropriate test to establish comparisons over time, although it is administered to 15-year-olds in schools and does not focus on elementary education. UNESCO tests that evaluated primary student achievement, PERSE[6] in 1998 and SERCE[7] in 2006, have significant differences that do not allow to compare students' performance between them or to make reliable inferences about the possible progress of countries (UNESCO, 2008, p. 26). Similarly, there are serious limits to validly compare between years the results of the ONE[8] test on academic performance obtained by the Ministry of Education in Argentina (Gvirtz, Larripa and Oelsner, 2006). Mostly for these reasons, we consider only PISA to analyze the academic performance of the Argentine educational system.

We will look at results obtained by Argentina in PISA Plus 2001, PISA 2006, and PISA 2009. PISA 2003 is not included in this analysis because Argentina did not participate that year. Every year PISA centers on a specific subject area. In 2000–2001 it was reading, and 43 countries or economies participated; in 2003 it was math, and 41 countries or economies took part; in 2006 it was sciences, and 57 countries or economies participated. In 2009 it concentrated once again on reading, and 65 countries or economies were involved.

Argentina did not participate in PISA 2000 but instead completed a test called PISA Plus in 2001, implemented in countries that had been unable to participate the year before. Argentina ranked 35th in the test in reading with 418 points, 34th in mathematics with 388 points and 37th in science with 396 points.

For each competence area, PISA has established achievement levels in increasing complexity levels from 1 to 6. Students attaining a certain level demonstrate knowledge and skills for that level as well as for those below it. For example, PISA Plus 2001 results on evaluation of reading literacy indicated 23% of students did not reach the minimum level set by the test. Level 1 was reached by 21% of students, which indicates "serious difficulties using reading literacy as an effective tool to advance and extend their knowledge and skills in other areas" (OCDE/UNESCO, 2003). The largest group of students, 25%, reached level 2, which means students are capable of basic reading tasks, such as locating straightforward information, making low-level inferences of various types, deciding what a well-defined part of the text means, and using some outside knowledge to understand it. Only 9% of students were in level 4 and 2% in level 5; in level 4 students are capable of difficult reading tasks and construing meaning from complex texts, and in level 5 students are capable of more sophisticated reading tasks.

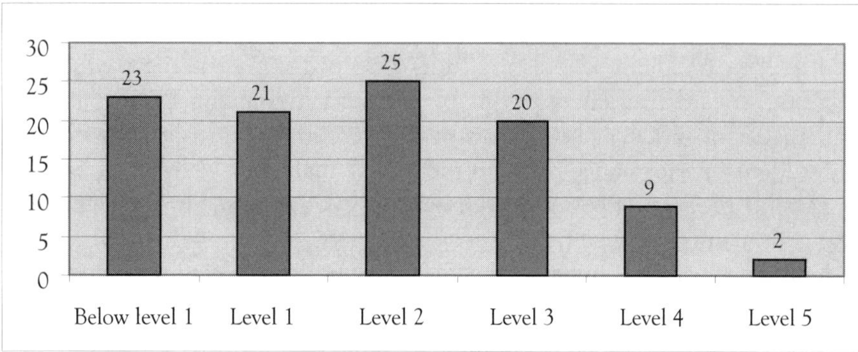

Figure 7.4: Proficiency levels in reading, PISA Plus 2001

In PISA 2006, Argentina obtained 374 points in reading, 381 in mathematics and 391 in science and was ranked in positions 53, 52, and 51, respectively, out of 57 participating countries or economies. In reading, 36% of students obtained results below level 1, 13% more than in 2001, and 22% attained level 1. Proportions of students falling into the remaining categories were all below 2001 levels: 22% in level 2, 14% in level 3,5% in level 4, and 1% in level 5.

Results in mathematics were worse than for reading since 64% of students were at or below the minimum level: 39% below level 1 and 25% at level 1. For the first group this means students will face serious difficulties in the future in order to use math as an effective tool to benefit from new education opportunities and life long learning. In the second case, students are able to solve problems that involve recognition of familiar contexts, in which all pertinent information is made available and questions are clearly stipulated. The proportion of students in the remaining mathematics levels was below reading levels in every case: 20% for level 2, 11% for level 3, 4% for level 4, and 1% for level 5. At level 2 students can interpret and recognize representations of mathematical concepts and begin to develop basic mathematical competences.

In the third level, students can execute clearly described procedures and are able to choose and to apply strategies to solve simple problems. Level 4 requires efficient work with a suitable model for concrete complex situations, and the selection and integration of different tools that link directly to real-life situations. And in level 5, students are expected to develop models and work with them in complex situations, selecting, comparing and evaluating adequate strategies to face problems of this type.

Finally, in science 56% of students reached or were below level 1: 28% were unable to show scientific competence required for the most simple daily life situations proposed by PISA, and a similar percentage of students had only limited scientific knowledge that they could apply in familiar situations, and present simple scientific explanations which were explicit from the evidence given in the study. Level 2 was reached by 26% of students, 14% reached level 3, and 4% reached level 4. This means more than 25% of students are able to give plausible explanations in familiar contexts or establish conclusions based on simple research; that less than 15% can identify scientific problems within a variety of contexts; and that under 5% can analyze problems and situations involving explicit phenomena on the role of science and technology in society.

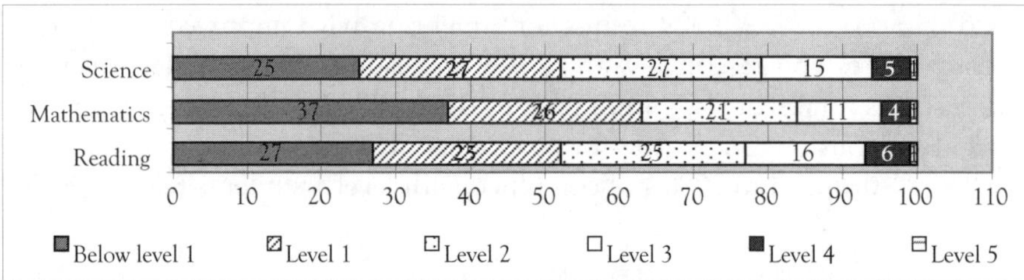

Figure 7.5: Reading, mathematics and science by proficiency levels, PISA 2006

Argentina's results in PISA 2009 improved both in terms of scores as well as ranking among participating countries or economies. In reading Argentina ranked 58th with 398 points, in mathematics 55th with 388 points, and in science 57th with 401 points. With respect to reading results, 27% of students were below level 1, which was 9% less than in 2006. The percentage of students in the remaining levels all increased in comparison to PISA 2006: 25% reached level 1, 25% level 2, 16% level 3, 6% level 4, and 1% level 5. Results for mathematics improved slightly and were distributed as follows: 37% below level 1, 26% level 1, 21% level 2, 11% level 3, 4% level 4, and 1% level 5. In science, improvements were observed given the fact that only 25% of students were below level 1, 27% were at level 1, 27% level 2, 15% level 3, 5% level 4, and 1% were level 5.

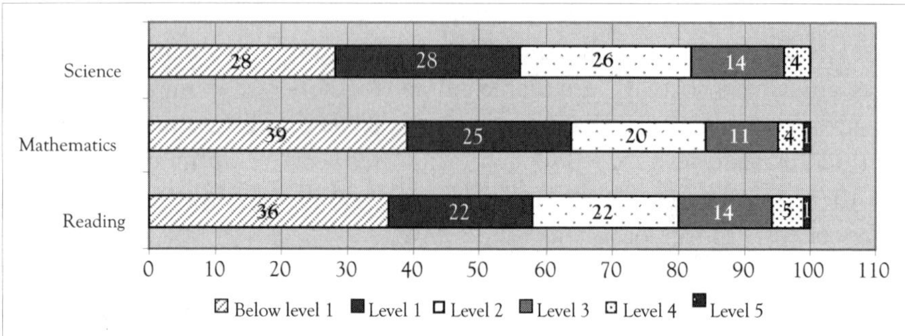

Figure 7.6: Reading, mathematics and science by proficiency levels, PISA 2009

Comparison of results between PISA Plus 2001 and PISA 2006 indicate the situation in Argentina worsened in all three subject areas evaluated both between tests, as well as compared to other countries participating in the evaluation. The most significant decline was seen in reading, where Argentina went from obtaining 418 points in 2001, to 374 points in 2006, and fell in rank from 35/43 to 53/57. This generates even more concern given the fact that 44% of students were level 1 or less in 2001, a figure which reached 57% in 2006. However, PISA 2009 results for Argentina have improved in all areas, both in scores and ranking. With respect to reading, for example, Argentina increased its total score by 24 points compared to 2006, reaching 398, and was ranked 58th out of 65 countries or economies. The percentage of students below level 1 dropped to 27% and combined with level 1 students reached 52%.

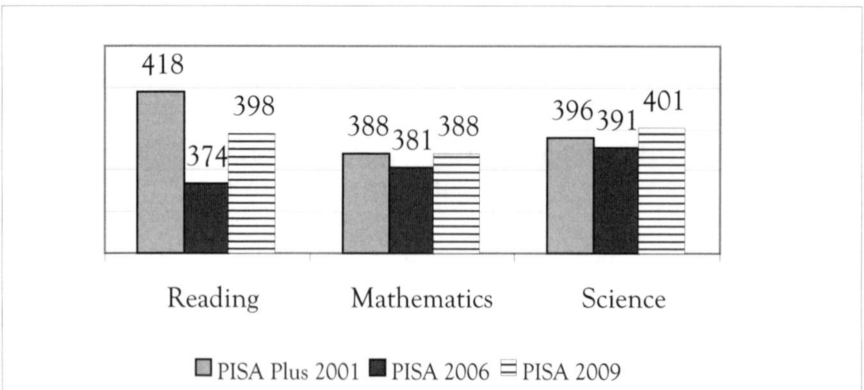

Figure 7.7: Reading, mathematics and science by score, PISA Plus 2001, PISA 2006 and PISA 2009

From the results of a well-established international evaluation instrument, we can affirm that academic performance in the Argentine education system underwent a decline in years following, and in proximity to the 2001–2002 crisis. A comparison between studies conducted by the OCDE before (PISA Plus 2001) and recently since the crisis (PISA 2006) showed a decline in performance in students completing basic school levels in all three subject areas evaluated, namely reading, mathematics and science. This said, data obtained during the most recent test (PISA 2009) indicate an improvement in academic performance vis-à-vis the prior evaluation. It is worth mentioning that after almost 10 years, results are (slightly) better than pre-crisis levels only in science.

c. *Material conditions that make teaching and learning possible*

In this final section we will refer to the effects of the 2001–2002 crisis on a third dimension: material conditions necessary for teaching and learning. As an example of these conditions, we will review education investment, calculated on public expenditure and instructional time estimated as school attendance according to hours and days a year during which classes are taught at schools.

During the 1990s, as well as during the first decade of this century, considerable efforts were made in Argentina towards investment in education, which in turn were clearly interrupted during the 2001–2002 crisis. A significant increase in government spending on education had materialized during the 1990s. Federal Education Law no. 24.195 passed in 1995, established in article 61, with certain laxity, criteria set to determine investment levels in education and ways in which it would be increased. Government spending in education starting at 3.4% of GDP in 1990, reached 4.3% in 1999, and investment in education as a percentage in social expenditure was equivalent to 24.7% in 1993, constantly increasing until reaching 26.9% in 1998. In this regard, Rivas, Vera and Bezem note it is remarkable that "in a stage of enrollment expansion...investment per pupil would have increased almost double in real terms, going from 660 pesos in 1991 to 1,140 pesos in 1998" (2010, p. 34).

The increase in education investment, which ceased during the years of economic recession prior to the 2001 and 2002 crisis, later plummeted, wiping out all the educational investment efforts made in more than a decade. Rivas and colleagues state that "between 2001 and 2002 there is not just a cutback in the education budget at nominal levels, but also an added impact from the strong devaluation which demolished educational investment in real terms after the return of inflation" (Rivas et al., 2010, p. 34). In 2003, investment dropped to 3.8% of GDP and 25% of social expenditure (Cosse, 2006, p. 5, table 6). After that year and as a result of exiting the crisis, investment in education began once again to rise.

The new investment stage in education materialized in principle after the Educational Finance Act no. 26.075 passed in 2005. The law proposed an increase in education, science and technology expenditure between 2006 and 2010 and improved efficiency in resource allocation with the aim to meet certain targets, both educational and financial, which were closely tied together in the norm. It addressed progressive budget increases designated for these areas to reach 6% of GDP by 2010. The figure was established based on assigning 4% of GDP to the area in 2005 and was expected to reach the investment percentage level accepted by UNESCO (6%) and OCDE participating countries (6.2%). In fact, investment in education rose sharply and, in 2007, surpassed historical figures to reach 5.4%, exceeding by 2009 the 6% objective proposed for 2010 and reaching 6.4% (Rivas et al., 2011, p. 8).

In recent years, length of time assigned to teaching, the second condition required, as well as its benefits, is being discussed more in depth. Benavot and Amadio, in Gillies and Jester Quijada (2008) sustain that school achievement increases when learning opportunities improve, particularly if time assigned to learning is maximized. The authors argue that investment in other variables, such as teachers, materials, curriculum, and so forth, are wasted if they are not applied during a reasonable time. According to a study by UNESCO (Gillies and Jester Quijada, 2008), in order to attain a reasonable quality of learning, the minimum number of school hours needed is between 825 and 1000 per year. The paper indicates an important gap exists between developed and developing countries, as the former dedicate three times more hours to schooling than the latter. Attaining this minimum number of hours is very difficult (if not impossible) if the school day is divided into two or three shifts. In some cases, the lack of information on just how many days a year schools are actually open and working, how many days students attend classes, level of teacher absenteeism, teacher to student ratio, and so on, is serious.

In the case of Argentina, for several reasons, sufficient instructional time was not provided for primary or secondary students before or after the 2001–2002 crisis, based on the number of school hours or days available. Prior to the crisis, a survey conducted by Mekler (2000) for the Ministry of Education compared the length of school days in Argentina to that of developed countries. The study presented the average numbers of class hours a year for students in the fourth grade as a reference for compulsory primary school and the ninth grade for secondary. Total number of hours a year naturally varied between countries, depending on the length of the school day (between 4 and 5 hours), the number of school days a week (5 or 6), and total number of school days in the year (between 175 and 220 days). The survey shows that Argentina offered, in 1998, an average of 175 school days, depending on the jurisdiction

(Mekler, 2000, p. 3). It also showed for primary school a total of 680 hours a year on average and a 4-hour school day. For secondary schools, this total was 880 hours a year on average and the school day lasted 5 hours (Mekler, 2000, p. 5). The time allocated to teaching offered to Argentine students is clearly inferior to other countries considered in the study, both in terms of the number of school days (France, Netherlands, Japan) as well as the hours a year (Netherlands, the United States, Korea).

During and after the crisis, time devoted to teaching was directly affected by numerous teacher strikes at the national and regional level, and in some jurisdictions, schools hardly opened. As a reference point, in some years certain schools had 50 days without class and others more than 70. From the end of 2000 onward, teachers (and university professors) called for strikes to protest against government policies of restricted investment in education during this period. A landmark decision related to government spending cuts in education was the elimination of the National Teachers Incentive Fund (*Fondo Nacional de Incentivo Docente* [FONID]), originally passed in 1999 after a hunger strike lasting more than a thousand days by teachers demanding guaranteed salary hikes. Once the crisis unfolded, teacher strikes continued as did demands of securing back pay, as well as ending wage cuts. Compensation conditions began to normalize early in 2003 and, with it, the number of school days. The next year, a law was passed (no. 25.864/2004) requiring the minimum school year to last 180 days. Bearing in mind that the primary school day is only 4 hours long, this is equivalent to 720 school hours a year, which does not meet the standard recommended by UNESCO. This situation was made worse by the fact that teacher strikes continued—the total number of teaching hours students were receiving continued to shrink. Between 2002 and 2008, 9 days of school were lost on average as a result of teacher strikes, a figure which surpassed 10 days average in many jurisdictions (Rivas et al., 2010, p. 106).

To conclude, material conditions necessary for adequate teaching and learning development were affected by the 2001–2002 crisis. On one side, the crisis clearly impacted levels of public spending on education, both with respect to GDP share as well as social expenditure, since the increase won during the 1990s spiraled and disappeared. On the other, instructional time clearly fell as a result of teacher strikes and absenteeism. Nevertheless, the facts show the matter of instructional time was yet not a subject worthy of debate. Only after the economy began to recover, the topic became part of the education agenda, so that in 2003, the norm imposing 180 days as the minimum school passed—although the total number of class hours has remained, before and after the crisis, below UNESCO recommended levels.

To Conclude

The most recent economic depression occurring in Argentina affected the political and social system as a whole, to such a degree that it has come to be known as one of the worse in the country's history. In this context, education was seriously jeopardized. In this study we analyze the effects of the crisis on the Argentine education system considering three dimensions simultaneously: internal efficiency, academic performance and material conditions. The first is fundamentally investigated in relation to repetition and inter annual dropout rates in primary and secondary schools and shows that, although increases were present in the two or three years preceding the crisis in both levels, these were more significant and constant during and immediately after it and more in secondary education. Academic performance analysis of the system based on comparison of PISA Plus 2001 results before the crisis to PISA 2006 after the crisis shows student performance at the end of compulsory schooling worsened in all three areas evaluated, namely reading, mathematics and science literacy. Nevertheless, results of PISA 2009 showed improvement in all areas vis-à-vis PISA 2006, but not yet compared to PISA 2001. Finally, analysis of variations in material conditions studied in relation to education investment and instructional time show both were clearly impoverished as a result of the crisis: GDP percentage directed to education plummeted, and a notorious increase in the number of school days (and hours) lost per year was observed as a result of teacher strikes.

We conclude that the three dimensions of the education system studied worsened considerably immediately following the 2001–2002 financial and economic crisis. Economic recovery would seem to require less time than educational recovery. Although the economy sustained a vigorous recovery in Argentina after 2002, the education system took much longer to bounce back and to show clear signs of improvement. Actually, the three dimensions considered appear to have different recovery times. The two material conditions studied show a different behavior: while investment in education increased from 2004, instructional time was affected by teacher strikes until at least 2008. Internal efficiency indicators studied, repetition and inter annual dropout rates, showed signs of improvement in both primary and secondary education only after 2005. Finally, academic performance showed a decline in student achievement in basic subject areas in 2006 and an improvement not until 2009.

Notes

1. All three dimensions of the educational system singled out can be studied at the national or provincial level. Thorough diagnosis of any educational system must also include the varying conditions of underlying subsystems. We would like to point out that for the purposes of this paper only the national level of the Argentine educational system was considered.
2. According to UNESCO (2011) the gross enrolment ratio (GER) is the total enrolment in a specific level of education, regardless of age, expressed as a percentage of the population in the official age group corresponding to this level of education. The GER can exceed 100% because of early or late entry and/or grade repetition.
3. The National Center for Quality of Education Assessment (*Dirección Nacional de Información y Evaluación de la Calidad Educativa* [DINIECE]) defines repetition rate as "the percentage of students enrolled in a given academic grade/year level enrolling as repeaters in the same grade/year level, the following academic year." (DINIECE-ME, 2003).
4. The National Center for Quality of Education Assessment (*Dirección Nacionalde Información y Evaluación de la Calidad Educativa* [DINIECE]) defines interannual dropout rate as "the percentage of students enrolled in a given academic grade/year level not enrolling the following academic year as new students, repeaters or re-enrollers." (DINIECE-ME, 2003).
5. Information on the education indicators selected is available starting in 1996. The National Center for Quality of Education Assessment (*Dirección Nacional de Información y Evaluación de la Calidad Educativa* [DINIECE]) does not have information on earlier years because national statistics underwent a period during which data were not registered between 1988 and 1994. The Ministry for Culture and Education began the first studies for Federal Education Information System reconstruction in 1994, conducting subsequent yearly surveys similar to the ones implemented in April 1996.
6. Primer Estudio Regional Comparativo y Explicativo (First Regional Comparative and Explanatory Study).
7. *Segundo Estudio Regional Comparativo y Explicativo* (Second Regional Comparative and Explanatory Study).
8. *Operativos Nacionales de Evaluación* (National Assessment Operatives).

References

Chudnovsky, D., López, A., and Pupato, G. (2003). Las recientes crisis sistémicas en países emergentes: las peculiaridades del caso Argentino. In C. Bruno, and D. Chudnovsky (Eds.), *Por qué sucedió? Las causas económicas de la reciente crisis argentine* (pp. 17-109). Buenos Aires: Siglo Veintiuno Argentina: Centro de Investigaciones para la Transformación.

Cosse, G. (2006). *El sistema educativo argentino entre 1995 y 2005 y los efectos de las crisis del 2001.* Buenos Aires: Ministerio de Educación, Ciencia y Tecnología.

DINIECE. (2003). *Sistema nacional de indicadores educativos.* Dirección Nacional de Información y Evaluación de la Calidad Educativa. Buenos Aires: Ministerio de Educación, Ciencia y Tecnología.

Gillies, J., and Quijada, J. (2008). Opportunity to Learn: A high impact strategy for improving educational outcomes in developing countries. Academy for Educational Development

(AED), Educational Quality Improvement Program 2 (EQUIP2).

Gvirtz, S., Larripa, S., and Oelsner, V. (2006). Problemas técnicos y usos políticos de las evaluaciones nacionales en el sistema educativo Argentino. Archivos Analíticos de Políticas Educativas, 14 (18) http://www.oei.es/evaluacioneducativa/problemas_tecnicos_usos_politicos_evaluaciones_sistema_educativo_argentino.pdf.

INDEC. (2003). Informe del Avance del Nivel de Actividad. In *Informe de prensa. Datos referidos al cuarto trimestre 2002.* http://www.indec.mecon.ar/nuevaweb/cuadros/17/pib_03_03.doc; http://www.indec.mecon.ar/nuevaweb/cuadros/17/pib_03_03.doc; http://www.indec.mecon.ar/nuevaweb/cuadros/17/pib_cua_06_03.xls; http://www.indec.mecon.ar/nuevaweb/cuadros/17/pib_cua_06_03.xls

Mekler. (2000). *Periodización del tiempo escolar en diferentes países. Documento Interno del Programa de Gestión Curricular y Capacitación.* Buenos Aires: Ministerio de Educación, Ciencia y Tecnología de la República Argentina.

Ministerio de Economía. (2003). *Informe 44: La Economía Argentina Durante 2002 y Evolución Reciente.* Buenos Aires: Ministerio de Economía.

OCDE. (2002).*Conocimientos y aptitudes para la vida. Primeros resultados del programa Internacional de evaluación de estudiantes (PISA) 2000 de la OCDE.* Paris: OCDE; México: Santillana.

OCDE. (2008a). *Informe PISA 2006. Competencias científicas para el mundo del mañana.* Buenos Aires: Santillana.

OCDE (2008b). *Programa internacional para la evaluación de los estudiantes. PISA 2006. Informe nacional. Resumen.* Buenos Aires: DINIECE, Ministerio de Educación.

OCDE/UNESCO. (2003). *Aptitudes básicas para el mundo de mañana. Otros resultados del Proyecto PISA 2000. Resumen Ejecutivo.* Paris: OCDE/UNESCO.

OECD. (2010). *PISA 2009 Results: What Students Know and Can Do. Students Performance in Reading, Mathematics and Science.*Vol. I. Paris: OECD.

PNUD. (2003). *El desarrollo humano en la Argentina del Siglo XXI.* Buenos Aires: PNUD.

Rivas, A., Vera, A., and Bezem, P. (2010). *Radiografía de la educación argentina.* Buenos Aires: CIPPEC, Fundación Arcor y Fundación Noble-Clarín.

Rivas, A.,Vera, A., and Bezem, P. (2011). *Monitoreo de la Ley de Financiamiento Educativo. Cuarto informe anual 2010, Informe de Monitoreo y Evaluación.* Buenos Aires: CIPPEC.

Saxton, J. (2003). Argentina's Economic Crisis: Causes and Cures. Washington, DC: Joint Economic Committee, United States Congress.

Sosa Escudero, W. and Petralia, S. (2010). I Can Hear the Grass Grow: The Anatomy of Distributive Changes in Argentina. Working Paper 106. CEDLAS, UNLP.

Tedesco, J. C. (1987). *El desafíoeducativo: calidad y democracia.*Buenos Aires: Grupo Editor Latinoamericano.

UNESCO. (2002). *EFA Global Monitoring Report.Is the World on Track?* Paris: UNESCO.

UNESCO. (2008). *Segundo estudio regional comparativo y explicativo. Los aprendizajes de los estudiantes de América Latina y el Caribe. Primer reporte de los resultados del Segundo Estudio Regional Comparativo y Explicativo.* Santiago de Chile: OREALC.

UNESCO. (2010). *EFA Global Monitoring Report.Reaching the marginalized.* Paris: UNESCO.

UNESCO. (2011). *EFA Global Monitoring Report. The Hidden Crisis: Armed Conflict and Education.* Paris: UNESCO.

• CHAPTER EIGHT •

Struggle for Agency in Contemporary Argentinean Schools

Ana Inés Heras

This chapter will reflect on what agency looks like when it is taken up by families at public, state-supported schools. In doing this, a tension between two different sets of ideas, *education as a right* versus *education as a commodity*, becomes apparent. When education is conceived of as a right, the guiding principle is *equal education for all.* This line of thought was prominent in Argentina over several decades, and the country had been known for its high literacy rates, high school attendance and high graduation rates. A different orientation has been pushed forward for more than two decades now, seeking to equate families to consumers and to frame education as being bought and sold within the market economy. This chapter argues that this logic is tied to the discourse on the benefits of globalization, which in Argentina was overtly taken up during the 1990s, yet was foregrounded prior to that decade and still prevails. In the midst of this ideological conflict over education, there was the economic crisis of 2001, which deepened and inflated the divide between those who believe that education is a fundamental right and those who follow free market economics. Therefore, to survive economic crises through education, one must bridge this divide and reconcile the rights of individuals to be educated with prevailing market conditions.

Argentina, Global Capitalism and Education

Argentina has had an intensely volatile political landscape over the last 35 years. From 1976 to 1983 a military regime abused political power and perpetrated murders, torture and the violation of human rights at a state-organized level. It was also during that time that Argentina's foreign debt increased, and those monies were used to subsidize projects taken up by the upper-class economic sector. The results were high rates of unemployment, high levels of violence, and a gap in cultural and political life because of the loss of a generation in the repression of 1976–1983. A clear orientation towards equating public policy with the capacity of *some* to maximize *their* profits was implemented, orienting national economic policies towards the interest of international capitalism.

After this regime, President Alfonsín (1983–1989) was elected by democratic vote. His mandate was plagued by the tensions inherited from the recent past and ended in a deep crisis. National elections were brought forward, and President Menem won the seat in 1989. During his campaign, Menem made it a point of using his rhetoric to establish the notion that his would be a process of radical change (*reforma*) and that Argentina would become part of the First World wealth and ways of doing things, while at the same time promising jobs and stability for all. Elected by vote, Menem governed the country during two consecutive periods, 1989–1994 and 1994–1998. While Menem's first and second presidencies aligned Argentina with hegemonic transnational capitalist values and practices, his promises were mostly unfulfilled.

An orientation towards the foundation of a *new order* characterized governmental discourse in all areas of policymaking (economic, health, education, etc.). In education, "The Reform" became the everyday idiom at use to name the changes implemented; it worked at different yet complementary levels: it meant changes associated with legal instruments and changes associated to discourses and practices at schools. "The Reform" became used as a placeholder, and it made common sense: in this line of thought, the Reform successfully installed a conception of schools as isolated, "management-type" units, associated with efficiency and with providing a *service* (Pérez and Alonso Bra, 1997). It also meant that, in educational matters, the discourse linked to choice, in turn tied to efficiency, achieved a prominent role during the 1990s. For example, Cardini (2005) has studied the initiative for charter schools in the Province of San Luis, Argentina, and has concluded that it is an example of

> the many attempts to restructure and deregulate state schooling that have characterised the educational policy arena during the last decades in many different countries. In the Argentine context, this policy...was the first attempt by a provincial government in the country to undertake an educational policy, aimed at enhancing market flexibility. It also sought to encourage privatisation and competition within state provision—all reforms which are generally associated with global policy trends. (p. 26)

During Menem's administration, the national government's discourse worked hard on two aspects: (1) to install the idea that these changes occurred democratically (by the passing of laws in Congress) and (2) to insist on that they were indeed significant and enlightened modifications (and thus the need to adopt the discourse related to "new foundation for the best"). These two aspects were very important at that time, since the memory of the military regime, 1976–1983, when democracy was nothing but a dream and Congress did not exist, was still fresh. Thus, any discourse that sought to be associated with change would be best received if it were done through the constitutional channels available. Educational policies associated with the Reform's conceptual turn affected everyday processes at public schools for more than a decade; the Reform's rationale, tied to the discourse of privatization, globalization, and capitalism, is still present today.

Normative Aspects of the Reform

The laws that have framed the normative aspects of the Reform may seem, at first glance, contradictory in that one places power in the hands of local decision-making structures, and the second one affirms the opposite. Law no. 24.049 (*Transferencia a las Provincias y a la Municipalidad de Buenos Aires de servicios educativos*, i.e., Transference of Educational Services to Provinces and to the City of Buenos Aires) mandated that educational services be transferred from national to provincial jurisdiction, thus establishing what was called a process of decentralizing education, a process similar to that of other Latin American countries in the same decade (e.g., México in 1992; Bolivia in 1994; Colombia in 1993, according to Rivas, 2004). Several analysts of this decentralizing process have pointed out that it was "decentralizing with no resources to make decentralizing possible," the hallmark of Menem's presidential rule in several policy areas (see, e.g, Smulovitz and Clemente, 2004).

Law no. 24.195 (*Ley Federal de Educación*, i.e., Federal Education Law) replaced Law 1420, which dated from 1884. This law, passed during April 1993, established that it would be the national state decision-making locus on mandated curricula, on formulating goals and on creating evaluation (testing) systems to measure their attainability. The national state was also the one who created compensatory policy measures to support specific processes in certain provincial jurisdictions. Therefore it can be said that the movement was in the opposite direction: decision-making power, and resources to implement these decisions, went from the local to the central state. As pointed out by Rivas (2004):

> The transference of educational services to the Provinces could be interpreted as a way to retain the macro-decision power, and to relegate to the Provinces an administrative role. In this way, the rationale underlying these changes is in the first place, a political one, perhaps economic, and educational as well—but probably in the

> last place. And this process can be said to exist during the XIX and XX centuries, so that it is hard to answer whether a National Educational System existed (or exists) at all. (p. 58, my translation)

The Reform Process and Beyond

A deep economic crisis took place in Argentina between 1999 and 2002 (with its peak in 2001), and a new administration was elected (President Kirchner from 2003 to 2007 and President Fernández de Kirchner from 2008 to 2011). The scenario has henceforth changed. For example, specifically in educational policy, a new national educational law, no. 26.206, passed in 2006, and the educational budget was increased.

However, the grounds for the fundamental tension between the notion of *education as a commodity* and *education as a right* are still present. This tension is visible in the social discourse (Angenot, 1999), and it is continually assumed by two different positions at the larger political arena: those who speak for a push for "privatizing" the educational system and conceptualizing it as a commodity in a market economy versus those who assume a discourse arguing for deepening the meaning of education as a public affair and as a right to which all should have access.[1] Thus, an analysis of the discursive practices at the larger societal level shows that explicit connections between "private" as "what is best" (or "private better than public") were and are being constantly made. This tension is identifiable in three tendencies still at play, defended by several sectors of the Argentinean population (e.g., policymakers who are lobbying for the privatization of all educational services; upper-class sectors who attend private schools; some confessional sectors):

1. Progressive restriction in resources to the public educational system (that dramatically contrast with resources allotted to the private system; see, e.g., Rivas, 2010).
2. Orientation to conceptualizing education as a service and a commodity, instead of viewing it as a right (Cardozo, 2009; Rodríguez, 2000).
3. Pressure towards administrative efficiency and results (e.g., testing) as more important than sustaining long-term, supportive educational contexts for students and families. (Pérez and Alonso Brá, 1997)

In order to reflect on these issues, I address the ways in which agency was taken up by families at public schools. The analysis focuses on two different yet complementary levels (everyday school life and societal larger arena) and on two different points in time and geographical locations. On the one hand, I interpret data from five middle and high schools in the city of San Pedro, a city of 50,000 inhabitants in the province of Jujuy (northwest area of Argentina). I show how a participatory action research project, taking place during 2005–2008, brought together teachers, administrators, students, and their families to reflect and act upon their everyday patterns of communication and how their capacity to reflect allowed them to discuss other issues not anticipated, yet very important. On the other hand, I discuss data from a process in which a self-organized group of families from different elementary public schools in the city of Buenos Aires have taken up their right to challenge current educational policies in the period running from 2009 to 2011. I write this article as an informed member of the two projects, although my role was different in each of them.[2]

Families, Schools, Challenges and Agency Building: Schools in the Northwest of Argentina

The action-research project in Jujuy was geographically located in the area of the Valley.[3] The original focus was on the communicative patterns amongst families, students, teachers, administrators and other school personnel. The guiding assumption was that schools were not open enough to acknowledging different communicative and cultural styles. Thus, some of the tensions associated with everyday school life could be looked at from a communicative perspective. Some of the teachers participating in this project had been documenting school life prior to formulating this project, because they had been working with me to understand their own practice. There was a need, however, as they stated it, to collaborate amongst more teachers and to include families and students in the process of reflection and understanding of school life. For all these reasons, when an open call for proposals was made by the national Ministry of Education to support in-school projects aimed at promoting meaningful change, we met with participants from five different schools and discussed the core ideas to design a project called "Communicating for Inclusion." We were selected as one of the winning projects.

Participation was voluntary, yet for those who decided to be part of the project, funds were available to support commuting (e.g., to meetings, to conduct observations, or to participate in other project activities) and basic research needs (e.g., pens, notebooks, xeroxing, audiotapes, tapes, batteries). Other funds were used to hire a specialist to document some of everyday school life interactions on video, produce some clips which were to be discussed during project meetings, and to teach students who wanted to learn how to use a video recorder to document school life.

Cycles of data collection and analysis were interwoven. Workshops open to teachers, administrators, other school personnel and researchers were undertaken during the first 18 months. The topics discussed were:

- everyday communicative patterns amongst students;
- different codes (e.g., colloquial, classroom talk, family-teacher interaction) used at school;
- perceptions about who uses what code, when and why;
- ways of documenting and understanding everyday school talk;
- different kinds of talk according to different spaces at school (e.g., talk overheard at the entrance, talk when adults seemed not to be regarded as audience, use of formal language for everyday greetings at the courtyard when students and teachers saluted the flag).

Some of the conclusions that we arrived at were that many students didn't differentiate all the codes used at school and that the majority of the adults at the schools (teachers, administrators, support personnel) didn't understand the different kinds of languages used by students. Moreover, they considered their repertoires poor, without understanding that there were several linguistic registers at play (Heras and Martínez, 2006; Heras, 2008). Some teachers, worried about sexist language codes used by male students to denigrate female students, delved in the study of these language patterns, and concluded that, as it was, everyday school life and organizational patterns didn't foster any kind of reflection on these interactions, and was silently supporting a discourse that devalued women. These lines of work were taken up by some of the participants to continue their work (see, e.g., Martínez and Peinado, 2010; García, 2005).

During the last 18 months of the project, we conducted a series of workshops oriented to work with families and students on some of these findings, and on opening up discussion to other topics that they might have found relevant. In these workshops, three issues were highlighted:

1. communication amongst schools and families was not as open nor fluent as it could be, thus creating a series of tensions which could be avoided;
2. families did not quite understand many of the difficulties related to teachers as workers (and the workshops helped clarify some but left some stated as questions);

3. the school buildings were deteriorated and families, teachers, administrators and students were worried about it, but did not know what to do.

It was in this context that we undertook a six-week workshop for students to teach them how to use audio visuals to document school life, specifically focusing on aspects related to space and to the buildings, since it was of their interest. A pattern clearly emerged: the buildings were deteriorated, and the material conditions of everyday school life were, to say the least, challenging. All participants paid attention to this issue, and thus they produced field notes, video clips, as well as some sketches and drawings. I quote the field notes taken by one of the teachers that illustrate connections between the state of the buildings, educational policy, and how the changes in economic policies affected education:

> The building where the school [he refers to what used to be the School of Arts] is located in a house that used to be an old mansion owned by a sugar cane plantation owner. Several different and unruly constructions were annexed to it over time [field notes describe extensively and in detail all the different buildings and spaces adjacent to the main house]. I reflect on what these buildings mean, who they house, what the educational changes were so that today we have co habiting in the same building several different educational tracks which are in turned housed in the same building and super imposed, so to speak. A progressive process of poverty has stricken the local population due to the national economic policies along the 1990s, i.e., neoliberal orientation and fiscal reduction. The once locally prestigious School of Arts is now empty since several families that once upon a time could afford this type of education for their children can no longer do so. Additionally, state resources to support the building were more and more scarce. The building deteriorated but paradoxically annexed other constructions. Since the Reform established a period in which changes had to be made, and tracks were to be implemented, the School of Art changed its curriculum and opened up to receive students who now ended their junior high school (a new track established by the Reform) and attended three years of high school at the newly opened Humanities and Social Studies track, housed also at the School of Arts. Thus in the same space/logic cohabited the high school students (3 years of schooling), the School of Arts students (5 years of schooling, equivalent to junior and high school), and sharing some of the space, also a school for mentally disabled students, which had no place to function and was assigned here. (My translation of RM field notes. His field-note taking process started in 2003 and continues until the present, since this teacher is one of the ones that has pursued his own line of research.)

Documenting the state of the buildings led to several actions:

1. Pictures and video footage were examined and a process of editing them started to construct audiovisual narratives by the students (with the help of one researcher and several teachers and administrators).
2. A line of interpretation emerged by which recent historical policy decisions were interrogated and questions about whose responsibility it was to attend to these issues were stated.
3. Families gathered and decided to petition the authorities for decent buildings (by presenting their findings on the local news, by organizing daily meetings at the school entrance, and by signing a petition to the school administration first and to the provincial administration later on).
4. The authorities were at the beginning not open to discussing these issues with families or students, and this was also documented and communicated by the students and their families.
5. Important questions were posed, such as: By virtue of whose decisions or why were the buildings in such a state? Who was to be asked about these specifics, and how could these be transformed? What was the specific history behind each of the buildings, and why were they now in such reduced condition? Participants established some connections between these issues and some of the main findings that had been discussed during the first 18 months of the project. Some of these questions and reasoning reached the local media (television), and thus visibility.

In this manner, a project that initially focused on communicative patterns, by virtue of interpreting the links between communication and space, turned as a springboard to make visible some (not so explicit) relationships between change in public policy, infrastructure, and a need for change. An analysis conducted by some of the teachers and the students revealed the link between the changes in national educational policies and the physical space, as follows:

- Schools used to be managed nationally, but they became to be provincial due to Law no. 24.049. This meant that resources had to come out of provincial budgets, which were not well enough resourced to support this change.
- Coupled with the fact that: The reform process, due to Law no. 24.195, established changes in mandated curricula and tracking. Thus there was a period (from 1994 on) in which several schools had to implement different tracks cohabiting in the same school space-building-system.

- Therefore: The buildings started to deteriorate severely, and by 2003 (10 years of the Reform process) most of them were in a very poor state.
- Buildings that once housed only one educational track now housed several, which caused a series of administrative, spatial and scheduling problems.

As a result of the process described above, families and students organized and promoted direct action by which they asked teachers to teach on the street, to show that they were not going to expose anyone to the health hazard posed by unstable roofs, walls or other dilapidated building structures; after a month of more or less direct confrontation, the provincial authorities agreed that a special budget plan was to be designed in order to meet at least some of the demands.[4]

Some important links were established across different levels of context, and these connections provided the local community with keys to understanding processes that otherwise remained obscure. Agency, as the capacity to see oneself as a full participant in a process and, thus, to see oneself—be that individual or collective—as capable of acting differently than it had been done or expected, was taken up because it was identified as a right.

The ability to learn how to pose simple questions at the right time is one of the most important learning experiences coming out of this process. For example, what are the long-term effects of public-policy decisions on students' and teachers' everyday school life? What do reforms look like, specifically? These are questions perhaps all actors should have in mind when participating in the processes in which they are a part—be it in their role as politician, policymaker, teacher, administrator, student, or other. This is a perspective taken up by researchers, most commonly post-factum (e.g., the area of analysis known as anthropology of public policy takes this stance). Less common, however, is that it is applied to processes while they unveil. In educational processes it is more common that teachers or administrators, or even students (by their representative bodies such as unions or student body committees) take action and see their right to do so. It is less common that families do that.

I have shown how a line of inquiry that started by asking about everyday communicative patterns at schools led to a thinking process by which participants sought to understand the crises in which they perceived their schools to be in. I end this section by pointing out that different results were achieved, at different levels, which show that when diverse roles come together, a capacity to see themselves as key actors may develop. Therefore, the results of this process affect differently at different roles, but all participants acted as full members of an educational *community*:

- by virtue of the joint participation some of these schools became eligible to receive funds to help with infrastructure;
- families were seen as key actors in local educational matters;
- students and teachers became aware of the possibilities associated with documenting and discussing everyday school life with other participants (policymakers, other teachers and administrators, families and researchers);
- teachers and administrators continued a process of learning how to do research, guided by their own questions and purposes.

Families and Schools in Buenos Aires

Familias por la escuela pública[5] is a self-organized group of families from very many different elementary public schools in the city of Buenos Aires. Since we gathered in 2009, we have agreed upon three core issues that guide our voluntary work. These are that:

1. the educational budget is set accordingly to guarantee that all children in the city of Buenos Aires are provided the right to be educated;
2. all schools access equal conditions, not only infrastructure (e.g., buildings, resources, etc.) but also the quality of their educational process;
3. all teachers should work under dignifying conditions (not only a salary according to their work, but also that they are treated in a nonauthoritarian way and that they are allowed the right to critically reflect upon their working conditions).

These three core principles were discussed at the beginning of our spontaneous gatherings, during the long teacher strike that took place in the months of March and April 2009, the beginning of that academic year. At that point, teachers agreed to boycott schools by calling strikes by what they termed the "surprise-factor tactic." It meant that during the first week, for instance, they would not attend schools during a Monday, the next week during a Tuesday and a Wednesday, and so forth, but without prior announcement (thus the families and governmental authorities did not know when teachers would indeed attend schools). There are around 14 teacher unions to which teachers belong in the city of Buenos Aires, and often their tactics differ and their strength is debilitated. During the beginning of the 2009 school year the unions cooperated and the strike was massive. Several families gathered to discuss the matter, in a spontaneous way, at the school entrances. We then started a process of connecting across schools in the city because the majority of us were in favor of supporting teachers in their demands, yet the consequences for our children and our family life were severe.

The city of Buenos Aires is the capital of Argentina and an urban setting with 3 million inhabitants; it is governed by a neoliberal administration (led by Mauricio Macri, chief executive and leader of the PRO political party). In the area of educational policy, this administration has augmented the breach between funding for public versus private education (in favor of private education). It has also divided school districts along lines of "richness and poverty," and has been selective as to supporting the north area of the city over the south area (the reader may guess that the north area is indeed richer compared to the south). Thus, this was the context in which, fuelled by the need to take a position towards the teacher strike, the families that gathered and discussed what to do, took those three already mentioned issues as our program for reflection and action.

Another issue has come to our attention since we started the process, one that has not been turned into a guiding principle but that we take into account by reaffirming our presence. The issue is that of challenging the mechanisms installed by the current administration to create a climate of persecution and fear, trying to set up an ambiance of guilt ("*por algo sera,*" the favorite statement during the military dictatorship and a well-known witch-hunting strategy) amongst teachers, families, students and administrators for taking up the right to participate in discussing public policy. For example, during the year of 2009, I participated in putting together a big open meeting in an open public recreational space called Parque Centenario. The meeting was called to discuss amongst whoever wanted to participate what were the most salient lines of educational public policy in place. In order to organize the gathering, we designed and xeroxed fliers to invite people. We asked the school principal administrator if those could be handed out to families at the school door or else by sending them home in students' communication notebooks (each student has a notebook where all communications to families are sent). The administrator agreed to both ways of spreading the news. During that week, she received an "unofficial" (termed as such) visit by the vice minister of the city of Buenos Aires (note the high-ranking officer the government sent) to admonish her that she had broken the law by virtue of communicating via the notebooks this gathering of families to discuss educational policies. The administrator asked the vice minister to make her visit official and to state in writing her admonishment so that she could to respond to it. The vice minister refused but advised the school administrator to "keep an eye on those two *subversive* mothers at her school," one of which is writing this chapter. Note the language used, that is, "subversive" is a key term in Argentinean politics since it was used by the military dictatorship to label participatory practices.

We interpreted these events as tactics for instilling fear and well-calculated, since the visit took place during a special date: it was during the day in which all administrators who were applying for promotion were not going to be at their schools because they had only that day to comply with all the administrative steps towards filing their applications. This, of course, was information known to the vice minister, as it was also known to her that the principal administrator would be at her school since she could not ask for promotion because she was retiring that same year. The principal called us (the two *subversive* mothers) to tell us what had happened and offered her explanation of why she had been visited that day: so that the other administrators would not be witnesses of the threat.

In this context, for families to gather, discuss and promote actions that critically reflect upon public policy, and that challenge the current administration, is a major step. Since our creation we have:

- collected 4,000 signatures backing up a list of demands that were presented in 2010 before the city representatives so that they commit to actively defending the three issues at the core of our work: (1) budget according to the needs; (2) high-quality schooling for all; (3) good working conditions for teachers. This set of demands was signed by citizens (we collected the signatures on the streets over a period of six months) and was also endorsed by other groups (such as ONG and other self-organized groups of parents);
- demanded that the city representatives be informed before discussing the 2011 budget (a process that took place from September to November 2010) by addressing a set of items that we presented before them to be taken into account (e.g., the differences we found between areas of the city, the fact that even if a certain budget was allotted to education the government failed to use it in 2009 and reassigned a portion to other areas, etc.);
- filed a law suit—which was decided in our favor—to stop the deviation of funds originally assigned to education and reassigned to other government areas during 2010;
- organized several open meetings to discuss public policies (we usually gather at open, public recreational spaces and we invite the people present at the moment to join us while we speak publicly, in an assembly type of gathering);

- participated in demonstrations in support of public education and in support of human rights.

In this process it seems crucial that we have taken up the right to think critically upon current educational policies and to act accordingly. This means that we have proposed a set of actions that in our eyes would be in the best interest of what state public policy is supposedly designed to do: provide equal access; guarantee the right of being educated to all students and their families; push forward the idea (and the practice) that discussing public matters publicly is a healthy practice.

As a group, we do not pretend to represent all families in state-managed, public elementary schools, and we reaffirm the status of each participant as direct family participants. This logic of practice has been termed *asamblearia*, which stands for direct, nonrepresentative, action driven by a constantly developing analysis type of participation (Fernández, 2007). From this perspective, no one represents anybody else, yet as families that are building up this process, we see ourselves entitled to propose and carry on actions. We see ourselves as full participants.

Discussion and Concluding Thoughts

Families who claimed a voice in favor of their children's education may be interpreted amidst a (maybe schematic, but real) push-pull, which in turn defines what counts as education during economic crises and described as follows: on the one hand, education can be considered as a public matter and as equity and access for all. Everybody has the right to be educated, and, thus, quality schooling for all is the main goal of this position. This means that public policies, public monies, and transparency of decision-making processes are the core guiding principles of this line of thought and action. In this scenario, families are full participants, and it is legitimate to gather, discuss, analyze, interpret public policy, and act accordingly.

On the other hand, education can be considered as a commodity and, as such, is sold and bought on the market. In this view, public policies may be manipulated at the benefit of sectors that, by virtue of their resources, may make their voices heard using "legal" channels in illegitimate ways. In this line of thought, only some do become full participants and anyone challenging this view is subject to being prosecuted.

As true as this portrayal may be, it is still schematic and does not account for all shades of opinion in real life. Matters can become more complex to analyze, and in fact they tend to remain not accessible for many. However, when families are faced with day-to-day situations they cannot understand or seem to change; some actions may indeed lead to an unexpected path. For example, taking up action and regaining confidence in their voice has proven to be a significant challenge to the status quo, as it was discussed in the Northwest schools. Or else a challenge posed by another sector (e.g., teachers calling a strike) may be a loud wake-up call to families that otherwise would not have reflected on teachers' rights, families' rights or the combination of the two.

At some point, however hard families may try, it is not in their hands to change the course of action. Yet if they are aware that they want to play a role in the educational arena, what are the lessons learned from the experiences analyzed in this chapter about agency in schools?

- Establish connections amongst layers of context that seem to be unrelated yet prove to add to understanding to the picture seems key. These connections may come from different sources, and what seems to be crucial is a space-time where-when to share them.
- Keep in mind that starting with an analysis of what may look as more simple, issues may lead to more specific, yet complex ones, that can be addressed by specific data gathering and analysis, when resources are provided (e.g., an action research project) or when circumstances push for voicing unanswered, puzzling questions at the forefront (e.g., what position to take in regards to a teacher strike).
- Keep the focus on "what these policy measures will look like" at everyday school life when planning, promoting or discussing policy changes.
- Establish connections amongst worldwide tendencies and local issues that are affected by them.
- Last, and very important: keep in mind that locally enacted actions also have lessons to teach, since history is what women and men do, every day. In this way, we may survive future economic crises through education.

Notes

1. These different and oppositional logics have been analyzed by the news press, for example, Tiempo Argentino, http://tiempo.elargentino.com/notas/denuncian-al-gobierno-porteno-contratacion-irregular-de-una-consultora. This is a process not only taking place in Western societies but also in other nations with different traditions, such as China or Japan, see Tobin et al. (2009, pp. 225–42).
2. In Jujuy I was one of the researchers and didn't have a role as a family member or as a teacher; in Buenos Aires I participate as the mother of two children who attend public, state-funded elementary school, and am a full member of the self-organized group of families. Along the process, I use my professional skills to document and reflect on our practice.

3. Jujuy is a small size province, yet very rich in geographic and cultural differences in its four areas: the Valley, the Yungas, the Quebrada and the Puna. The largest cities are in the Valley area.
4. It is interesting to note that this process took place between 2005–2008, preannouncing a similar one that took place later on in Buenos Aires in approximately 28 schools from different neighborhoods of the city. It ended three months later, after an intense boycott to the city administration in 2010, when the City Ministry of Education signed an agreement with students and families to devote monies to take care of deteriorated buildings, a process that is yet to be completed, and over which the struggle continues.
5. http://www.familiasxlaescuela.org.ar/

References

Alonso Brá, M. (2008). El sentido de la universidad a partir de las transformaciones en su historia presente. *Revista de la Educación Superior*, 3(147), 77–87.

Angenot, M. (1999). *Interdiscursividades. De hegemonías y disidencias.* Córdoba, Argentina: Universidad Nacional de Córdoba.

Cardini, A. (2005). The influences of globalisation in education policy-making: The case of the charter schools in the Province of San Luis, Argentina. *Education, The Journal of Educational Research*, 5(1), 26–38.

Cardozo, N. D. (2009, June). *Políticas educativas argentinas en perspectiva comparada. El rol del Estado en la Ley federal de educación y la Ley de Educación Nacional.* Paper presented at the 3rd National Congress & 2nd International Meeting of Comparative Studies in Education, "Contemporary Educational Reforms: Continuity of Change?" Buenos Aires, Argentina.

Fernández, A. M. (2007). Lógicas colectivas, subjetividad y política. In Y. Franco, H. Freire, and M. Loreti (Comps.), *Insignificancia y autonomía. Debates a partir de Cornelius Castoriadis* (pp. 45–49). Buenos Aires, Argentina: Biblos.

García, V. O. (2005). La escuela entre el suelo estatal y la fluidez del mercado. *Revista Iberoamericana de Educación,* 36(12). Retrieved April 2011, from http://www.campus-oei.org/revista/1167.htm

Heras, A. I. (2008). Configuraciones dinámicas y géneros discursivos de los estudiantes de escuela media: Un estudio en Jujuy, Argentina. In *Transformaciones, Prácticas Sociales e Identidad Cultural* (pp. 347–367). Tucumán, Argentina: Universidad Nacional del Tucumán, Departamento de Publicaciones de la Facultad de Filosofía y Letras.

Heras, A. I., & Martínez, R. A. (2006, March). *Efectos de lugar. Una investigación etnográfica en escuelas medias de Jujuy.* Paper presented at the Educational Ethnographic Research—21st Interamerican Symposium, Humanities and Social Sciences School, Buenos Aires University, Buenos Aires, Argentina.

Martínez, R. A. (2005, November). *Escuela, calabozo y política de encauzamiento.* Paper presented at the 2nd Meeting in Educational Research. Organized by the Teacher Education Program, San Pedro de Jujuy, Argentina.

Martínez, R. A., & Peinado, E. (2010). The uses of sex in school or how the school field is a space where the patriarchal habitus "deepens," *Cuadernos FHyCS-UNJU, 38*, 127–143.

Pérez, H. O., & Alonso Brá, M. (1997). La actual reforma educativa argentina y la institucionalización del espacio escolar: ¿De la administración burocrática a la gerencia educativa? In CLAD-UNESCO, *El tránsito de la cultura burocrática al modelo de la gerencia pública: perspectivas, posibilidades y limitaciones* (pp. 9–62). Caracas, Venezuela: CLAD-UNESCO.

Rivas, A. (2004). *Gobernar la educación. Estudio comparado sobre el poder y la educación en las provincias argentinas.* Buenos Aires, Argentina: Granica.

Rivas, A. (2010). *La ruta hacia la justicia y la transparencia de los aportes estatales a la educación de gestión privada* (Public Policies Document). Retrieved from http://www.cippec.org/Main.php?do=documentsDoDownload&id=440

Rodríguez, L. (2000). Tendencias privatizadoras. *Boletín Número 4*. Buenos Aires, Argentina: Instituto de Investigaciones Pedagógicas de la CTRA.

Ruiz, G. (2008, November 27). Recurrentes y recientes reformas educativas en la Argentina. *Quaderns Digitals, 55*. Retrieved from http://www.quadernsdigitals.net/index.php?accion Menu=hemeroteca.VisualizaArticuloIU.visualiza&articulo_id=10813

Senate and Representatives Resolution No. 24.049. (1991). *Transference of Educational Services to Provinces and to the City of Buenos Aires.*

Senate and Representatives Resolution No. 24.195. (1993). *Federal Education Law.*

Senate and Representatives Resolution No. 26.206. (2006). *National Educational Law.*

Smulovitz, C., and Clemente, A. (2004). Descentralización, sociedad civil y gobernabilidad democrática en Argentina. In A. Clemente and C. Smulovitz (Comps.), *Descentralización, políticas sociales y participación democrática en Argentina* (pp. 39–89). Buenos Aires: Instituto Internacional de Medio Ambiente y Desarrollo—IIED-AL.

Tobin, J., Hsueh, Y., & Karasawa, M. (2009). *Preschool in three cultures revisited. China, Japan, and the United States.* Chicago: University of Chicago Press.

• CHAPTER NINE •

Education and Governmentality in Degraded Urban Territories: From the Sedimented to the Experience of the Actual

Silvia Grinberg & Eduardo Langer

> Capitalism therefore liberates the flows of desire, but under the social conditions that define its limit and the possibility of its own dissolution, so that it is constantly opposing with all its exasperated strength the movement that drives it toward this limit. (Deleuze and Guattari, 2004, p. 153)

Introduction

Like a science fiction story come true—a story that does not grow less real as it grows more virtual—since the final decades of the twentieth century, crises have become a neuralgic part of our daily life. The call to change, to become subjects in a constant state of transformation and adaptation, are the specific and unwavering appeals of the society in which we live. Thus, in recent years we have grown so accustomed to speaking of crisis, change and uncertainty that we treat those terms like an objective description of a given reality. Yet, we understand, in keeping with Deleuze and Guattari, that this "given" reality is, in fact, the specific logic of capitalism, the displacement and codification of flows of desire that it creates but also fears.

In the framework of governmentality studies (Peters, Besley, Olssen, Maurer and Weber, 2009; Rose, O'Malley and Valverde, 2006; Dean, 1999), we understand that the idea of crisis is a component of the rationality of the government of population in the management age (Peters, 2001). We will discuss the particularities of school life in societies that, like Argentina, have experienced successive social and economic crises since the 1980s. These crises have meant changes in the currency and devaluations, as well as a traumatic impoverishment of the population. This has meant, among other things, the constant growth of shantytowns where three generations currently live (Grinberg, 2011).

In regions like Latin America, and particularly in countries like Argentina, the call to decodification became a part of daily reality. Indeed, since the end of the twentieth century, it has become not only the crux of a *sui generis* (divine calling), but a neuralgic part of the government of the population (Foucault, 1991) in the educational system. In a less than a twenty-year period starting in the 1990s, for instance, the educational system in the Buenos Aires province[1] has undergone three structural reforms. These reforms entailed, among other things, the redefinition of educational cycles and attendant change in the physical location where classes are given, change in authorities and curricula. While many of these changes were applied throughout the country, the way different educational institutions were affected varied greatly. This is due both to the federal nature of the country and the simultaneous deepening of the gap between social sectors, which acts in very specific ways in each school. Those institutions that grew in the midst of the systematic impoverishment of the population that has been taking place since the 1970s are affected by this permanent production of crisis in various ways.

In this chapter, we offer some reflections born of the research that we have been carrying out in contexts of extreme urban poverty in the Buenos Aires metropolitan area since 2004.[2] More specifically, the project is being done in schools located in extremely degraded urban territories (Davies, 2007) that, as stated above, have grown ceaselessly since the late 1980s. While we have worked in a number of institutions, here we will discuss widely fieldwork done in a secondary school.

Thus, in the perspective of governmentality studies and in keeping with the work of Deleuze and Guattari, we will describe forms of state regulation as well as noncodified flows of desire as they exist in these urban areas. In the words of Tamboukou, "Resistance is immanent in *dispositifs* of non-juridical models of *power...lines of* flight and *becoming* are immanent in *agencements*" (2010, p. 693). Thus, we undertake this reflection with a keen awareness of the population's potential for life and the way these subjects inhabit and exist in their neighborhoods and institutions. We are particularly interested in students, their concerns and desires, and the particular modes of regulation that are enacted in these schools.

It is in this context, this paper delves into the particularities of pedagogical devices in extremely degraded urban territories in the age of management during years marked by crisis, reform and counter-reform. We will address the ways that the school, after years of social and educational crisis, has become a place where students place their hopes and desires for the future. As will be discussed below, incidents like a student jumping over the wall to get into his school express what we believe to be the complex fabric of school life in these urban spaces. How can we understand these situations? We suggest that in times of permanent crisis, schools—in the midst of and despite all the contradictions and tensions experienced therein—constitute the most stable institutions in these communities. And that is not a minor fact. The question, then, becomes how survival is possible and what remains of schools and subjects in a context where crisis has become the norm. We will offer first a brief conceptual reflection and then delve into a discussion of the research.

Governmentality and Pedagogical Devices in the Management Age

Foucault used the notion of device especially when he began to discuss what he called "governmentality" or "the government of men" (Agamben, 1998). In his reflections on Foucault's notion, Deleuze (1990) stated that we were witnessing a process of transformation in both the ways power is exercised and the processes of subjectification. Deleuze maintained that the forms of discipline described by Foucault "are the history of what we gradually cease to be, and our present-day reality takes on the form of dispositions of overt and continuous *control* in a way that is very different from recent closed disciplines." Foucault agrees with Burroughs, who claims that our future will be "controlled rather than disciplined" (Deleuze, 1992, p. 164). Similarly, in the lectures that Foucault (2007) gave at the College de France, which were published under the title *The Birth of Biopolitics*, he spoke of configuration of enterprise society to address the changes beginning to take place in the government of the population. Thus, the term *management society* (Grinberg, 2008) refers to the new dynamics in the government of the population.

One of the essential traits of management societies is that the government of the population is no longer conceived as a totality. Society ceases to be envisioned as a body that, at least on the narrative level, should function as an organic whole and where, therefore, the actions of government tend toward that ideal. As authors like Durkheim maintained, that ideal also served to define the margins of school action. It is no longer a question of homogenizing populations; indeed, the narrative of government is constructed as the very opposite, as the tolerance of diversity, as the glorification of the Self and its individual potentials.

Urban life constitutes one of the clearest crystallizations of this logic. Indeed, in recent years we have witnessed an ever-growing fragmentation of urban life. These are times of "selective" metropolization (Prevot Schapira, 2002), characterized by the participation of cities in excellence and worldwide chains of command, on the one hand, and a heightening of inner ruptures at the heart of urban spaces, on the other. This tension furthers discourses based on the empowerment of communities as a "solution." In this context, education has ceased to be a space for the normalization of behavior and is, instead, a space for grouping and homogenizing differences to the point of becoming the key social space for selective metropolization. Indeed, such processes constitute at present a neuralogical part of the rationality of the government of population.

These transformations are associated with the reformulation of strategies for the government of economic life, the specification of subjects of government in terms of an ethic of action that establishes new divisions between those citizens who are competent and those who are not. This is a reformulation of the relations between expertise and politics that implies the emergence of an array of new technologies for expert government (Rose, 1996). The community is thus rendered the locus of government, and in times of crisis, it must manage permanent adaptation to change and resolve questions as diverse as identity and belonging, safety, poverty, solidarity and responsible citizenship. This is because a fragmented metropolis requires decentralized organs of government—diverse, superimposed and diffuse institutions that must become agents of solidarity and take responsibility for the life of subjects and neighborhoods. These new modes of assemblage (Deleuze and Guattari, 2000) entail combining responsibility, autonomy and election, which are the cornerstones of individual freedom and its exercise. The school, in contexts of extreme urban poverty, becomes a privileged center of multiple demands. Thus, here we will attempt to describe the processes of reterritorialization that have taken place in and through the educational system and schools.

School Life in Contexts of Extreme Urban Poverty: Power, Desire and Resistance

Since the late 1970s, Argentina has experienced a number of economic crises. Periods of hyperinflation, changes in the name of the currency and its devaluation have led to, among other things, the constant impoverishment of the population and its correlate, the ceaseless growth of what are commonly called shantytowns. The shantytown is the territorial expression of the increase in extreme urban poverty. In shantytowns, the occupation of the lands is individual, called *hormiga*.[3] Each family or individual arrives to the land on its own and builds its house as best it can; there is no urban organization in the shantytown; there are no streets, just passageways. The lands in the urban registries are considered empty lots.

Although the emergence of the shantytown can be traced back to the early twentieth century, the growth of this sort of space has been constant since the 1970s. They have grown especially in times of crisis or economic upheaval, which produces a mass influx of people to these neighborhoods. Thus, the demographic growth of shantytowns came along with the foreign debt crisis of the 1980s, the privatization of state-owned companies in the 1990s, and the crisis at the beginning of the twenty-first century, which was driven, among other things, by the constant growth in the country's risk rating. It is important to point out that these sorts of sites are not limited to a specific space in the city and its surroundings; they are found in public lands and in an array of neighborhoods, from the affluent to the lower-middle class, from downtown to the outskirts. The shantytowns were once temporary places of residence, but, in recent decades, they have become more and more established sites where people live.

In this context, the schools, like the neighborhoods in which they are located, bear the markings of urban decay and poverty. The metropolitan area in which this research is under way has been stigmatized historically. In the words of one student and principal:

> On TV, the only time San Martin is mentioned is when something bad happens, when they killed somebody. In the shantytowns there are also good, hard-working people. They never show that. They always show the bad side. (Female student, 2010)

> This school was also looked down on...like the school for the shantytown....We are combating that image. (Principal of the secondary school)

Management logic takes on a certain specificity when it comes to the administration of the life of the population that Foucault (2007) so aptly called liminal: subjects are called on to make themselves, and the school—reinterpreted as a community institution—is left to its own devices. In the twenty-first century, those who attend schools in extremely degraded urban territories are children of welfare plans, of parents who get by performing odd jobs and rummaging through the trash for recyclable goods, of families who eat whatever they can find at the *quema*[4]; these are unemployed people whose bodies are no longer required to be docile or, at least, not in the same way they had been in the framework of industrial capitalism. The liminal population of which Foucault spoke has become the abject population (Kristeva, 1988; Butler, 2002).[5] These subjects, as well as the areas where they live, constitute uninhabitable, yet densely populated, areas. In keeping with Kristeva, the abject places us at the limit of the tolerable and of the conceivable, of the assimilable, and hence, it is prone to being rejected. Thus, it is disturbing and the object of forgetting. In the words of one of the students at the school:

> What we are showing here is what there is in the Carcova.[6] We are showing something hidden that was there but that no one, no government, no one at all, has paid attention to. Something that doesn't exist because for people, that is, people with money, it's like the Carcova doesn't exist; it's a trash dump where we live, but that's not how it is because it is where we grew up. There are people. (Interview with a student, *Re Copada* video,[7] 2008)

Significantly, the right to the city (Lefebvre, 1978) is called into question in shantytowns on a daily basis. This is because these areas have either very precarious or no access to the sewage system, potable water, electricity and trash collection. The housing, layout of the streets, and educational establishments, recreational and green areas are equally precarious. In Agamben terms (1998), these are zones of exception, and the schools are included in this exception, first, because the educational system took shape alongside the process of selective urbanization that ensued in the metropolitan area of the city of Buenos Aires. While this exclusion from the right to the city is by no means new,[8] it has grown worse due to the particularities of life in extremely degraded territories. Second, the impact of the crises and educational reforms on these schools has been very particular. Indeed, the schools where this research is being done express the deepening of social inequalities on a daily level. Some indicators directly linked to the deepening of this process of social fragmentation include:

1. An increase in the levels of truancy[9] as the year progresses, an increase in the rate of changes in school shifts[10] and in changing schools—in fact, it is common for students to change schools three or four times during their school careers—and an increase in the drop out rate.
2. Increase in the rate of teacher absenteeism for different causes and an increase in the turnover of teachers in schools over the years.
3. The deterioration of the school premises themselves. This sometimes means sewage covers that flood over as soon as it starts drizzling; classrooms whose walls are under construction; schoolyards in deplorable conditions—some of whose walls can actually have electric currents. For these situations to be taken care of it is necessary that the school administration actively protest and so, in many case, they aren't resolved.

Both these neighborhoods and schools are the manifestation and result of the social and economic crises that have affected Argentina since the late

1980s. School life is a constant back-and-forth and, of course, its administration is a juggling act. Hence, if there is no fire, so to speak, no imminent danger, and if no one shouts very loud, life just goes on as usual. Given the im-impossibility of tending to everything, school life just ensues, and subjects and institutions are left to their own devices; they must find the way to survive. Under the logic of syndromic surveillance (Fearnley, 2005), the question is being able to control events so that things don't get out of hand, guiding things toward a predetermined end. Schools are faced with institutional difficulties when it comes to addressing a vast range of problems, conflicts and needs. Significantly, many of the social policies geared toward communities (Rose, 1996), policies that are part and parcel of the logics of population government in the age of management, are enacted through schools. The luck of the school, of those who work in them, of the students and of their families depends on individual will and what the sum of those wills is capable of doing. Along these lines, one of the new characteristics of school life, particularly in extremely degraded urban territories, entails how subjects are called upon to take responsibility for themselves and to participate actively in the regulation of their own conduct. Indeed, these strategies of government attempt to create individuals who do not need to be governed by others but can govern and manage crisis by themselves, subjects free to take full advantage of their own existence through the responsible management of their lives. That is, subjects who must take care of themselves and whom schools are called on to protect, though of course they lack the resources to do so. Hence, there are daily struggles for survival at home and at school.

Hence, school has become one of the institutions where individuals are instructed on how to become active subjects of their own government. Although the state is still responsible for regulating and financing education, there is, to use Foucault's terms (1991), a sort of "disinvestment" or policy of energy conservation that makes use of the subjects themselves to enact more efficacious government. Thus, for example, the scant resources schools in extremely degraded urban areas do have only serve to generate situations of powerlessness. The following is one of the many situations that manifest these dynamics:

> At the beginning of the term, work to improve the building gets underway. Two months in, the computer room still cannot be used; it is now up to the principal to yell loud enough so that the company in charge of the work comes back to the school to finish up. Meanwhile, neither the teachers nor the students can use the room, nor do they know when they will be able to. (Field notes)

Something that began as the responsibility of the state (improving school premises) becomes a crescendo of responsibilities that must be assumed by subjects. For the teachers, this is manifest in an array of situations. Below, a teacher speaks of a field trip and its implications for teachers and students:

> We work with the kids a great deal. And since they didn't have any money, we helped the girls to get dressed for the outing. We all met at the Suárez train station and we motioned to the kids to get on the train. In Retiro,[11] we all chipped in to pay for the taxi to the Law School. (Interview with a female teacher, 2010)

Due to these situations, teachers often vacillate between an almost religious devotion to their work and abject fear (Deleuze and Guattari, 1997), which is expressed as complaints about the failures and deficiencies of students and their families:

> This school has always been a school for teenagers from the shantytown, and the type of teens who lives in shantytowns has changed. Fourteen years ago, excellent, extremely grateful kids would come to this school. They all became lawyers, doctors, psychologists....But that has changed...I am pretty disappointed....They are totally lazy; I see a total lack of enthusiasm. And no values either. They don't know right from wrong. And that saddens me deeply. (Interview with female teacher, 2010)

> There are all sorts, as always. There are idealistic young people who look to the future, who study, and others who don't study. Young people today are more direct, more sincere; they are not hypocrites. They say what they think, and I think that's good. When they don't like something, they come right out with it, and I think that's healthy. And when there is a teacher who they think is, as they say "jiving them," who doesn't know what he or she is talking about, they also come out with that. And I think that's good. I also see that they don't give it their all; they could do more, they just sit back. Actually, the fact that they don't do much is not their fault. Often, there is no model at home, regardless of their social class. I am not talking about perfect, nuclear families here. (Interview with a female teacher, 2010)

Indeed, it is likely that the loneliness that, according to the teacher, the students feel describes how the adults at these schools feel, the ones who have stayed on through changes, crises and reforms. They experience situations for which they were not trained, situations in which their role is not clear. It is, then, difficult for them to approach and connect with their students. This is expressed in many ways that go from frustration and a feeling of powerlessness to stigmatization and abject fear. Phrases like "Let's do something for the kids" and "You can't do anything with these kids" may seem contradictory, but in fact characterize the ways that teachers inhabit these urban spaces. According to Ehrenberg (2000), expressions that fluctuate between euphoria and depression characterize these times. Not surprisingly, teachers' working conditions constitute an essential component of their states of despair. "One teacher told us that he mixed up the day of the week and took the wrong bus. After traveling for almost an hour, he ended up at the school he was supposed to be at the next day."[12] This sort of disorientation constitutes an integral part of how pedagogical devices take shape in these spaces in the age of management. But how do students experience this?

Beyond the abject fear, the stigmatization and the messianism in these urban spaces, we find the potential for life of these young students, desire and resistance.

When we walk into the school, we find "a student [being] punished for jumping the school wall. That is, he jumped the wall to get into the school." This is just one of the many strange situations experienced at these schools every day: a student enrolled in the school who does not attempt to escape but to get in. On the basis of this episode, one might wonder about the desires and interests of the students. In this case, the student most certainly wanted to get in, just not by traditional means. So one might ask, "How do we understand these facts?" Are they only reactions or also forms of resistance? What is the status quo that is resisted in schools? Practices like jumping the wall to get into school hardly conform to traditional school practices, even practices of rebelliousness. Such practices constitute the lines of subjectification, of fissure or breakage of which Deleuze (1992) speaks in all *dispositifs*.

In times of crisis, where it seems that there is no place for an important group of the population, this episode expresses its opposite. Although with a naked eye it is about nonsense (Deleuze, 1994), it is precisely for that reason that, paradoxically, it turns full of sense.[13] A student climbing a wall not for escaping but to enter school produces a feeling of estrangement in relation to what is normally considered poor behavior. It also confronts us with the power of someone who fights to have a place.

These practices do not suggest the image of hopeless poverty. Faced with the abjection and impossibility usually attributed to these students, this one jumps up impulsively as if to say, "I am here." This constitutes an incident that dramatically opposes abject fear, and it questions the notion that the students at this school don't care about anything.

It is often difficult for teachers to communicate with their students, both in informal conversation and in the classroom. This leads to class situations that resemble a comedy of errors and lead to conflict or negation:

> We also mess up. But they shouldn't come over and scream at us. They are our teachers, not our parents. They are right about something: we talk back, we don't show respect, we don't do what we are supposed to. The thing is, sometimes we are bored and we start goofing off, talking and that's when they write something on the board. That's when they start coming after us. (She changes her tone of voice.) "You never do anything. You just come here to pass the time" "Why don't you just stay home" and stuff like that. (Female student, 15 years old)

As this young woman relates, many situations in school life that start out with boredom and turn into disorder or violence are derived from the search for something that is so simple: teachers that teach and students that learn.

In keeping with Deleuze and Guattari (2004), abject fear does not express a molar need in the subject but rather "the molar organization deprives desire of its objective being" (p. 29). Thus, in this scene we find subjects that have something to say:

> I want to keep studying languages. I want to be a chef. Study to be a hairdresser. Get a job and pay for cooking school. And maybe even work in a cruise or a hotel. I want it all. (laughter)

> I love reading. That's what I like most. I like reading out loud.

> I want to be a cop, a police officer. To go to the Carcova and get the purse-snatchers, the junkies who hang out in the back. I also want to be a sexologist. I like that job. But I don't know if I will be able to because you have to study for a long time.

> I want to finish school, so that tomorrow I will be somebody, not a number on a document. I don't want to have a kid until I am thirty.

"I want it all." "I like." "I want." Far from lacking enthusiasm, they speak of what they do like and desire. So one might ask to what extent the nihilism—or is it, in fact, the "nihilization" that is used to describe these neighbors and subjects—constitutes a form of regulation, a part of the molar operation, of the codification of flows of desire. In other words, apathy is the basic term used to refer to young people who live in shantytowns. Indeed, the notion of resilience (O'Malley, 2009) is often used to explain poverty in regions like Latin America. It is also a crucial notion in working in these neighborhoods where schools attempt to elevate low self-esteem in order to help young people overcome these situations. In time of crisis, the negation of desire and diagnoses of apathy increase because they serve to explain that which has no explanation: thousands and thousands living in a state of exception. Nonetheless, on the ground we find just the opposite: if subjects manage to survive and reproduce their daily lives in these contexts, it is precisely because they are highly capable of overcoming adversity.

It is important to emphasize the multiplicity of situations observed in these schools that address the life of subjects and the dynamics of school life itself, especially their students. We believe that desires undermine the reigning order and resist "established forms of pleasure, its modes of distribution and, by this same action, sets off the production of social machines" (García Hodgson, 2005, p. 72). Thus, these students, whose lives are so often negated and—as they themselves point out—hidden, come on the scene not as tragic figures but as subjects determined to consider and express their desires.

Closing Remarks

As Deleuze pointed out, "Michel was amazed by the fact that despite all the powers, their underhandedness and their hypocrisy, we can still manage to resist. On the contrary, I am amazed by the fact that everything is leaking and the government manages to plug the leaks. In a sense, Michel and I addressed the same problem from opposite ends" (Rabinow and Gandal, 1986, p. 21). These opposite ends, which we believe are increasingly present in times of crisis, are exactly what we have attempted to describe here. This implies, among other things, covering up the sewage drains in an act of negation and abjection, on the one hand, and students insisting on their wants and desires as they fight in and for the school, on the other.

Thus, in times of crisis we come upon the configuration of these new ways of exercising power through technologies of the self-founded in a spirit of freedom and responsibility. These define a new framework in which we are called to take responsibility for, direct and redirect a self that is always already at the border. We have attempted to show how this new configuration and its contradictions are expressed in the daily life of schools located in shantytowns.

The first observation occurs: when everything melts away, the struggle lies in staying put, in being present, in counting on the existence of an institution that consists of something more than an isolated individual. When crisis becomes the most stable state of affairs, we find students who struggle for the continued existence of schools as well as a place for themselves in them, students who get angry and argue and, above all, desire. Second, before the images of abjection and apathy that are so often bestowed on these neighborhoods and the demand to foster resilience, we find young people who jump walls to get into school; these young people do not passively accept the negation that weighs them down and attempts to undermine their existence as subjects with a future. In the face of abject fear, it is essential for these students to make visible aspects of their lives that are hidden even when we all know about them.

Many of these daily situations in schools make us think not only about frustration, powerlessness and limitations but also about desiring and wanting, and, fundamentally, about the act of desiring as political action, as statement, *énoncé*. The codification of the flows of desire that capitalism releases also tirelessly threatens. Maybe that is why the fight is not to play hooky, to get away, but to get in, to be there, to occupy that space.

In conclusion, in times of crisis where nothing would seem permanent, the struggle is for schools to perdure. Abject fear constitutes a neurological part of the codification of these flows of desire, the fear of noncodified desire, and the "I want's" uttered by the students are the primary threat. Nihilism, the hypothesis of low self-esteem as a response to that threat, is a hypocrisy, a low blow,

Deleuze would say, that does not anticipate anything but rather serves to cover up the sewage drains in societies where subjects fight, struggle and, above all, desire. And those "I want's" constitute modes of perduring, insisting and resisting.

Notes

1. Argentina's political system is federal such that the provinces are autonomous and can dictate, reform, and create their own structures. Thus, for instance, though two national laws on education have been passed in recent years that mandate far-reaching structural changes, the city of Buenos Aires has not, at the time of the writing of this article, passed any law in that direction. On the other hand, the province of Buenos Aires has passed and enacted three reforms that changed school structures, curriculum and so forth in the past twenty years. The schools discussed here fall under the jurisdiction of Buenos Aires province.
2. "Dispositivos pedagógicos y producción de subjetividad en emplazamientos urbano/marginales. Un estudio en caso en la Enseñanza Secundaria Básica del Partido de Gral. San Martín." PICT 2005, Proy. No. 33413, Sede UNSAM. Agencia Nacional de Promoción Científica y tecnológica, Argentina.
3. Literally "ant"- this term refers to the way used to arrive to these areas: one by one.
4. *Quema* [burn] is the term used in the neighborhood to describe one of the largest trash dumps in the area.
5. The notion of *abject* is used here to refer to the relative position occupied by subjects in social life; that is, the relationship between the inside and the outside of areas often called *shantytowns* (Grinberg, 2010, 2011).
6. Carcova is the name of the shantytown where this research is being done. In other writings, we describe the neighborhood (Grinberg, 2011).
7. The documentary video workshop discussed here has been under way since 2008 in a public secondary school located in the outskirts of the city of Buenos Aires, in a town called José León Suárez that has a number of shantytowns. This project, which is for students between the ages of twelve and seventeen approximately, is aimed at generating a space to problematize, document and narrate daily life in the school and the neighborhood. To that end, the work entails linking the production of documentary videos to the aims of the curriculum and the teachings at school; teaching secondary school students techniques and concepts related to film production by means of which they can then document and communicate their lives (needs, desires, projects); and allowing teenagers (secondary school students) to conceive of themselves as historical subjects communicating their ideas, thoughts and feelings through documentary videos.
8. See Baudelot and Establet (1971) regarding France; Bowles and Gintis (1981) regarding the United States; and Braslavsky (1985) and Llomovatte (1990, 1991) regarding Argentina. These are key works to identifying the existence of qualitatively different informal circuits within educational systems.
9. This situation, which we call fluctuating enrollment, works as follows: some students stop attending schools for long periods of time during the school year; others attend erratically; and others stop attending to return, in many cases, the following year. The reasons for this sort of truancy are manifold.

10. In Argentina, students and families can choose whether to go to school in the morning or the afternoon; high school students can also attend at night.
11. A train station in downtown Buenos Aires.
12. In Argentina, it is common for teachers to work at several different schools.
13. In Deleuze terms, "sense is thus inseparable from a new kind of paradox which marks the presence of nonsense within sense, just as the preceding paradoxes marked the presence of nonsense within signification...In short, sense is always an effect" (1990, p. 70).

References

Agamben, G. (1998). *Homo Sacer. El poder soberano y la nuda vida*. Madrid: Pre-textos.

Arendt, H. (1996). *La condición humana*. Buenos Aires: Paidós.

Baudelot, Ch., and Establet, R. (1971). *La escuela capitalista en Francia*. Df México: Siglo XXI.

Bowles, S., and Gintis, H. (1981). La instrucción escolar en la America capitalista. Buenos Aires: Siglo XXI.

Braslavsky, C. (1985). *La discriminación educativa en Argentina*. Buenos Aires: Grupo Editor Latinoamericano.

Butler, J. (2002). *Cuerpos que importan. Sobre los límites materiales y discursivos del sexo*. Buenos Aires: Paidós.

CEPEC-UNSAM-ESB32. (2008). Re-copada. Video. Bs. As.

Davies, M. (2007). *Planeta de ciudades miseria*. Madrid: Ediciones Foca.

Dean, M. (1999). *Governmentality: Power and Rule in Modern Society*. London: Sage Publications.

Deleuze, G. (1987). *Foucault*. Buenos Aires: Paidós.

Deleuze, G. (1990). *The Logic of Sense*. New York: Columbia University Press.

Deleuze, G. (1992). What is a dispositif? In *Michel Foucault Philosopher* (T. Armstrong, Trans.). (pp. 155-163). New York: Routledge.

Deleuze, G. (2005a). *La imagen tiempo*. Buenos Aires: Paidós.

Deleuze, G. (2005b). *Derrames entre el capitalismo y la esquizofrenia*. Buenos Aires: Cactus.

Deleuze, G., and Guattari, F. (1997). *Rizoma*. Madrid: Pre-textos.

Deleuze, G., and Guattari, F. (2000). *Mil mesetas. Capitalismo y Esquizofrenia*. Madrid: Pre-textos.

Deleuze, G., and Guattari, F. (2004). *Anti-Oedipus: Capitalism and Schizophrenia*. Minneapolis: University of Minnesota Press.

Ehrenberg, A. (2000). *La fatiga de ser uno mismo. Depresión y Sociedad*. Buenos Aires: Nueva visión.

Fearnley, Lyle. (2005). From Chaos to Controlled Disorder: Syndromic Surveillance, Bioweapons, and the Pathological Future. ARC Working Paper, no. 5, March 25, 2005.

Foucault, M. (1977). El juego de M. Foucault. Ornicar. *Saber y Verdad* 10, 171–202.

Foucault, M. (1988). El sujeto y el poder. In H. L. Dreyfus and P. Rabinow (Eds.), *Michel Foucault: más allá del estructuralismo y la hermenéutica* (pp. 227–44). DF México: UNAM.

Foucault, M. (1991). *Tecnologías del Yo. Y otros textos afines*. Barcelona: Paios/I.C.E–U.A.B.

Foucault, M. (2007). *Nacimiento de la biopolítica*. Buenos Aires: Fondo de Cultura Económica.

García, R. (1999). *La anarquía coronada. La filosofía de Gilles Deleuze*. Buenos Aires:

Puñaladas/Colihue.

García Hodgson, H. (2005). *Deleuze, Foucault, Lacan. Una política del discurso.* Buenos Aires: Ed. Quadrata.

Grignon, C., and Passeron, J. P. (1991). *Lo culto y lo popular.* Buenos Aires: Nueva visión.

Grinberg, S. (2006). Gubernamentalidad, vida escolar y violencia en emplazamientos urbano marginales. *Claroscuro* Revista del Centro de Estudios sobre diversidad cultural. FHyA. UNR. Año V, No. 5, 93–115.

Grinberg, S. (2008). *Educación y poder en el siglo XXI. Gubernamentalidad y Pedagogía en las sociedades de gerenciamiento.* Buenos Aires: Miño y dávila Editores.

Grinberg, S. (2010). Schooling and Desiring Production in Contexts of Extreme Urban Poverty. Everyday Banality in a Documentary by Students: Between the Trivial and the Extreme. *Gender and Education* 22, no. 6, 663–78.

Grinberg, S. (2011). Territories of Schooling and Schooling Territories in Contexts of Extreme Urban Poverty in Argentina: Between Management and Abjection. *Emotion, Space and Society,* Elsevier, 1e12 doi:10.1016/j.emospa.2011.01.001 (Article in press).

Kristeva, J. (1988). *Poderes de la perversión.* Buenos Aires: Siglo XXI.

Lazzarato, M. (2006). *Políticas del acontecimiento.* Buenos Aires: Ed. Tinta Limón.

Lefebvre, H. (1978). *El derecho a la ciudad.* Barcelona: Ediciones Península.

Llomovatte S. (1990). *La educación media y el trabajo en la Argentina.* Buenos Aires: Propuestas Educativas.

Llomovatte, S. (1991). *Adolescentes entre la Escuela y el trabajo.* Buenos Aires: FLACSO/Miño y Dávila ed.

O'Malley, P. (2009). Resilient Subjects: Uncertainty, Warfare and Liberalism. *Economy and Society* 39, no. 4, 488–509.

Peters, M. (2001). Education, Enterprise Culture and the Entrepreneurial Self: A Foucauldian Perspective. *Journal of Educational Enquiry* 2, no. 2, 58–71.

Peters, M. A., T. Besley, M. Olssen, S. Maurer, and S. Weber. (Eds.). (2009). *Governmentality Studies in Education.* Rotterdam: Sense Publishers.

Prevot Schapira, M. (2002). Buenos Aires en los años '90: Metropolización y desigualdades. *EURE* 28, no. 85, 31–50.

Rabinow and Gandal. (1986, Spring). The Intellectuals and the Politics: Foucault and Prison. *History of the Present,* no. 2, 20–21.

Rose, N. (1996). Identidad, genealogía, historia. In *Cuestiones de identidad cultural,* compiled by S. Hall and P. Du Gay (pp. 214–250). Buenos Aires: Amorrortu editores.

Rose, N., O'Malley, P., and Valverde, M. (2006). Governmentality. *Law & Society Annual Review,* 2–83.

Tamboukou, M. (2010). Charting cartographies of Resistance: Lines of Flight in Women Artisti's Narratives. *Gender and Education* 22, no. 6, 679–96.

Wacquant, L. (2007). *Los condenados de la ciudad. Gueto, periferia y Estado.* Buenos Aires: Siglo XXI.

Youdell, D. (2011). *School Trouble: Identity, Power and Politics in Education.* London: Routledge.

• PART THREE •

Educational Theory and Economic Crisis

Doing Work as a Reflection of the Other: Notes on the Educational Materialism of Deleuze and Guattari

David R. Cole

> She was a vampire incarnate and she led more people astray than the Pied Piper led children...It was only when credit was taken from her that she appeared in her true colors. Then it found that her eyes were hard, her lips cruel, and her body a mere empty shell. (Smitley, 1933, p. 8)

Introduction

This chapter will analyze recent economic crises and the vampirism as described above, through a philosophical lens provided by the ideas of Gilles Deleuze and Félix Guattari (1988), and that coincides with the quote from Smitley (1933). This lens allows us to focus on the 'regimes of work' associated with the crises and their connections to education as a practice (Schatzki, 1996). Regimes of work are increasingly being sieved and processed through the mechanics of a deterritorialising, postindustrial, global capitalism. This digitized, 'machinic' influence reaches into the subjectivating heart of what it means to exist in regimes of work, how to escape if necessary, and how to formulate and sustain questions of freedom from within these regimes. This chapter will analyze such a multilayered situation using the connections to educational practice as a frame of reference, and as a way of understanding how the forces at work are organized. The pivotal text that will be used in this writing as a platform for connecting regimes of work with educational practice is *A Thousand Plateaus*, by Deleuze and Guattari (1988). This chapter includes understanding the immanent materialism that Deleuze and Guattari formulate through *A Thousand Plateaus*, and relating this to the 'regimes of work' and interconnected educational practice. The work of high school English teachers will be given as an example of educational practice. The writing presented in this chapter takes the ideas of Deleuze and Guattari seriously as a philosophical means to explaining the ways in which capitalism currently functions, and with reference to this book as whole, helps us to understand how economic crises, exemplified by the global financial crisis (GFC) of 2008, have definite and lasting interpersonal effects beyond financial loss. This chapter also builds on previous works that explain literacies and multiple literacies (e.g., Masny & Cole, 2009), and functions to connect educational practice with regimes of capitally differentiated and digitalized work.

October 2008: The Reflection Process—Office Work

What is a regime of work? Factory workers know that they have to arrive at their clock-in station at a certain time, remain in their position for their paid hours, and leave the workplace after attending to their functions in the factory. This 'regime of work' is ordered, repetitive and clockwork. The worker fits into the system as another cog in the machine—and as such they are drained of creativity, individuality and flair. Joining the union might help to keep the workers' wages above the minimum, yet the worker has no decision-making opportunities, no input in terms of product design, and no understanding of the economic situation and capital flows that determine the life of the factory. This picture of what constitutes a regime of work has not ceased, though most sweatshop style factories have now moved to 'developing countries', where wages are lower and people may still be happy to do factory work. In 'developed' countries the regimes of work have, to a large extent, changed. Digital technology has empowered workers to become designers, to control flows of capital via computer screens, to sit in offices and communicate by e-mail, to work from home or to have flextime schemes (e.g., Barnes, 2006). These digital regimes of work have given rise to a new reality that has also changed education, in that it is now seen less as being a preparation for factory life and more as a means to producing the next generation of 'e-workers' (see Peters, Marginson & Murphy, 2009).

In the recent sequel to the 1987 film *Wall Street*, the young protagonist, Jake, is an example of a contemporary e-worker that education is now mandated to produce. He is a specialist in alternative sources of energy, and this knowledge acts as an ideal outcome and dénouement to the current phase of accelerated capitalism (or the green bubble). At one point, the film's hero gets out of bed in his pristine New York apartment and wanders over to a triptych of screens that have been set up in a space adjoining the bedroom. The screens are already turned on, the character can immediately reenter the markets, which are beginning to register a fictional account of the October 2008 financial crash. One can see that the regime of work has transmigrated from the office and into the apartment. There is no escape from market engagement. Even when this engagement could mean an end to employment, or the search for another job, market analysis is still operant—the agent can never switch off. Of course, one may head for what remains of the country and try to live a solitary or communal life closer to nature and in an echo of 1960s hippies' movement, though few of us have the power to sustain such a dull existence. Most of us in developed countries now live in this market-driven world, which invades our homes through TV reports or directly relates to the ubiquitous digital workplace that must in some way deal with the latest market trends.

The events of October 2008 impinge upon consciousness as part of the market invasion. Education, which must now produce e-workers, should also include understanding the experience of financial crashes. This is because the ways in which the GFC worked has lasting effects in terms of developing new strategies and tactics for 'crash survival'. Jake from *Wall Street* changed jobs and became involved with a deal to use Chinese money to fund his green energy proposal in a new position. Most of us will experience unemployment, the search for new work, the erosion of certainty, and patterns of repeated volatility in the markets. This is because ubiquitous global market economics, driven by digital technology that steers 24/7 capital investment, is also still dependent on base products such as oil, coal and food prices. The digital technology that now channels the global economy runs on electricity that is usually still fired by coal. Therefore, any changes in the price or production of coal will be fundamentally registered by the global economy and evoke new investor strategies. Office work is now a reflective and cognitive process (see Liu, 2004) that involves manipulating large amounts of data and making connections of a radical and multiple nature. The first task, therefore, is to try to understand what happens to the agent in this complex, breakdown situation.

Economic Crisis and Subject Breakdown[1]

Complete engagement with interrelated and changing global market forces and understanding the precise reasons for GFC events as they happen is rare, if not impossible. Most of us live in a void that has been created due to a growing separation between the digitally accelerated reality of market surges and depreciation and the lived reality of processing this situation (as it happens). The *Wall Street* sequel ends happily with the hero receiving investment monies from his estranged father-in-law, the ruthless Gekko character. In contrast, and if one wants to understand the void, one needs to bring into the frame a character that fills out the contemporary accelerated movement between volatile market conditions and lived reality:

> Soon everything seemed dull: another sunrise, the lives of heroes, falling in love, war, the discoveries people made about each other...There wasn't a clear, identifiable emotion within me, except for greed and possibly, total disgust. I had all the characteristics of a human being—flesh, blood, skin, hair—but my depersonalization was so intense, had gone so deep, that the normal ability to feel compassion had been eradicated, the victim of a slow, purposeful erasure. I was simply imitating reality, a rough resemblance of a human being, with only a dim corner of my mind functioning. (Ellis, 1991, p. 282)

This monologue is by Patrick Bateman in the novel *American Psycho*. Bateman is a psychopath and ruled by irrational demons whilst manipulating the markets and working in a high-pressure trading environment. To understand such a character, one needs to relate the forces at work in disparate market control and events such as the GFC, with those of the death drive. Deleuze (1997) acknowledges that for Freud the death drive can never be a pure principle. It always appears as one entwined aspect of a qualitative duality, it is always a combination of two drives—those of Eros and Thanatos. Despite this interwoven character, Deleuze (1997) observes that the death drive can result in either an outward sadism—under the governance of Eros, or an erotogenic masochism—libidinally bound within the organism (e.g., Bateman). Furthermore, the death drive can be turned against the organism and result in a passive form of masochism. Initially, perversion is characterized by a desexualization and later by a resexualization entailing both 'defusion'[2] and combination of the two drives, although this action is achieved through a displacement of the energies at the service of Thanatos. Deleuze (1997) points out that Freud's two accounts of defusion relate, respectively, to narcissism and to the formation of the superego, as is the case with the *American Psycho*.

In *Beyond the Pleasure Principle*, the death drive is more complicated. Deleuze notes (1997, 1989) that Freud continues to espouse a monism of the drives for which all apparent exceptions are reconciled, including unpleasure, circuitousness, games of mastery applied to unpleasant experiences, and transference phenomena. However, Eros does not have final authority because a second-order (transcendental) principle accounts for the compliance of the field with the (empirical) first-order erotic principle. This dualism is expressed in two forms of repetition or market realization. First, the operations of Eros achieve a binding of excitations making them resolvable into pleasure through subsequent discharge. Deleuze (1997) says that this phenomenon may be characterized as a 'repetition', insofar as it has responsibility for constituting (as a holding together) through reiteration, both the moment of life (paying dividends) and the union of its elements. While the pleasure principle depends on both a moment of binding-linking and one of elimination-destruction, there is a third repetition that either saves or fails to save. In the synthesis of time not only is there a repetition of the present instant, and a repetition of what was before it, but also a third moment of anticipation of what is to come (futures speculation). Deleuze (1997) follows Freud in describing this complicating moment, or 'the groundlessness of the Ground', as one underpinned by difference of rhythm or amplitude, and in the market, this is investment patterning or hedging.

Deleuze (1997) goes on to consider the phenomenon of the defusion of the Drive, noting that Freud applied this concept to the formation of both the narcissistic ego and the superego. Significantly, Deleuze (1997, 1989) also links the third moment of repetition and the attendant defusion of the drives to Hume's analysis of the psyche. He notes that defusion occurs through a process of desexualization, through which a certain quantum of the libido becomes neutralized, undifferentiated, and freely mobile, as happens in dispersed market analysis. With respect to Freud, this neutral energy sets in motion a process of idealization (responsible for the power of imagination in ego) or identification (responsible for the power of thought in superego). The effect that defusion has on the workings of the pleasure principle includes both functional disturbances and the sublimation of the drives. Nevertheless, in all this, the pleasure principle is not invalidated, and Freud continues to argue that wish fulfillment still motivates dreams (market upsurge). Deleuze (1997) raises the prospect of a third alternative to the constitution of both ego and superego, related less to their interdependence than to a functional divide between them. He notes that in perversion, the phenomenon of desexualization is more pronounced, removed from sublimation and disturbance and retained during the process of resexualization—thus explaining the apathy and coldness of the perversions that one sees in the market control of Bateman.

Deleuze (1997) turns to Nietzsche by stating that if pain and suffering have any meaning it is because they are enjoyable to someone: either pleasing to the gods (investor strategists), or pleasurable to the one who inflicts or suffers. However, pain only acquires significance in relation to the types of repetition that condition (market tendencies). In achieving separation from the pleasure principle, the force of repetition becomes an idea, or an ideal independent of any previous pleasure. Deleuze observes (1997) that there is a kind of otherness in perversion; for the greater the renunciation, the more impressive are the resulting gains. Repetition ensures that a resexualized Thanatos holds sway over a desexualized Eros, where pain is merely an effect and pleasure must be renounced and, henceforth, recovered as a reward (market payouts).

Deleuze (1997, 1989) sees little difference in each of Freud's interpretations of sadomasochism (market control). In the first, the existence of primary masochism is only implied, but in the second, while explicitly acknowledged, it is interpreted as sadism and 'turned around' against the subject. In contrast, Deleuze (1997) argues that there is pseudosadism in masochism and pseudomasochism in sadism. In summary, he claims that:

1. Sadism is speculative-demonstrative, whereas masochism dialectical-imaginative;
2. Sadism operates with the negative and pure negation, masochism with disavowal and suspension;
3. Sadism operates by means of quantitative reiteration, whereas masochism by means of qualitative suspense;
4. There is a masochism specific to the sadist and equally a sadism specific to the masochist;
5. Sadism negates the mother and inflates the father, while masochism disavows the mother and abolishes the father;
6. The role and function of the fetish and the function of the fantasy are totally different in each case;
7. There is an aestheticism in masochism, while sadism is hostile to the aesthetic attitude;
8. Sadism is institutional, whereas masochism contractual;
9. In sadism the superego and the process of identification play the primary role, whereas masochism gives primacy to the ego and to the process of idealization;
10. Sadism and masochism exhibit totally different forms of desexualization;
11. Finally, there is the most radical difference between sadistic apathy and masochistic coldness (Deleuze, 1997, p. 134).

Patrick Bateman personifies these eleven points above and shows how they relate to market control. The rupture points of economic crises serve as a release for sadistic and masochistic drives as they fill the void between market manipulation and living through such a reality. This reality is permeated by the death drive that destroys the subject from within. To understand further how such subject breakdown works, one has to extend the analysis of the death drive and resulting sadism and masochism, and look at the immanent materialism of Deleuze and Guattari (1988). The sexualization of the regimes of work within and through digital markets, the concomitant social realities and subject breakdown (death) is given fresh impetus through this philosophical approach. Immanent materialism helps to connect the type of subject breakdown that one sees in Bateman with education as a regime of work.

Immanent Materialism and the Analysis of 'Flow'

The plateau of October 2008, which may be located through the events of the GFC, is rippling in the global economy in terms of national debt crises in Greece, Ireland, and Portugal and increased international financial regulation. These 'flows' also define the desires of the populations caught within the repercussions of the GFC. For example, the dreams of young architects in Ireland have been altered, Greek civil servants fight for their basic rights, and credit and debt landscapes for new projects in Portugal have been curtailed. In the terms of Deleuze and Guattari (1988), these flows may be understood as immanent materialism. *A Thousand Plateaus: Capitalism & Schizophrenia II* is constituted by very specific moments in history and in the complex throughlines that bisect these moments. *Capitalism & Schizophrenia II* explores themes such as the unhuman elements of becoming that are involved with human action, and the nonlinear nature of history, whereby capitalism can reproduce itself through bifurcation and microassemblage. The perhaps bewildering aspect of immanent materialism is that it introduces research into biological and physical models of becoming into the thesis about capitalism and schizophrenia. These models are designed to disrupt humanistic assumptions about selfhood in the thesis, which their first joint book (1984), *Anti-Oedipus: Capitalism & Schizophrenia*, began to unravel yet retained in terms of critique and revolutionary force. This is why the materialism of *A Thousand Plateaus* constitutes immanent materialism, because it does not construct a transcendental outside to capitalism but looks to deconstruct its formations from within. Immanent materialism simultaneously unhinges phenomenology as a possible state-science in order to understand consciousness and experience as a type of multiple 'matter-flow' (Deleuze & Guattari, 1988, pp. 410–12). Deleuze's engagement with phenomenology does not end in *A Thousand Plateaus*, yet it does constitute a zenith in repeated salvos against a 'cherished opponent' (Beaulieu, 2009). Deleuze needs phenomenology to write against and to show how immanent materialism works. For example, Husserl's (1983) writing on immanence does foreground and entangles with many of Deleuze's workings out of immanence in his oeuvre that peaks in *A Thousand Plateaus*:

> Then there is an altogether different plane, or an altogether different conception of the plane. Here, there are no longer any forms or developments of forms; nor are

> there subjects or the formation of subjects. There is no structure; any more than there is genesis. There are only relations of movement and rest, speed and slowness between unformed elements, or at least between elements that are relatively unformed, molecules and particles of all kinds...Nothing subjectifies, but haecceities form according to compositions of non-subjectified powers or affects. We call this plane, which knows only longitudes and latitudes, speeds and haeccities, the plane of consistency or composition (as opposed to the plan(e) of organization or development). It is necessarily a plane of immanence and univocality. (Deleuze & Guattari, 1988, p. 266)

Deleuze and Guattari (1988) think immanence through to its limit. Husserl (1983) stops in his thinking through of immanence by retaining its relationship with transcendence. This is characteristic of the construction of metaphysics that Deleuze and Guattari are keen to avoid, and the reason they do so is in order to free up the notion of immanence beyond metaphysics to make it applicable for variant explorations (in this chapter, immanence joins the GFC with regimes of work and education). The plane of immanence is associated with abstract machines in *A Thousand Plateaus* and these populate a vast array of historical strata. Abstract machines make things happen in terms of mathematical formula, sketches in notebooks and the workings out of writers, philosophers and artists. For instance, Leonardo da Vinci left notebooks with sketches and drawings of machines and nature that have inspired and intrigued generations of artists, engineers and scientists. If one thinks these sketches through to the limit, one can say that they constitute an abstract machine (a da Vinci machine); it is as if we have access to the workings of da Vinci's mind through a plane of immanence that connects us with his ideas through the many processes of working out of his ideas that we can still see in his notebooks and unfinished sketches. In contrast to *Anti-Oedipus*, that is populated by the unconscious workings of monstrous others, *A Thousand Plateaus* lines up a series of great thinkers to help us understand the connections between capitalism and schizophrenia. Madness and becoming are tied to genius in *A Thousand Plateaus* rather than to the sexual and, at times, perverse proliferations of *Anti-Oedipus*. Immanence encourages a community of thinkers through a plane of consistency, rather than as a revolutionary force born out of sexual liberation. Immanent materialism has also been explained with reference to cybernetics (Mullarkey, 1999, pp. 72–76).

In *A Thousand Plateaus* consciousness does not exist alone but is a series of relative processes that pass through bodies randomly arranged in time. There is no perception of objects nor transcendental 'I', only the world and history of the world as described through the lens of an immanent materialism, collective assemblages rising and falling according to inextricably entangled fields of force. In corollary, one could state that the thesis of immanent materialism is cybernetic in that the machinations of society mesh with modes of organization borne out of organic complexity. This cybernetics is nonreductive as it is a 'wholly abstract framework of a general system theory' (Mullarkey, 1999, p. 78), given the empirical and chaotic elements of the framework as nonorganic life may also take on a life of its own according to Deleuze (an open-systems theory or machine). This type of cybernetics also helps to explain the politics of immanent materialism that rests on Marx's (1976) statement: 'Capitalist production seeks continually to overcome [these] immanent barriers, but overcomes them only by means that again place these barriers in its way and on a more formidable scale. The real barrier of capitalist production is capital itself' (p. 50). The immanent barriers of the system are explained as a means to production in *A Thousand Plateaus*, or as a cybernetic appropriation and play of force. The problem of capital is dealt with by capitalism through abstract machines that organize debt structures and virtual loans (as seen in the GFC). These machines are immanent to contemporary social life, and they orchestrate nexus points of control and submission. In *A Thousand Plateaus* these points become entangled with state-run mechanisms, war machines and machinic enslavements such as watching television or using a computer. State control of social life in terms of the construction of an apparatus of capture of the 'socius' through history comes in for particular attention in *A Thousand Plateaus*, which has made some wonder about the *realpolitik* behind immanent materialism (see Patton, 2000). However, the overwhelming message of immanent materialism is to question capitalist modes of production, not through critique and transcendence but by activating forms of nomadism that burrow through sedentary overlays of capitalist codes and subjectivation immanently. Deleuze and Guattari (1988) call this process rhizomatics (pp. 3–26) in the introduction to *A Thousand Plateaus*, and rhizomes are characterized by subterranean connections and as a form of politics. This politics is applicable to educational practice. Education is caught in the flows that emanate from the GFC, and is part of their reproduction as capitalism has taken over many of the ways in which teaching and learning now operates. Immanent materialism demands that we analyze the flows from within.

Selected Moments in the Anatomy of Learning—English Teaching and Multiple Literacies

The work of high school English teachers is changing. This fact has been recognized in academic literature and in practice since at least the 1990s. The changes are driven by new regimes of work and their intersection with digitally mediated forms of communication (see Cole, 2007). Of course, there are conservative reactions to the changing practice of teaching English, and these reactions are characterized by calls for back-to-basics teaching, with an emphasis on grammar, spelling and 'the classics'. However, the impetus for change, and the idea that high school English teaching should prepare students for new forms of digital socialities (Kress, 2006), has continued to grow over the last twenty years. In 1996, the New London Group published a manifesto for the changing work of English teachers under the banner *Multiliteracies: Designing Social Futures* (New London Group, 1996). This new pedagogic approach was meant to take into account and incorporate the regimes of working that were opening up due to the latest in digital technology; at the time this was primarily the Internet. This approach has lately been taken up by the new literacies movement (see Coiro, Knobel, Lankshear & Leu, 2008), which has argued that digital technology now dominates many aspects of adolescence in postindustrial countries and should, therefore, be incorporated into teaching and learning curricula as a basic sociological fact and new communicative option. The new literacies are also greatly expanded through mobile technology, whereupon access to digital mediation is made ubiquitous, leading to the development of M-Space, within which the agent can navigate through cyberspace without interruption. One of the most recent developments in literacy comes in the shape of multiple literacies theory (MLT), whereby the notion of literacy is almost entirely uprooted from the tradition of reading, writing, speaking and listening in analogue print:

> Multiple literacies refer to literacies as a construct—machinic assemblages: social, medical, economic, etc. Literacies consist of words, markings, gestures, attitudes, and ways of communicating, human and non-human. Accordingly, literacies constitute ways of becoming: becoming with the world. They involve texts in the virtual that actualize as sense emerges. They are taken up as visual, oral, written, tactile, olfactory, and in multimodal 'digitality'. Literacies constitute texts, in a broad sense, for example, music, visual arts (painting, sculpting), physics, mathematics, digital remixes. Texts are assemblages of events. Moreover, literacies fuse with socio-political, cultural, economic, political, gendered and racialized contexts. This is how literacies are coded. These contexts are not static. They are fluid and transform literacies, and that produce speakers, writers, artists, digital avatars: communities. (Masny, 2011, personal communication)

This description of multiple literacies theory brings us closer to the connection between changing regimes of work and current educational practice. This is because the new regimes of work cannot be overlaid on top of traditional English classes by, for example, taking students to the computer lab and asking them to write essays on 'Word'; new regimes of work flow through the very practice of education. Corporate practice, as characterized by the breakdown of the subject above, market analysis and the following of money flows, set up by events such as the GFC, and is reproduced in schools. This is because current forms of capitalism, which are energized by digital technology, duly invade youth markets for expansion. One cannot designate a transferable identity between corporate practice and teaching practice but that the influence comes from within. Teachers, administrators and students in state-run systems struggle for funding and therefore reproduce the power relation of debt through their practice (see Cole, 2009a). Privately funded schools reproduce capital flows in the 'given-ness' of choice and experimentation in educational practice, which reproduces the lightness of touch and control available to the CEOs of thriving companies. It is as if there is symmetry between the new regimes of work and educational practice, a symmetry that can be understood through multiple literacies:

> Literacies are actualized according to a particular context in time and in space in which they operate. Given the nomadic tendencies of literacies; they are not wed to a context, but are taken up in unpredictable ways across various contexts. Reading is both intensive (disruptive) and immanent. Literacies involve constant movement in the process of becoming other. There is potentiality in releasing literacy from its privileged position as the printed word by not allowing it to govern all other literacies. In this way, literacies open themselves to what is not already given. In short, literacies are about reading, reading the world, and self as texts. (Masny, 2011, personal communication)

English teachers trying to hang on to the old ways of working with print text may be caught out by this situation. Not least because the students may find mono-print literacy pedagogy boring and out of touch with new multiple realities that are flowing through them (e.g., Cole, 2009b). In fact, the atmospheres in schools and colleges is currently affected by the ways in which multiple literacies are defining new senses of teaching and learning practice; and these are simultaneously shifted or 'othered' by the new regimes of work. For example, the immediacy, speed and mobility of the new multiple literacies leave behind the necessity to repeat exercises in order to get them right. Furthermore, students can upload a video on YouTube, make a Wiki or create a podcast to express their ideas. Compare this with the laborious task of writing a formal essay out by hand. New capitalism demands new literacies, and they must be multiple and driven to cope with dispersed market conditions. English teachers need to change their practice to cope with these multiple transformations and to allow their lessons to deal with future regimes of work as they impinge upon the educational practices of today.

The Future of Work: Accelerated Schizophrenic Capitalism (ASC)

The work of English teachers is put under pressure and destabilized by multiple literacies. In Deleuzian terms this is because of the duration that is present in contemporary teaching and learning, where the multiple becomes realized in time (Bergson, 1965). It is as if students are agents of the future, carrying with them the new regimes of work into the classroom; and as a consequence, they cannot engage or sustain traditional forms of reading, writing, speaking and listening. Yet perhaps it is too narrow to speak about agency in this context. Students are synonymous with the ways in which culture is changing; new forms of capitalism and the consequent regimes of work therefore put the context of education under pressure. One consequence of this pressure is that the category of work itself has changed—from the factory to the office, and now from the office into everyday life. This latest transformation takes, for example, the flows of money and consequent matter from the GFC and asks the fundamental question: What is the point of work and education now (under the conditions of an unstable financial system)?

> A consummate libidinal materialism is distinguished by its complete indifference to the category of work. Wherever there is labor or struggle there is a repression of the raw creativity, which is the 'a-theological' sense of matter and which—because of its anegoic[3] effortlessness—seems identical with dying. Work, on the other hand is an idealist principle used as a supplement or compensation for what matter cannot do. (Land, 1994, p. 90)

This quote comes from 1990s theorist Nick Land, who examined capitalism from an accelerated, negative perspective. He associated the immanent materialism of Deleuze and Guattari (1988) with libidinal materialism, in a reference to the influence of Freud and the analysis of the unconscious. The point here is that the old, 'heroic' category of work has changed and given way to new, disguised regimes of work, regimes that function *sans travail.* The sweaty efforts of the past are replaced by cool, impersonal interactions and dispersed networks. One could say that it is not that work is now associated with being, but that itself has changed under pressure from digitalization. The unemployed labor of the past is now 'ionized matter particles that shift in clouds' (see Gee, 2005). Attitudes have also changed from alienation, defiance and potential revolution against the exploitation of labor, to an abstract, global creativity that is only accessed through engagement with the ways in which the future clashes in the present (e.g., Kelly, 1999). As we have seen above, this dark creativity as vital commodity necessitates subject breakdown and the release of energies such as sadism and masochism, exemplified in characters such as Patrick Bateman and events such as the GFC. This release mechanism, also changes the notion of greed that one can associate with present and future forms of capitalism:

> The obsolete psychological category of 'greed' privatizes and moralizes addiction, as if the profit-seeking tropism of a transnational capitalism propagating itself through epidemic consumerism were intelligible in terms of personal subjective traits. Wanting more is the index of interlock with 'cyber-positive' machinic processes, and not the expression of private idiosyncrasy. What could be more impersonal—disinterested—than a *haut bourgeois* capital expansion servomechanism striving to double $10 billion? And even these creatures are disappearing into silicon viro-finance automatisms, where massively distributed and anonymized human ownership has become as vacuously nominal as democratic sovereignty. (Land, 1993, p. 478)

This quote is exemplified through the *Wall Street* films and the Gekko character. In the first film, he was the epitome of greed and ego, using greed as the primary drive and means to exploitative and financial power. In the second film, Gekko has been to prison, written a book, and deals with his daughter's boyfriend to get his fortune back. The difference between the two fictional representations of the same character is that the older version has inculcated reflective practice. He is still 'greedy' because he schemes to secure his old money for himself, yet his means to power are more circumspect, disguised and ultimately expedient as he does share his wealth with his family. In terms of education, this designates a change in motivation for students that are living through the current situation. If greed is not personally motivating, what does drive them to seek qualifications and to strive to do their best at study? The answer lies in having the capacity to 'fit in' with the new forms of capitalism as they emerge around the globe and to use these forms to one's advantage. I would like to name this form of capitalism as *Accelerated Schizophrenic Capitalism* (ASC), after the groundbreaking work of Nick Land (1993, 1994) and in line with the immanent materialism of this chapter. ASC is a development in capitalism that includes the self-reflexive breakdown of events such as the GFC that have in no way slowed down the processes of capitalist development, but have in many ways accelerated them by creating new markets of debt and misery in places such as Greece, Ireland, Portugal, and so forth. These new markets are ripe for capitalist exploitation. The tendency towards democracy in the Middle East is also ultimately driven by ASC, in that the desire for freedom from tyranny will result in being controlled by the concerns of credit, debt and money. ASC is a complicated mixture of commercial values and digital distribution, territorial gains coupled with psychological tremors. To quote Land once more:

> 'Digito-commodification' is the index of a cyber-positively escalating techno-virus, of the planetary techno-capital singularity: a self-organizing insidious traumatism,

> virtually guiding the entire biological desiring-complex towards post-carbon replicator usurpation...The reality principle tends to a consummation as the price system: a convergence of mathematico-scientific and monetary quantization, or technical and economic implementability. This is not a matter of an unknown quantity, but of a quantity that operates as a placeholder for the unknown, introducing the future as an abstract magnitude. Capital propagates virally in so far as money communicates addiction, replicating itself through host organisms whose boundaries it breaches, and whose desires it reprograms. It incrementally virtualizes production; 'demetallizing' money in the direction of credit finance, and 'disactualizing' productive force along the scale of machinic intelligence quotient. The dehumanizing convergence of these tendencies zeroes upon an integrated and automatized cyber-positive techno-economic intelligence at war with the 'macropods'.[4] (Land, 1993, p. 479)

This fascinating description of the future as being present in current tendencies brings us closer to understanding ASC. Numbers on stock exchange boards currently organize the world. This was illustrated by the GFC, where the run on companies and credit lines nearly sunk the entire globally interconnected financial system. It is not a question of How much? anymore, as the numbers are often too large to imagine. The questions that one should ask have now changed to those of future market tendencies and politicosocial questions connected to the emergence of new markets and the ways in which these new markets may be manipulated and used (to make money). It is in this regime of work (as nonwork) that ASC exists. Questions of power, agency and responsibility are all mixed up in this space. It is impossible to know who (or what) is really in control, because the function of ASC is to introduce elements beyond nonrational control into any relatable equation. ASC defines a situation as E {x + y}. One might say that there is continually something else to consider and multiply, making research fluid and sedentary location impossible. If one tries to define these exigent elements, for example, by using ideas of sentiment or fear, ASC has the capacity to inculcate these explanations into its functioning and to use them for market realization purposes (see Moran, 2005). Education is crucial in this process, as was demonstrated though the example of high school English teaching and learning above, whereby multiple literacies now stream through the digitally augmented consciousness of the classroom. Trying to defend one's practice against this tendency is futile; it is better to get with the program and to understand and study ASC, the GFC and any relevant questions that flow through these postindustrial singularities and precursors to everyday life.

Conclusion

This chapter has argued that ASC brings us closer to understanding the ways in which current regimes of work impinge upon educational practice. This is because ASC includes the self-reflection of events such as the GFC, along with the manipulation of its consequences, to create wealth. Education is often seen as a means to producing metacognitive events in the agent so that thinking might happen and understanding deepen (see Cole, 2010). Of course, this is exactly the type of new task and regime of work that is encouraged through ASC (even if it is a category of dispersed or disguised nonwork). The problem for education is that ASC works on a deeply irrational level, as well as responding to rational directives in language and to the mathematical proofs of economists. Therefore, if education is to provide the means to surviving events such as the next GFC, it must as a practice delve into culturally dormant unconscious assumptions. The example of high school English teachers, now confronted by an array of multiple literacies, which student cohorts carry with them, is a good example of how this might work. The point is not that English teachers suddenly abandon concerns about grammar and spelling or formal reading and writing but that they confront the multiple in literacy as a serious means to student engagement and coming closer to ASC as a contemporary regime of work. Teachers should understand that this is not a superficial concern of their cohorts, but part of the new shifting reality of being an adolescent in post-industrial Western countries. The student's creativity and sense of freedom now lies in the multiple, as ASC permeates every action and thought that is conceivable. There is no outside to ASC, as every trend and unconscious desire is codified even before it emerges into full-scale product exploitation. ASC is a drug that we are all taking, living off and living through. If we stop taking the drug, madness ensues (ASC is madness). The only choice is to keep up the dosage and to make ASC a fully integrated part of life. In education, this means dissecting the mechanics of events such as the GFC and teaching and learning through their component parts. The unknown aspect of this plan is whether or not ASC sustains into the future, and if it does dissemble, what will take its place.

> Operating in the mode of a macho hard-edged realism, what accelerationism attests to is the poverty of a theoretical imagination unable to reconstruct any rationality in the present and instead content to wallow in the fantasmatic residues of capitalism's own irrationalisms. (Noys, 2010, p. 7)

Notes

1. I would like to thank James Juniper (2010) for explaining the connections between Deleuze's reading of Freudian drives and market manipulation.
2. Freud used the terms 'fusion' and 'defusion' (Mischung and Entmischung), in the context of his second theory of the instincts, to account for the 'mixing' and separation of the life instincts and the death instincts. Throughout his work, Freud relied upon the notion of an instinctual dualism; an opposition between two fundamental kinds of instinct that explains the conflict inherent in mental life. In his first theory of the instincts, he contrasted sexual instincts, on the one hand, and self-preservative instincts (or ego instincts) on the other. In his second theory, the life instinct, or Eros, stood opposed to the death instinct, and Freud emphasized that the antagonistic relationship between the two reflected their essential nature. The life instinct, for its part, was a force that strove to unify, and this included unifying the two fundamental instincts themselves; their intimate fusion came about through their simultaneous cathexis of the same object, which rendered them well-nigh indissoluble. At the same time, the death instinct, which promoted dissolution, worked to defuse them through a decathexis of the object, thus threatening the unity of the psyche itself.
3. Meaning without an ego or any sense of 'I'.
4. PODS = Politically Organized Defense System

References

Barnes, P. (2006). *Capitalism 3.0: Enriching ourselves by enhancing our commons*. San Francisco: Berrett-Koehler.

Beaulieu, A. (2009). Edmund Husserl. In G. Jones & J. Roffe (Eds.), *Deleuze's philosophical lineage* (pp. 261–282). Edinburgh: Edinburgh University Press.

Bergson, H. (1965). *Duration and simultaneity* (with reference to Einstein's Theory) (L. Jacobson, Trans.). Indianapolis: Bobbs-Merrill.

Coiro, J., Knobel, M., Lankshear, C., & Leu, D. (Eds.). (2008). *Handbook of research on new literacies*. New York: Lawrence Erlbaum Associates.

Cole, D. R. (2007). Virtual terrorism and the Internet e-learning options. *E-Learning*, 4(2), 116–127.

Cole, D. R. (2009a). Indexing the multiple: An autobiographic account of education through the lens of Deleuze and Guattari. In D. Masny & D. R. Cole (Eds.), *Multiple literacies theory: A Deleuzian perspective* (pp. 119–132). Rotterdam: Sense Publishers.

Cole, D. R. (2009b). The power of emotional factors in English teaching. *Power and Education*, 1(1), 57–70.

Cole, D. R. (2010, December). The reproduction of philosophical bodies in education with language. *Educational Philosophy and Theory*, 42 (8), 816–829.

Deleuze, G. (1989). *Coldness and cruelty* (J. McNeil, Trans.). New York: Zone Books.

Deleuze, G. (1997). *Essays critical and clinical* (D. W. Smith & M. A. Greco, Trans.). Minneapolis: University of Minnesota Press.

Deleuze, G., & Guattari, F. (1984). *Anti-Oedipus: Capitalism and Schizophrenia* (R. Hurley, M. Steem, & H. R. Lane, Trans.). London: Athlone Press.

Deleuze, G., & Guattari, F. (1988). *A Thousand Plateaus: Capitalism and Schizophrenia II* (B. Massumi, Trans.). London: Athlone Press.

Ellis, B. E. (1991). *American psycho*. New York: Vintage Books.

Gee, J. P. (2005). Semiotic social spaces and affinity spaces: From the age of mythology to today's schools. In D. Barton & K. Tusting (Eds.), *Beyond communities of practice: Language, power, and social context* (pp. 214–232). Cambridge: Cambridge University Press.

Husserl, E. (1983). *Ideas pertaining to a pure phenomenology and to a phenomenological philosophy: First book* (F. Kersten, Trans.). Boston: Martinus Nijhoff Publishers.

Juniper, J. (2010). Deleuze, Lacan and the philosophy of affect. *Australasian Society for Continental Philosophy*. Annual Conference 2010, University of Queensland, December 3–5.

Kelly, K. (1999). *New rules for the new economy*. London: Fourth Estate.

Kress, G. (2006). Reimagining English: Curriculum, identity and productive futures. In B. Doecke, M. Howie, & W. Sawyer (Eds.), *'only connect'* (pp. 31–41). South Australia: Wakefield Press.

Land, N. (1993). Machinic desire. *Textural Practice*, 7, 471–482.

Land, N. (1994). Making it with death: Remarks on Thanatos and desiring-production. *Journal of the British Society for Phenomenology*, 24, 75–91.

Liu, A. (2004). *The laws of cool: The culture of information*. Chicago: University of Chicago Press.

Marx, K. (1976). *Capital, Vol.* 3. In Marx/Engels Collected Works. London: International Publishers. Available online at: http://www.marxists.org/archive/marx/works/1894-c3/ch15.htm

Masny, D. (2011). Definition of multiple literacies. Personal communication (e-mail).

Masny, D., & Cole, D. R. (Eds.), (2009). *Multiple literacies theory: A Deleuzian perspective*. Rotterdam: Sense Publishers.

Moran, J. (2005). *Reading the everyday*. London: Routledge.

Mullarkey, J. (1999). Deleuze and materialism: One or several matters? In I. Buchanan (Ed.), *A Deleuzian Century?* (pp. 59–85). Durham, NC & London: Duke University Press.

New London Group. (1996). A pedagogy of multiliteracies: Designing social futures. *Harvard Education Review*, 66(1), 1–30.

Noys, B. (2010). The grammar of neoliberalism. *Accelerationism Workshop*, Goldsmiths, London, September 14, 2010.

Patton, P. (2000). *Deleuze and the Political*. New York: Routledge.

Peters, M. A., Marginson, S., & Murphy, P. (2009). *Creativity and the global knowledge economy*. New York: Peter Lang.

Schatzki, T. R. (1996). *Social practices: A Wittgensteinian approach to human activity and the social*. Cambridge: Cambridge University Press.

Smitley, R. L. (1933). *Popular financial delusions*. Philadelphia: Fraser Publishing.

• CHAPTER ELEVEN •

The Crisis of Mutative Capitalism: Holey Spaces, Creative Struggle and Educative Innovations

Robert Haworth & Abraham P. DeLeon

Introduction

In 1999, students at the *Universidad Nacional Autónoma de México* (UNAM) occupied and eventually shut down one of the largest universities in the Western Hemisphere for 292 days. These actions took place not only because of the Mexican government's aggressive moves to impose tuition fees but also because students were actively contesting the larger neoliberal policies that were attempting to privatize public institutions (Rhoads & Liu, 2009). After the passage of the North American Free Trade Agreement (NAFTA) in 1994, the pressure to repay the high interest bailout money to the International Monetary Fund (IMF), international creditors and the private sector caused Mexico to introduce new legislation into law that called for the opening of education and public health sectors to private investment (Delgado-Ramos & Saxe-Fernández, 2005). During the strike, university students not only demanded stoppages to neoliberal policies and the pillaging of public spaces, but they also called on the government to recognize Article 3 of the Mexican Constitution. This Article stems from the Mexican Revolution in the early twentieth century and lays the groundwork for education as a democratic right (Rhoads & Mina, 2001). Because of the forceful push of the IMF and the demand for economically restructuring public spaces, the students' demands were outright denied by the ruling party (PRI), and in 2000 federal officers forced the students out of UNAM and the strike ended.

More recently, in 2010, students in the United Kingdom smashed the front windows and occupied the Conservative Party's campaign headquarters to demonstrate against the preposterous raises in tuition and funding cuts to universities. Students strongly declared this was just the beginning for organizing opposition movements to contest neoliberal economic and educational policies. In March 2011, an estimated 400,000 UK students and public workers fulfilled their promise that these movements were not isolated (http://www.edu-factory.org). Protesters marched and contested their "double taxation" when the public was asked to bail out banks and, at the same time, were being told to take the brunt of the major cuts to education, health care and wages to public employees.

The United States has not been immune to these public dismantling maneuvers. Conservative governor Scott Walker, along with billionaire conservatives and market fundamentalists David and Charles Koch, have worked diligently in setting a nationwide precedence to eliminate collective bargaining for public employees, while at the same time making major tax cuts for corporations and wealthy individuals. New legislation has led to some of largest massive demonstrations in Wisconsin's history. Unfortunately, the "union busting" bill has begun to penetrate the daily lives of public workers by gutting public education funding, raising the costs of medical care and slashing retirement benefits. At the same time, these policies have inspired other conservative governors around the country to make similar attempts to undermine and pull down organized labor.

At first glance it would seem that these brief examples would give a sense of frustration and futility. From another perspective, however, the rise of alter-globalization movement(s) could be considered a refreshing alternative to unbridled profiteering. Students, public sector workers and university professors creatively disrupting the relentless push for open and unregulated markets are a welcome sight when wealthy and political elites attempt to tread on public spaces. For university students, it is already a well-known reality that grants and other financial support are scarce and, in many cases, nonexistent. In fact, students are taking on an extraordinary amount of debt, and, according to the *Wall Street Journal*, student debt has now surpassed credit card debt (Pilon, 2010). As debt for poor and working families has led to large-scale housing foreclosures and bankruptcies, we continue to see market speculators scour the planet in search of new ways to profit while shifting the economic burden on the public. Although such reactionary shifts by the larger global financial institutions have led to our current economic crisis, according to Chomsky (1999) "the economic consequences of these policies have been the same just about everywhere" (p. 8). The brief vignettes we have emphasized are just a few of the examples of how neoliberalism and economic restructuring has had negative consequences on public spaces. But these examples also point to how capitalism and, in particular, neoliberal capitalist policies have mutated or transformed (Deleuze & Guattari, 1987). No longer can the marketplace be viewed as a stagnant system of deterministic goals and outcomes. According to Vandenberghe (2008) it is important to construct more elaborate and emerging concepts and analyses of how capitalism operates, and where it "feeds, as it were, on its own problems and in the process it changes itself and mutates" (p. 878). Therefore, if capitalism is transforming or becoming other than, it is important that the economic crisis be discussed in much more complex ways—where individuals and collective organizations expose the illegitimacy and mutative qualities and mechanisms of the system, and thus contest the oppressive nature of capitalism through direct actions and other micropolitical fronts (Best & Kellner, 1991; Foucault, 1980).

In this chapter, we look at the mutative characteristics of capitalism, the economic crisis's brutal dismantling of public spaces, and why, even under most oppressive practices by corporations and the state, subjects desire to become what Deleuze and Guattari (1983) described as *Oedipedalized subjects*. The current narrative is that the only solution to the economic crisis is privatization, corporate populism, and, of course, more free-market values. By contesting desired neoliberal movements, we will draw upon Deleuze and Guattari's (1987) work regarding the *smith* and *nomad* as potential subjectivities for transformation, not only in their capacities to contest capitalist mutations, but also in their ability to create political and educational experiments or imaginaries outside of formations of global capitalism.

Mutative Capitalism

If there is one thing that can be learned from the economic crisis, it is that neoliberalism has enabled capitalism to become highly flexible, thus enabling it to infiltrate our daily lives. DeLeon (2010) describes these shifts regarding the spatial and unrestricted movement of capitalism stating,

> Capitalism has free reign over the entire globe in a series of vast, open networks that give it the possibility of uninhibited movement, while at the same time limiting the movement of bodies and labor. In this way, neoliberal capitalism spreads through social and topographical networks harnessing a new form of embodiment for capital itself. (p. 54)

The "open networks" and "uninhibited movements" of capitalism demonstrate the fluid and expansive nature of the "creative economy" (Peters, 2009). Moreover, Peters attributes the shift in the economy to one that is "based on the growing power of ideas and virtual value chain—the turn from steel and hamburgers to software and intellectual property" (p. 45). Therefore, the drive to invest in large industry is de-emphasized. This has shifted the economy into virtual spaces and social-networking environments. Although industrial models are not completely dismantled, they become less favorable within the current creative economy. Capital is acquired through purchasing islands in the virtual world of *Second Life* or the proprietorship of finding new ways of data mining consumer information to cross advertise and reach a larger global audience. Thus, capitalism becomes much more inventive and productive—it is invasive in our everyday lives (Vandenberghe, 2008).

Similar to Foucault (1980), Deleuze and Guattari's (1983, 1987) works also highlight the importance of recognizing the relationships between macro- and microeconomics and politics that contemporarily enable more complex understandings and critiques of neoliberal and global capitalism. Primarily, their work steers our analysis away from being entrenched in deterministic binaries or what they describe as "aboreal" (linear, hierarchical) ways of thinking, which in many cases has directed us to tenacious beliefs about how power operates (Dimitriadas & Kamberelis, 2006). Rather than perceiving power in its binary construction of "good" or "bad," Deleuze and Guattari (1987) view it as being productive and created in multiple capacities through different lines of flight. Just as revolutionaries attempt to take up different lines of flight, the desiring machines of capitalism also take on different and complex forms and mutations. In fact, the complex paths that power operates in and around are why Vandenberghe (2008) argues that the twenty-first century is Deleuzian: "[It is] empiricist and materialist, pragmatic and performative, heterogeneous and machinic, chaosmotic and rhizomatic, hypercomplex and hypercapitalist" (p. 878). These mutative qualities enable capitalism to function differently, not only in recognizing individuals as human social capital, but also envisioning individuals as guided consumer citizens embedded in 'techno-romanticized' lifestyles under the creative economy (Peters, 2009).

If, in fact, Vandenberghe's (2008) interpretations of Deleuze and Guattari are accurate, and capitalist flows are *becoming other* or mutating through complex and decentralized mechanisms, then a more intricate and critical analysis of its transformations are needed. One example of these mutative qualities comes from economic fluctuations or what Vandenberghe describes as "flexible accumulation." Within these traits, capitalism functions more heterogeneously and fluid and has become what he describes as "leaner" and "meaner" (p. 880)—leaner in a sense that the economy does not rely solely on older factory models and infrastructure, but is dependent heavily on social and virtual networking to infiltrate markets; "meaner" in a sense of transforming the workplace. He explains:

> The principles of the market were progressively introduced in the organization, unions were sidelined, wages were individualized, contracts liberalized and labour

> time flexibilized, with the result that, 30 years later, the individualized, casualized and contractualized flexi-worker is confronted with insecurity and delivered to a completely restructured, radically flexibilized labour market on which she or he has to sell not only her or his labour force, but also personality, self and ultimately perhaps also soul. (p. 880)

Becoming more cognizant of movements and mutations of capitalism lends us to take on new and multiple forms of understanding the restructured workplace as well as emerging speculative market desires. More important, we should also ask the question: In what capacities can we resist these particular ongoing oppressive flows under capitalism, when there is ongoing desire for more accountability to the marketplace (Giroux, 2004)?

Desire and the Oedipedalized Subject

Part of the mutative characteristics of capitalism involves the social, as well as the intricacies of desire. Deleuze and Guattari (1983) point out that capitalism does not limit desire, but attempts to control its functions—its lines of flight. It is the assemblages of the capitalist machinery that attempt to territorialize or tame desires of liberation outside the function of the state. If the desiring-machines of capitalism are in constant flow, they are *becoming other* through transforming assemblages and networks (Newman, 2002). In this case, subjects "plug into" assemblages and lines of power leading to larger machines. The impulses and drives within these assemblages become saturated and overcoded within the confines of capitalism. According to Smith (2007) desires are "constructed, assembled, and arranged in such a manner that your desire is positively invested in the system that allows you to have this particular interest" (p. 74). In other words, your desires of social transformation are based solely within reforming the system and only within the limitations of capitalism.

This is where we turn to Deleuze and Guattari's (1983) discussions surrounding the *Oedipedalized subject*—a desire for the state. The Oedipedalized subject desires the parent-child relationship of the state as well as capitalist flows, where she/he is at home in striated spaces (Day, 2005). For example, in an interview Deleuze (1995) comments, "People got hard-ons for Hitler, for the beautiful fascist machine" (Lothringer, 1995). Similarly, Oedipedalized subjects desire the interworkings of the state and the capitalist machine, and they also have a desire for their own repression (Best & Kellner, 1991; Deleuze & Guattari, 1983). Whether it is the fascist state or the capitalist system, desire within the Oedipedalized subject plays an important role in how we understand our relationships to state or corporate entities. This is evident under contemporary managed and state-centered democratic practices, along with corporate media outlets, where there is a constant chattering for more free market interventions. Under state and corporate attempts to control, capitalist networks become desired by the striated spaces of the Oedipedalized subject. The consistent efforts to privatize, to uphold marketplace values, and the unending desires of consumerism and entrepreneurship are the desiring-machine's results through controlling lines of flight. For example, we can conceive how desires for liberation are cut off or limited through the recent market shifts to green capitalist illusions and environmental ethics. This shift alludes to the false notion that Wall Street concerns itself with issues surrounding global warming and the environment. These ludicrous prospects of engaging in capitalist ethics also fall short within the flexible investments of corporations in the "green economy." As Oedipedalized subjects, desire shifts to reform environmental laws to curtail global warming within the confines of "aboreal" thinking under capitalism. For instance, GE makes concerted efforts to invest and produce a "green" corporate identity, while simultaneously subsidizing nuclear energy and clean-coal technology. Hence, capitalism seeks to cut off and reterritorialize spaces and lines of flight that create collective and ecological arguments, as well as actions outside the formations of the mechanisms of capital. In fact, capitalism creates new lines of flights and machines that redirect desire from these liberatory actions.

More Capitalism Please!

> In the grander sense, we choose the private space over the diversity of the public space. (Kincheloe, 2006, p. 222)

As we have discussed earlier, capitalism is mutating and consistently attempting to control desiring-machines. Because these networks pass through the macro- and microlevels of society, education is not immune to these controlling mechanisms. In fact, capitalism's productive power to infiltrate educational spaces is expanding. Dokuzović and Freudmann (2009) point out that even investors in the music industry are shifting their energies to education, highlighting that "knowledge is a tradable commodity and considered profitable." The focus to not only shift speculation but also to privatize and profit from education and the knowledge economy are part of those movements to economically restructure society under neoliberalism. From the militaristic and hypercompetitive scare tactics of the Reagan administration's report titled *A Nation at Risk*, to Barack Obama's shift to aggressively support privatization, discussions regarding educational policies in the United States have steadily argued for more competition and capitalist interventions.

Whether it is competition between nation-states or within the context of the marketplace, education reform is discussed within the particular confines of these capitalist assemblages. Business class educational positions are not surprising as neoliberal policies produce the desire for more privatization of public spaces and capitalist flows. At a national level, this ushered in the unrealistic measurable goals of No Child Left Behind that supported private takeover (educational management organizations) of failing public schools. The Obama administration has also weighed in as it pushes for more charter schools and for funneling money into public-private ventures. Moreover, the move to privatize education becomes more dominant, polices corral teachers into being judged, and, driven by efficiency models and intensifies connections with marketplace values (Cole, 2011; Olssen & Peters, 2005; Saltman, 2007).

Although by early 2000 the move to privatize education in the United States was considered a failure, the desire for "more capitalism" and, as Saltman (2007) argues, "backdoor privatization" enacted individuals to falsely accept that the ultimate solution to issues regarding public education and public spaces, in general, is a desire for more privatization, deregulation and hyper-competitivism. But these actions should not be surprising considering that "capitalism does not prevent the desire-flows of bodies, but instead seeks to ensure that those flows are always already functioning for capitalism" (Hickey-Moody & Malins, 2007, p. 15). Therefore, the lines of flight to transform education outside of desiring-machines and the formations of capitalism are controlled and mutated into production and consumption.

The film *Waiting for Superman* (2010) is another example of how capitalism redirects and controls lines of flight to embrace competition, accountability and meritocracy and the representations that emerge to support these larger discursive realities. One example of this occurred during the opening weeks of the film's debut. Twenty-four-hour news networks, including MSNBC, who led an educational "teach in" titled "Education Nation," discussed the concerns brought up in the film about public education. In the MSNBC program, Geoffrey Canada, CEO of the highly recognized charter schools the *Harlem Children's Zone*, and Michelle Rhee, who was the former chancellor of Washington (D.C.) public schools (and recently was accused of falsifying test score outcomes) were touting meritocracy, accountability and creativity, while American Federation of Teachers union president Randi Weingarten was highly criticized and in many cases cut off by both the guests and corporate moderators. Thus, leaving the public to accept that Canada's and Rhee's arguments for more competition, accountability and meritocracy are desired solutions and outcomes to issues regarding public schools. Throughout the show, connections between corporate and privatized solutions were seamless. While individuals latched on to Canada's slogans of educational change, the discourse maneuvered in and out of the promotion of his charter schools through American Express Members Project commercials. Moreover, Canada's and Rhee's language is very interesting to note. Their notions of flexibility enveloped a coded language for "management flexibility," where superintendents need versatile ways of "hiring and firing" employees as they see fit. In this case, creative ventures and management flexibility are valued in how well you can compete for limited corporate resources and build relationships with market ventures. The interactions, language and discourse become part of the controlling mechanisms that redirect and reterritorialize spaces that have any transformative potential or ways of moving beyond market ideologies.

Contesting Capitalist Desire and the Neoliberal Citizen: Nomads, Vagabonds and Smiths

As we have argued, capitalism makes vicious attempts to control desiring lines of flight, but because these lines of flight are constantly being redirected and diverted, capitalism is unable to have total or universal control. Therefore, systems are not totalizing as there are machines that are not commanded—ones that have potential to challenge capitalism (Deleuze & Guattari, 1987). Deleuze and Guattari see these transformations of individuals as emerging assemblages of different networks of desiring-machines. Subjects transform into something different, something outside of the constraints of capitalism or oppressive structures. As Newman (2002) illustrates,

> Becoming is a process of evolution of two or more separate entities—a process of assemblage and connection. Subjects are linked to the state through a series of lines, and if we are to resist this subjectification we must refuse who we are and become other. (p. 103)

Recognizing and dismissing ongoing assemblages or machines that desire capitalism and the state is not deterministic in nature. In many instances the complex mechanisms and assemblages of desire are difficult to detect and decode because they are constantly in flux. According to Masny (2005) this is why it is critical to not only understand "how transformations occur, but more importantly how they are taken up" (p. 150). In *A Thousand Plateaus*, Deleuze and Guattari (1987) describe how these lines of flight are "taken up," particularly through the interrelated subject-machines regarding the citizen, nomad and smith. We will focus primarily on how the nomad and smith take up transformations and innovations in educational spaces.

Looking for Lines of Flight: Nomads and Vagabonds

When we think about possibilities for escape or lines of flight, we can think of the necessity that rethinking subjectivity would need to be a component of this process. Because capitalism tries to control the movement of bodies by harnessing affective desire and enclosing the possibilities for lines of flight, there are characters that have transcended these state mechanisms of control. Nomads, like those living in the Saharan desert, to Western formations, such as artists or drifters, move through space and boundaries in ways that do not give credence to borders or other supposedly "legitimate" lines of demarcation that arise from state-sanctioned discourses. The key subjective experience for nomads would appear to be movement; movement being a signal for a new configuration of bodies that is rooted in change and instability. Although constructed as static in the West, our conceptions of the individual cannot be separated from the larger market-driven ideological framework and practices that seem to guide our understandings of what bodies can do. To reassert Spinoza's questions to indeed question what the limits of a body are in society, the movement of nomads appears to help transcend the limits of what we think our own reality can or should mean. Although not explicitly speaking of a nomadic existence (although this is part of her analysis), Erin Manning (2007) explores the radical potentials of movement by examining the dance of the tango that arose in Argentina but has transcended this by becoming a global phenomenon. But, for Manning, the key idea will always be about bodies that move and the tango helps to represent the importance that movement serves and the importance that touch plays for rethinking our own boundaries. As she claims, "Through the tango, I have attempted to make the point that touch is not simply the laying of hands. Touch is the act of reaching toward, of creating space-time through the worlding that occurs when bodies move. Touch...is not simply an addendum to an already-stable body" (p. xiv). Through movement and through touch, subjectivities can be reforged through new ways of (en)countering the world.

Another character also emerges that incorporates the importance of movement that nomads have established. Vagabonds, emerging in European society with the rise of market capitalism, were also a strange character to the self-ordered bourgeois body that sought a Protestant work and life ethic. Traditionally, European society kept strict control on movement through various social, economic, and geographic policies that attempted to contain certain characters or classes of people. Influenced by events like the Enlightenment, to the reorganization of medicine and medical understanding that Foucault bemoaned in his own studies, and the Protestant work ethic that was guided by economists like Adam Smith, European society frowned upon idleness and those who refused the menial tasks of back-breaking labor that was given to the poor and working classes. The development of disciplinary practices that both (re)produced specific forms of subjectivities and bodies along with it would guide many interpretations of those that sought a life outside of this constructed and manufactured reality. Vagabonds resisted the concept of work and sought a life free from the constraints that a market society placed upon their bodies. They moved, resisted, played, and attempted to subvert the idea of labor and work through *bodily and spatial practices*, a key component when thinking about resistance in light of the draconian social measures that currently exist seeking to control and discipline our bodies. "In vagabondage we see a paradigmatic image of the constant drift out of biopolitical discipline, a drift which simultaneously forced the development of some of the core strategies for the control of migration which we encounter today" (Papadopoulos, Stephenson & Tsianos, 2008, p. 43). In this way, the vagabond not only produced a new affect, a new experience for the vagabond, but it also elicited a strong response for those in control, demonstrating that "capitalism's survival depends on recapturing those in flight. Workers must work and produce value. Capital must exploit them" (Holloway, 2005, p. 205). However, this shows the radical potential of bodies that resist traditional subjectivities and ways of being and the fear they elicit from the state.

But the nomad and the vagabond are historically situated figures and archetypes. This is not an effort to de-historicize these characters nor is it an attempt to try to build a "program" or "plan" using tactics that are historically, spatially, and culturally specific. However, when taken together, the nomad and vagabond provide an interesting way to think about escape and finding what we have repeated is necessary for resistance in a networked capitalism: lines of flight, escape, and the possibilities for resistance that emerge through what John Holloway (2010) calls the "cracks" of capitalism, because in the end "we want to create a different world" by what he calls "breaking" or "seizing the initiative" and refusing to "submit our lives to the rule of money" (p. 3). This places these two characters in an interesting social space because of their rejection of one of the principles of life in the West. But, as Deleuze and Guattari (1987) claim, "the life of the nomad is the intermezzo" because the space(s) in which they occupy are open and resist a preimposed path or direction (p. 380). Brian Massumi (1992) reminds us that

> "nomad thought" does not lodge itself in the edifice of an ordered interiority; it moves freely in an element of exteriority. It does not repose on identity; it rides difference. It does not respect the artificial division between the three domains of representation, subject, concept and being; it replaces restrictive analogy with a

conductivity that knows no bounds. Rather than reflecting the world, they are immersed in a changing state of things. (p. 5)

Nomads and vagabonds resist the concept of normalcy: the bourgeois work ethic that demands long hours, civility, narrowly defined ethics and a "business as usual" approach to living (Papadopoulos et al., 2008). "Pulled forward by hope untested, pushed from behind by hope frustrated...the vagabond is a pilgrim without a destination: a nomad without an itinerary" (Bauman, 1993, p. 240). They move, crossing boundaries in a line of flight that does not follow a preimposed path. They are not bound to the rules of the state and, instead, "journeys through an unstructured space; like a wanderer in the desert" (Bauman, 1993, p. 240). Space becomes temporary, a movement that resists the status quo because "the vagabond structures the site he [*sic*] happens to occupy at the moment, only to dismantle the structure again as he [*sic*] leaves" (Bauman, 1993, p. 240). In essence, the combination of bodies, subjectivity, space, movement, and the imagination are expressed through the figures of nomads and vagabonds and demonstrate the potential of rethinking the limits of our bodies, returning to Spinoza's impetus to rethink the limits of the body and what it can accomplish.

Holey Spaces and the Smith

Another potential way subjects may take up and challenge of the desiring-machines of capitalism are through the experimental traits of the *smith*. As Day (2005) highlights, Deleuze and Guattari's discussions regarding the *smith* have not been as prevalent as the citizen and nomad. Part of it stems from constant deterritorializing and reterritorializing, as well as the interrelationships that the citizen and the nomad have within contested spaces. Alternatively, the traits of the smith are hybrid since they are not within the limitations of the smooth spaces of the nomad or the sedentary spaces of the citizen—the smith has potential to construct possibilities and seeks innovative ways and opportunities to intervene in and around structures (Day, 2005, p. 174). Moreover, since the smith is hybrid, she/he is able to communicate and act within these spaces in unique ways. According to Day, the smiths' innovative metallurgical practices attempt to create holes and different subjectivities within the totalizing efforts of the capitalist system. Day concludes that "the activities of *smiths* show us that no matter how totalizing a system might be, it is impossible to create a system with no outside, even a system that appears to cover an entire planet" (p. 175). The holey spaces that the smith produces are temporary and "in between" spaces that are "always on the way to becoming one state or another" (Frichot, 2007, p. 175). Additionally, Frichot illustrates the movements of these holey spaces and how they are "composed of passages forged through smooth nomadic space and sedentary space without stopping at either one" (p. 175). Therefore, the smith creates holey spaces that are not linear and facilitate unique communication, as well as actions between nomadic and sedentary terrains (p. 175). Day describes the "hackers" and the "monkey wrencher" as examples of becoming smiths, but there are other instances where the holey spaces of the smith and the smooth space of the nomad are located, particularly within educational experiences.

From the vignettes that we laid out in the beginning of the chapter, it is important to not only recognize that state-run educational systems are falling prey to neoliberal policies of privatization and global capitalism, but to also better understand how subjects are contesting these movements. It is apparent from the (alter) globalization movements that students, university professors, union workers and other community members are taking up lines of flight that are challenging the neoliberal citizen and the sedentary. In differing capacities these subjects are taking up the characteristics of the smith and the nomad. For example, students who are involved in contesting tuition hikes and neoliberal policies within state-run institutions are also engaged in creating nonhierarchical and mutual learning spaces outside of the university and the productions of capitalism. In some cases, the students are not asking to "go back" to some romanticized period of the university. Conversely, they are constructing possibilities or potential in transforming the university. In other words, as Shukaitis (2009) argues, "One can find ways to use the institutional space without being *of* the institution, without taking the institution's goals as one's own" (p. 167). At the same time, there are nomadic subjects involved in creating collective and participatory spaces, *Free Skools* and other critical learning spaces in the UK and in Canada (Motta, forthcoming; Shantz, forthcoming). These individuals and collectives not only see the importance of exposing and contesting neoliberalism and global capitalist movements at the university and public spaces in general, but they also see the urgency of constructing ongoing avenues and pathways of learning differently and becoming anti-Oedipedalized or liberated subjects who attempt to operate outside current capitalist structures.

Finding Lines of Flight: Where Can We Escape?

We close this chapter with the affect produced by the possibilities of escaping dominant reality or institutions that do not allow for rethinking the conditions in which we live, work, play, and love. The nomad moves so as to resist state ordering, and the vagabond escapes by questioning bourgeois ethics of work and being. At the same time, the smith uses her/his innovations to drill holes into the landscape of the capitalist system. Despite these oppressive realities, escape is always present and a possibility, whether through the cracks of capitalism that Holloway (2010) discusses or through the lines of flight that Deleuze and Guattari offered us. What is important to learn from these different lines of flight is that contemporary political experimentations and movements to liberate desire are based in permanent struggle. Therefore, subjects need to engage in critical and reflective responses to what networks are plugged into at the social, political, economic and cultural levels as well as at the level of desire that drives struggle in the first place.

As Foucault (1980) and others have argued, power needs to be contested through multiple fronts because of the varied ways in which struggles for power emerge. This is a significant insight that many of the current movements against neoliberalism have considered. Moreover, power does not emerge or operate outside of subjects and the libratory spaces they inhabit. Individuals who are involved in collective actions in the streets and universities of Mexico, Puerto Rico, Greece, the United Kingdom and the United States are continuing to develop critical and reflective strategies to contest the onslaught of global capitalism at both the micro- and macrolevels. Deleuze and Guattari understood this and warned that even within revolutionary struggles there are microfascists ready to crystallize at any moment. This is why they argued for political groups to "wage permanent struggle within their own ranks" in order to avoid taking on the oppressive characteristics of systems which they are fighting against (Best & Kellner, 1991, p. 95).

For the nomad, vagabond and smith, creating experiments in living and working outside the oppressive state can be difficult because of the alluring and seductive characteristics of capitalism. Therefore, it is not only important to engage in political struggle and collective action against the state and global capital, but, at the same time, be concerned with liberating desire. This means that we must pay more attention to the affective desires produced by deterritorialized networks of capital. Without considering the liberation of the social and desiring machines as ongoing and interconnected struggles, groups potentially reproduce and take up the hierarchical and authoritarian processes they oppose (p. 95). This reality makes the (re)production of oppression a complex struggle that must be met with an equally sophisticated response.

From an educational standpoint, the nomad, the vagabond and the smith offer potential alternatives to corporate institutions and marketplace values. As Guattari and Negri (2010) argue, the new lines of alliance and new subjectivities are based in "articulating the different dimensions of mass intellectuality" and, at the same time, "actively neutralizing the destructive power of capitalist arrangements" (p. 79). Not only are dominant conceptions of the body thrown into question, but also are our own subjectivities and how this is tied to larger power struggles occurring locally, nationally, and internationally. These new movements form educative innovations and creative struggle in and around, as well as outside of, oppressive structures–enabling experiments and the emergence of new forms of subjectivity (Day, 2004, p. 740). Just as we saw in Seattle, Washington, and now within our contemporary movements against neoliberalism, an affinity between workers, environmentalists, teachers and other organizations demonstrate there is capacity to create individually and collectively even within crisis and the challenges of mutative capitalism.

References

Bauman, Z. (1993). *Postmodern ethics.* Maldon, MA: Wiley-Blackwell

Best, S., & Kellner, D. (1991). *Postmodern theory: Critical interrogations.* New York: Guilford Press.

Chomsky, N. (1999). *Profit over people: Neoliberalism and global order.* New York: Seven Stories Press.

Cole, D. R. (2011). Matter in motion: The educational materialism of Gilles Deleuze. *Educational Philosophy and Theory* (in press).

Day, R. J. F. (2004). 'From hegemony to affinity'. *Cultural Studies, 18*(5), 716–748.

Day, R. J. F. (2005). *Gramsci is dead: Anarchist currents in the newest social movements.* Toronto: Between the Lines.

DeLeon, A. P. (2010). Reporting from the realm of the absurd: Rethinking space in a neoliberal world. *Theory in Action, 3*(4), 38–58.

Deleuze, G., & Guattari, F. (1983). *Anti-Oedipus: Capitalism and Schizophrenia.* Minneapolis: University of Minnesota Press.

Deleuze, G., & Guattari, F. (1987). *A Thousand Plateaus: Capitalism and Schizophrenia.* Minneapolis: University of Minnesota Press.

Delgado-Ramos, G. C., & Saxe-Fernández, J. (2005). The World Bank and the privatization of public education: A Mexican perspective. *Journal for Critical Education Policy Studies,* 3(1), Retrieved from http://www.jceps.com/index.php?pageID=article&articleID=44

Dimitriadis, G., & Kamberelis, G. (2006). *Theory of education.* New York: Routledge.

Dokuzović, L., & Freudmann, E. (2009, November). *Creating worlds. Squatting the crisis: On the current protests in education and perspectives on radical change.* Retrieved from http://eipcp.net/projects/creatingworlds/dokuzovic-freudmann/en

Edu-Factory. (March, 2011). Retrieved from http://www.edu-factory.org/wp/klf-days-of-action-london-march-26th-reports/

Foucault, M. (1980). *The history of sexuality.* New York: Vintage Books.

Frichot, H. (2007). Holey space and the smooth and stratiated body of the refugee. In A. Hickey-Moody & P. Malins (Eds.), *Deleuzian encounters: Studies in contemporary social issues* (pp. 169–180). New York: Palgrave-MacMillan.

Giroux, H. A. (2004). *The terror of neoliberalism: Authoritarianism and the eclipse of democracy.* Boulder, CO: Paradigm Publishers.

Guattari, F., & Negri, A. (2010). *New lines of alliance, new spaces of liberty*. New York: Autonomedia/Minor Compositions.

Guggenheim, D. (director). (2010). *Waiting for Superman* [film]. Beverly Hills: Participant Media.

Hickey-Moody, A., & Malins, P. (2007). Introduction: Gilles Delueze and four movements in social thought. In A. Hickey-Moody & P. Malins (Eds.), *Deleuzian encounters: Studies in contemporary social issues* (pp. 1–15). New York: Palgrave-MacMillan.

Holloway, J. (2005). *Change the world without taking power: The meaning of revolution today*. London: Pluto Books.

Holloway, J. (2010). *Crack capitalism*. London: Pluto Books.

Kincheloe, J. L. (2006). A critical politics of knowledge: Analyzing the role of educational psychology in educational policy. *Policy Futures in Education*, 4(3), 220–235.

Lothringer, S. (Ed.). (1995). *Chaosophy*. New York: Autonomedia/Semiotexte. Retrieved from http://www.generation-online.org/p/fpdeleuze7.htm

Manning, E. (2007). *Politics of touch: Sense, movement, sovereignty*. Durham, NC: Duke University Press.

Masny, D. (2005). Multiple literacies: An alternative OR beyond Friere. In J. Anderson, M. Kendrick, T. Rogers, & S. Smythe (Eds.), *Portraits of literacy across families, communities, and schools: Intersections and tensions* (pp. 171–184). Mahwah, NJ: Erlbaum.

Massumi, B. (1992). *A user's guide to capitalism and schizophrenia: Deviations from Deleuze & Guattari*. Cambridge, MA: MIT Press.

Motta, S. (forthcoming). Notes towards a systemisation of the praxis of the Nottingham Free School. In R. H. Haworth (Ed.), *Anarchist pedagogies: Collective actions, theories & critical reflections on education*. Oakland: PM Press.

Newman, S. (2002). *From Bakunin to Lacan: Anti-authoritarianism and the dislocation of power*. Lanham, MD: Lexington Books.

Olssen, M., & Peters, M. A. (2005). Neoliberalism, higher education and the knowledge economy: From the free market to knowledge capitalism. *Journal of Education Policy*, 20(3), 313–345.

Papadopoulos, D., Stephenson, N., & Tsianos, V. (2008). *Escape routes: Control and subversion in the 21st century*. London: Pluto Books.

Peters, M. A. (2009). Education, creativity and the economy of passions: New forms of educational capitalism. *Thesis Eleven*, (96), 40–63.

Pilon, M. (2010, August 9). *Wall Street Journal*. Retrieved from http://blogs.wsj.com/economics/2010/08/09/student-loan-debt-surpasses-credit-cards/

Rhoads, R. A., & Liu, A. (2009). Globalization, social movements, and the American university: Implications for research and practice. In John C. Smart (Ed.), *Higher education handbook of theory and research*, Vol. 24. New York: Springer Netherlands.

Rhoads, R. A., & Mina, L. (2001). The student strike at the National Autonomous University of Mexico: A political analysis. *Comparative Education Review*, 45(3), 334–353.

Saltman, K. (2007). Schooling in disaster capitalism: How the political right is using disaster to privatize public schooling. *Teacher Education Quarterly*, 34(2), 131–156.

Shantz, J. (forthcoming). Spaces of learning: The Anarchist free skool. In R. H. Haworth (Ed.), *Anarchist pedagogies: Collective actions, theories & critical reflections on education*. Oakland, CA: PM Press.

Shukaitis, S. (2009). Infrapolitics and the nomadic educational machine. In R. Amster, A. DeLeon, L. A. Fernandez, A. Nocella, & D. Shannon (Eds.), *Contemporary anarchist studies: An introductory anthology of anarchy in the academy* (pp. 166–174). New York: Routledge.

Smith, D. W. (2007). Deleuze and the question of desire: Toward an immanent theory of ethics. *Parrhesia: A Journal of Critical Philosophy* (2), 66–78.

Vandenberghe, F. (2008). Deleuzian capitalism. *Philosophy & Social Criticism, 34*(8), 877–903.

• CHAPTER TWELVE •

The Current Dynamics of Professional Expertise: The Movable Ethos, Pathos, and Logos of Four Norwegian Professions

Torill Strand

Introduction

Worldwide economic crises have led many countries to reconsider their educational priorities, particular in regards to higher education. At this phase of the global recession there is not only a question whether higher education offers value for money. There is also a question about the purpose and priorities of educational institutions. The most pressing issue is not how to help economic recovery. Rather, the most pressing issue concerns ways of conceptualizing and promoting robust knowledge cultures (OECD, 2010). Consequently, a debate on how to conceptualize and build professional expertise is now being re-evoked.

Taking the current crisis, professional expertise now undergoes transformations. But what are the characteristics of these changes? And to what degree are they produced by the epistemic ruptures generated by economic crisis and the ways in which global-local symbolic economies now interact, converge, and convert? I here address these questions by exploring findings from an extensive theoretical and empirical study on the altering expertise of Norwegian nurses, teachers, auditors and computer engineers—ten from each group—over a span of eight years (2003–2010). In the initial years of the study, these nurses, teachers, auditors and computer engineers were followed in their transition from pre-service training to work.[1] However, I here put emphasis on the last phases of the study since my ambition is to outline how these professions now reshape their knowledge and skills in accordance with current demands: If reconsidering the purpose and priorities of higher education, such knowledge is needed. It should be said, however, that the four Norwegian professions cannot be considered representative, since Norway has experienced a shallower recession than other countries. Norway has a productivity lead over most OECD countries, and the labor utilization is also high (OECD, 2011, p. 126). Nevertheless, the shifting expertise of the four Norwegian professions helps to illustrate some dynamics that influence working life in most knowledge-intensive societies. So, what happens to professional expertise in the current situation?

In general, "expertise" denotes some trustworthy faculties for judging, deciding and acting rightly, justly or wisely (ethos); some jointly defined and acquired capabilities given public authority and status according to a specific domain (pathos); and a set of productive procedures, techniques, and skills (logos). However, such expertise is not here considered as some identifiable features of an individual specialist. Contrary, in this chapter professional expertise is seen as some emergent characteristics of the epistemic culture of a professional group. While cutting across the intellectual landscape of philosophy and the social sciences, my aim is to disclose some current dynamics of such expertise.

In the first part of this chapter I adopt a sociological outlook while emphasizing the movable ethos—credibility—of the expertise of Norwegian nurses, teachers, auditors and computer engineers. I here compare and contrast how the social missions of these four professions now seem to be renegotiated according to the new divisions of epistemic labor in society. In the second part of the chapter I adopt a discoursive[2] outlook while highlighting the movable pathos—public appeal—of the tangible work of Norwegian nurses, teachers, auditors and computer engineers. In the third part of the chapter, however, I adopt a semiotic outlook that put the epistemic dimension of the productive expertise of Norwegian nurses, teachers, auditors and computer engineers into focus. In summing up I again ask: In what ways does professional expertise now undergo transformations? And how should we read the alterations? But let me first briefly portray the current situation.

Professional Expertise in the Present

A great many recent studies document how professional expertise and its theoretical representations now undergo deep-seated transformations. First, recent studies point to how the tools and technologies of a networked knowledge society have made knowledge and information vital components of public life. Conventional divisions of epistemic labor thus seem contested: On the one hand, some authors speak of an emerging 'epistemification' of everyday life (Paavola & Hakkarainen, 2005; Nerland, 2010). Such 'epistemification' is parallel to the new mode of knowledge production, which implies that scientific productions now diffuse into other sectors of modern societies and opens up for multiple participations (Knorr-Cetina, 2007; Nowothny, Scott & Gibbons, 2001). On the other hand, active participation in contemporary knowledge societies call for a new type of 'epistemic citizenship'; a form of public epistemic literacy that implies competencies in how to engage with, confront and produce flows of knowledge and information. Or in other words, there is a new social contract between knowledge and society that implies "a new type of collectivity which defines and delimits itself more completely by its capacity to produce and mobilize knowledge" (Elam & Bertilsson, 2003, p. 234). These changes create a new context for professional work. But in what ways may the new division of epistemic labor affect the missions, and thus the required expertise, of the professions? Do the new divisions of epistemic labor call for a renewed professional ethos?

Recent studies also point to how the fast flows of knowledge, information and resources seem to trouble the very architecture of professional cultures and their expertise (Noordengraaf, 2007; Strand, 2011a; Sajor, 2005; Tynjälä, Välimaa & Sarja, 2003). Most studies tend to focus on the output of these flows. By contrast, Sassen (2001, 2006) calls attention to the tangible work of those producing the flows, while exploring ways in which the global era of informationalism is dependent on locally rooted work cultures. In fact, transnational flows of knowledge, information and resources are dependent on the "capabilities" of the rooted work cultures "for servicing, managing, and financing the global operations of firms and markets" (Sassen, 2001, p. 359). Thus, location matters to sophisticated flows of information. But even more important seems the "capabilities" of these locations to collectively produce, process, and handle information and resources. Such capabilities are "collective productions whose development entails time, making, competition, and conflicts, and whose utilities are, in principle, multivalent because they are conditioned on the character of the *relational* systems within which they function" (Sassen, 2006, p. 7, my emphasis). But in what ways and to what degree may this common call for communal and rooted "capabilities" affect the very architecture of professional cultures and their expertise? Does this new situation provide some scaffolds for the professions? Or will the current situation, by contrast, undermine the public appeal of the professions and their expertise?

Third, several authors underline that a vital characteristic of the new era are the ways in which global-local epistemologies now interact and convert (Burawoy, 2000; Castells, 2004; Urry, 2002). Marginson, Murphy and Peters

(2010) point to how the emerging "image of the world as a single sphere" (p. 9) is generated by an extraordinary dynamism of the current symbolic economies: On the one hand, global synchrony and convergence have been changing the conditions for ways of imagining, producing and sharing productive work in different spheres: global, transnational and local. On the other hand, the new and emerging global dimension—in terms of its communication, culture, and productive knowledge—is itself a human product, continuously in the making. So, as flows of knowledge, information and resources are no longer constrained by geographical proximities or institutionalized boundaries, they "intimately connect the local and the global" (Becher & Trowler, 2001, p. 2) by offering new incentives, opportunities and openings (along with new disincentives, dangers and limitations). Furthermore, these flows are themselves generated by and generating a symbolic logic that not only opens possibilities of innovative ways of retrieving, sharing, and archiving knowledge and information, but also of creative images, aspirations, and epistemic forms of practice marked by a new era in the making. So what happens to professional expertise in this situation? To find out, let us take a closer look on the movable ethos, pathos and logos of four Norwegian professions.

Movable Ethos

Classic sociological analyses draw attention to the ethos—or credibility—of professional expertise. Here, the attributions of professional knowledge and skills (*phronesis*) are combined with their trustworthiness (*arête*) and perceived goodwill (*evnoia*) (Hartelius, 2008). Focus is the relation between a profession's expertise and its social mission—and the ways in which this mission is being generated, upheld, adjusted and renegotiated in relation to the divisions of epistemic labor in society. Taking a sociological outlook, it is thus pertinent to ask in what ways, and to what degree, the new divisions of epistemic labor affect the missions, and thus the required expertise of the four Norwegian professions studied. Do the new divisions of epistemic labor call for renewed professional ethos?

In our study, the group of Norwegian nurses now speak of an "evidence-based practice"; the Norwegian teachers embrace the rhetoric of public education as "knowledge promotion"; the auditors speak of a renewal of their methodology; and the computer engineers seem to be shifting focus from how to *process* to how to *produce* knowledge. Such shifts may be signs of a new type of collectivity "which defines and delimits itself more completely by its capacity to produce and mobilize knowledge" (Elam & Bertilsson, 2003, p. 234). Moreover, these shifts may also signify how the four professions now renegotiate their expertise in the intersection of the traditions versus the new. If so, the very missions of the four Norwegian professions and the credibility of their conventional expertise seem to be at stake.

To Durkheim (1957) the mission of a profession is generated and justified socially and, next, producing and justifying certain ways of thinking and forms of practice within that profession (or guild). Durkheim saw professional expertise as a "social fact," which "consists of manners of acting, thinking and feeling external to the individual" (Durkheim, 1901, p. 52). Consequently, the very existence of a profession is based on and justified through its expertise, which again is socially structured. A somewhat naïve example is the group of auditors, whose very existence and professional status is based on and justified through the trustworthiness of their faculties, techniques and skills in performing their mission, namely auditing. Durkheim thus helps to stress the social formations, functions and credibility of institutionalized expertise—and by implication how the tradition of a profession is vital to its ethos: A profession always "carries the mark of the social conditions that brought it into being" (Durkheim, 1957, p. 24). Comparing and contrasting the altering ethos of the four Norwegian professions, we should thus consider how their traditional ethoses are marked by quite different social conditions and, by implication, different and somewhat contrasting social visions and missions. To the Norwegian nurses, it seems significant that the healthcare profession was first defined by Florence Nightingale (1820–1910); to the teachers it is probably influential that their profession received certification with the establishment of a Norwegian teacher-training program already in 1826; the ethos of the auditors is possibly marked by the fact that Norwegian auditing was professionalized as late as in 1951; and to the ethos of the Norwegian computer engineers it is relevant that their profession is as young as the ICT industry itself (their very first educational training program was established in the United States in 1971). When meeting the new ways of the symbolic economies of today, these four professions' ways of renegotiating and renewing their expertise inevitably happen quite differently according to their distinct tasks, traditions and missions.

One example is the altering expertise of the group of Norwegian computer engineers: When interviewed in 2009, the computer engineers portrayed an emerging agile work style, which contrasts their earlier "torrent" style that demanded specific skills in the fast flows of problem-solving procedures. They now tend to stress the importance of sharing their expertise with colleagues in and beyond their workplace; they have access to, and use daily, a multitude of knowledge resources, databases, and centers, which seems to have improved considerably the last few years. More than previously they also stress the importance of an oral exchange of ideas; they attend more international forums and conferences than before; and they cooperate continuously with international research centers. These are signs that the individual computer engineers we interviewed have now acquired skills and competencies that demonstrate their progress from "advanced beginners" (as when interviewed in 2005) to "proficient" experts (e.g., Dreyfus & Dreyfus, 1986). Moreover, when taking into consideration that professional expertise should be read as some emergent characteristics of the *epistemic culture* of a professional group, these are also signs of the epistemic development of a profession as young as the ICT industry itself: The group of Norwegian computer engineers now seems to be experiencing a shift from a focus on how to *process* information over to a focus on how to *produce* knowledge.

However, compared to the other groups, such an emerging ethos of knowledge creation seems to parallel the ways in which the Norwegian nurses now speak of an "evidence-based practice"; the Norwegian teachers of "knowledge promotion"; and the auditors of a renewal of their methodology. In this way, the movable ethos of the four professions studied may relate to the emergent "epistemification" of everyday life in knowledge-intensive societies, which not only implies a new division of epistemic labor. It also implies a form of public epistemic literacy that involves competencies in how to engage with, confront and produce knowledge and information. Hence, the traditional gap between professional expertise and common knowledge is being radically narrowed. To the present-day professions, the conventional mantra of 'knowledge on knowledge' (mirroring an epistemic reflectivity) may seem insufficient: To gain credibility within a knowledge-intensive society, a profession should also comprise knowledge (and skills) on how to produce and mobilize knowledge.

In sum, the above examples illustrate how the expertise of these four Norwegian professions cannot be separated from their social missions. Also, how these missions are being renegotiated parallel to the current contestation of the conventional divisions of epistemic labor in society. A sociological outlook thus offers a fruitful framework and some analytical tools for exploring altering professional expertise in relation to the divisions of epistemic labor in society. However, the implications of the tangible *work* of the four professions studied should not be overlooked.

Movable Pathos

A discoursive outlook draws attention to the movable *pathos*—or public appeal—of professional expertise. Here, the social recognition of the tangible work of a profession is conceived as a vital vehicle in the discoursive configurations and reconfigurations of such expertise: On the one hand, the social recognition of the substantial, skilled work of a profession is at the very heart of the social power, position and legitimacy of this professional group. On the other hand, the call for social recognition is vital to the discoursive configurations of the expertise of a profession, since this call generates images of appropriate work identities and performances. Thus, while focusing on the distributed power relations within social interactions, institutions and bodies of knowledge, this outlook helps to reveal how discoursive configured and social recognized images of professional expertise contribute to the shaping, reshaping and justifying of the expertise of a profession, both from within and at a distance.

Consequently, taking a discoursive outlook, it is pertinent to ask in what ways and to what degree the current situation troubles the very architecture of professional cultures and their expertise. In what ways, for example, may the fact that advanced economies are totally dependent on the "capabilities" of rooted work cultures "for servicing, managing, and financing the global operations of firms and markets" (Sassen, 2001, p. 359) affect the images of appropriate work identities and performances? Is there now an emergent public appeal of the tangible work of professional groups? And if so, what kind of expertise seems to be recognized? Let us look to the Norwegian teachers.

When interviewed in 2005, the group of Norwegian teachers[3] came forward as a unified group of professional workers, carrying a distinct collective teacher identity. But when interviewed again in 2009, their individual professional identities seemed more manifest. More than earlier they now emphasized the importance and value of testing school results; they portrayed some systematic routines for developing, updating, and evaluating their teaching skills; moreover, all teachers depicted the World Wide Web as a vital arena for retrieving, sharing, and updating their knowledge. Overall, the teachers—when interviewed in 2009—expressed a higher confidence in collective standards and procedures and a more transparent teacher role (as most of them now invited external evaluators into their classrooms). They justified their work in accordance with the new national curriculum (the "knowledge promotion") which was implemented in 2006, embracing the government's aim to "promote Norway as a leading knowledge based and innovative society" (Norwegian Ministry of Education and Research, 2008). Overall, the teachers now adopt the rhetoric of public education as "knowledge promotion". However, Norwegian teachers now seem to outsource some vital aspects of their long-established expertise, as they welcome, adopt, and expose confidence in educational directives, instructions and ready-made lesson plans handed over to them by the school management, local municipalities, and the government. But are these signs of an altered public appeal of the expertise of Norwegian teachers?

Emphasizing the relative autonomy of professional expertise, Fournier (1999) explores the ways in which the call for public appeal of such expertise "potentially allows for control at a distance through the construction of 'appropriate' work identities and conducts" (p. 281). Next, she argues that the common appeal to "professionalism" should be seen as a disciplinary logic, a "conduct of conduct", made intelligible and practicable by the professionals themselves. Evetts (2003; 2006) further elaborates on Fournier's perspective, pointing to the gap between the myth and reality: The myth is that professionalism includes exclusive ownership of an area of expertise and knowledge, the power to define the nature of the problems within that area, as well as the control of access to potential solutions. The reality, however, is "very different" as the discourse of professionalism—meaning "the ways in which occupational and professional workers themselves are accepting, incorporating and accommodating the idea of 'profession' and particularly 'professionalism' in their work"—is generated by and generating occupational change and social control at both macro- and micro levels (Evetts, 2006, p. 139). Thus, to Norwegian teachers, the current situation is of importance, since local, national, and transnational educational policies inevitably generate altered images of teaching expertise, both within and beyond the profession itself. However, to understand the discoursive reconfigurations of the expertise of the Norwegian teachers, it is pertinent to explore the ways in which the teachers themselves portray their tangible work.

The expertise of the Norwegian teachers seems to be closely related to, inscribed in, and dependent on a network of cooperative functions and accountabilities. This is illustrated by the ways in which the group of Norwegian teachers now embraces the rhetoric of "knowledge promotion" while simultaneously "outsourcing" vital aspects of their work. "Knowledge promotion" designates a comprehensive curriculum reform, implemented in 2006. This reform carries a rationale for teaching and learning that sharply contrasts the rationale that lies at the heart of Norwegian teachers' long-established ways of teaching. The "knowledge promotion" rationale focuses on basic skills and outcome-based learning, while the earlier rationale came close to the idea of liberal education and the methods of reform pedagogy. When interviewed in 2009, most teachers mentioned this contrast and pointed to the fact that their preservice teacher training had not qualified them for the new ways of teaching. To reduce complexity and to cope with the new, they welcome, adopt, and expose confidence in directives, instructions and ready-made lesson plans handed over to them by the school management, local municipalities, and the government. Most teachers also invite external evaluators into their classrooms. So, as the qualities of teaching and learning are becoming increasingly complex, the group of Norwegian teachers seems to admit some shortcomings of their long-established expertise. Hence, it may seem smart to outsource some tasks, since the public appeal of their expertise may rather be strengthened than weakened by the fact that they now acknowledge the new demands and the relative autonomy of their conventional expertise.

In sum, the discoursive outlook sees the social recognition of professional work as a vehicle in the cultural machineries of the altering expertise of the professions. On the one hand, the social recognition of the tangible, skilled work of a profession is at the very heart of the social power, position and legitimacy—and thus the very existence—of this profession. On the other hand, the call for social recognition is a vital aspect of a profession's expertise, as it contributes to the construction of "appropriate work identities and conducts" (Fournier, 1999, p. 281). In analyzing the connections between "discoursive practices" and the wider sets of "nondiscoursive" activities and institutions, the underlying material resources that make discourses possible needs to be taken into account. The aim is to reveal ways in which and to what degree a particular discourse reproduces or transforms the material world. Consequently, this outlook offers a fruitful perspective on the altering expertise of contemporary professions, including the ways in which these alterations relate to other social objects, such as the state, transnational policies, or economic processes. However, this way of conceptualizing the current dynamics of professional expertise may be in danger of overlooking a crucial matter, namely the vital dynamics of *knowledge* itself.

Movable Logos

A semiotic outlook draws attention to the movable *logos*—epistemic dimension—of professional expertise, since this outlook focus on the processes of knowledge creation. In short, semiotics is the study of the action of signs and sign systems. It is an interdisciplinary field of study, containing several branches that offer theories on the generative logic of signs and analytic tools to reveal the ontological and epistemic shifts created. Since semiotics takes a nonpsychologistic perspective of the generative action of the flows of signs, the subjects are here seen as semiotic entities, not social actors, structures or forces. In this way, the dynamic qualities of the epistemic dimension of professional expertise are placed at the forefront. The semiotics of C. S. Peirce (1904, 1907) offers a fruitful way of modeling these dynamics.

To Peirce, knowledge is "a living historic entity", acquired through experience, mediated through signs, clarified by the pragmatic maxim, and validated by the final consensus. Professional expertise is a verb and the flows of signs (semiosis) are the very generative principles of the alteration and creative powers of such expertise. Focus is the ways in which "the actions of signs"–which happens through everyday, lived experience–generate a deep-seated remaking of common sense. To Peirce, "common sense" is a notion used to tress the sociality of knowledge, as it denotes a universe of discourse, having community as a product and common understanding as an effect. A remaking of common sense does not only promote a reorientation but also deep-seated transformations that reconstruct worldviews, experiences, and habits of thought and action–and restructure our ways of learning (Strand, 2011a, 2011b). Consequently, the dynamic flows of signs (semiosis) may contribute to a reconstruction of our ways of seeing the world, and thus ways of making the world, and by implication the ways of the world themselves.

To Peirce, semiosis–the creative acts of the flows of signs–does not happen as translations, but in trans*actions*. Semiosis is not an action between two, for example, between an agent and a phenomenon or between a phenomenon and a representation of that phenomenon. "By semeiosis I mean, on the contrary, an action, or influence, which is, or involves, a cooperation of *three* subjects, such as a sign, its object, and its interpretant, this thri-relative influence not being in any way resolvable into actions between pairs" (Peirce, 1907, p. 411). In other words, flows of signs do not mediate, represent, or carry external phenomena. On the contrary, these flows are nothing but the very phenomena themselves. Professional expertise does by no way mirror an external reality. Contrary, the dynamics of professional expertise are *in* the very flows of signs–which are flows of experience, thought, action and creation. Thus, when–for example–the Norwegian nurses speak of their "evidence-based practice", "systematic investigation", and ways of relating to knowledge and information at "the research frontier", they do not speak of how they observe external phenomena. Contrary, they portray an engagement with the very phenomena themselves. Knorr Cetina (1999, 2007, 2009) helps to further explore these dynamics.

Following Knorr Cetina, a profession can be studied as "those sets of practices, arrangements and mechanisms bound together by necessity, affinity and historical coincidence which, in a given area of professional expertise, *make up how we know what we know*" (Knorr Cetina, 2007, p. 363, my emphasis). Next, she conceives expertise as an "epistementality", which appears first, as the particular forms of knowledge use, distribution, validation and production characteristic for that profession. Second, the epistementality of a profession becomes visible through the *knowledge ties* relating to that profession's epistemic object. Such objects are objects used in the everyday life of the professionals, such as the problems they need to solve, the models they create, the tasks they have to fulfill, the reports they write, or the information systems they employ. However, epistemic objects are "processes and projections, rather than definite things" because they are open and question generating: The more they are explored, the more they increase their complexity. Consequently, a profession's relationship to its epistemic objects—or that profession's "*knowledge ties*"—is defined "through the notion of a lack and a corresponding structure of wanting" (Knorr Cetina, 1997, p. 12). The quality and nature of these knowledge ties generate the epistemic culture's specific forms of practice, mediate and facilitate the exploratory characteristics of these forms of practice, and serve as a driving force for learning loops, processes of inquiry, and the knowledge production of that culture. Consequently, the quality and nature of the knowledge ties of a profession are vital to that profession's characteristic expertise. However, the emergence of new and globalised symbolic economies now contest conventional "object-relation regimes", and thus the knowledge ties and the very design of the expertise in question. As flows of knowledge, information and resources are no longer constrained by geographical proximities or institutionalized boundaries, these flows offer new incentives, opportunities and openings (along with new disincentives, dangers and limitations) in regards to the epistemic dimension of professional expertise. Furthermore, since these flows are generated by and generating a symbolic logic, they open possibilities of innovative ways of retrieving, sharing, and archiving knowledge and information. Moreover, they generate creative images, aspirations, and epistemic forms of practice marked by a new era in the making. The interviews with the Norwegian nurses illustrate this case.

Norwegian nurses make a highly specialized and differentiated professional group. When interviewed in 2009 the nurses revealed some exceedingly focused and short-lived epistementalities of a professional field of "fast knowledge", picturing themselves as concurrently observers to and participants in the fast-moving changes now happening. They all described epistemic forms of practices characterized by some highly developed and consistent routines for a systematic inquiry, for sharing their expertise, developing and updating their procedures, and for an uninterrupted and systematic validation of their labour, their disciplined inquiry, and their ways of evaluation. When describing the epistemic cultures and practices at their workplaces, they used the rhetoric of science, not only speaking of an "evidence-based practice" but also of "systematic investigation", "the research frontier", and "research tools". Overall, the nurses portrayed their epistementalities as based on a research interest and carried out through a highly focused and orderly set of systematic routines. This kind of epistementality seems to be generated by the urgency of their work: When one of the interviewees was asked "What if you do a mistake?" she promptly responded: "No, no. No, I can never do any mistakes. If I do, the patient will die".

Remaking Professional Expertise

So in what ways does professional expertise now undergo transformations? And how should we read the alterations? Overall, the three discourses on professional expertise presented above point to how the expertise of a profession is never given. Rather, it is a relational and constantly shifting entity, generated, justified, shaped and reshaped according to the altering dynamics of social institutions, changing societies, and symbolic economies. The three discourses—emphasizing, respectively, the *ethos*, *pathos* and *logos* of such expertise—mirror these dynamics.

The sociological outlook emphasizes the movable ethos—credibility—of Norwegian nurses, teachers, auditors and computer engineers. The professions studied now seem to be renegotiating their missions according to the new divisions of epistemic labor in society: The group of Norwegian nurses speak of an "evidence-based practice"; the Norwegian teachers have adopted the rhetorics of public education as "knowledge promotion"; the auditors speak of a renewal of their methodology; and the computer engineers seem to be shifting focus from how to *process* to how to *produce* knowledge. Are these shifts signs of an emerging ethos of knowledge creation? If so, the movable ethos of the four professions may signify the insufficiency of the conventional mantra of 'knowledge on knowledge' (mirroring an epistemic reflectivity): To gain credibility, professions operating in a knowledge-intensive society should also comprise knowledge (and skills) on how to produce and mobilize knowledge. Consequently, a way of promoting robust knowledge cultures is to educate professionals with knowledge on how to produce and mobilize knowledge.

The discoursive outlook highlights the movable pathos—public appeal—of the tangible work of Norwegian nurses, teachers, auditors and computer engineers. On the one hand, the social recognition of the substantial, skilled work of the professions is at the very heart of their social power, position and legitimacy. On the other hand, the call for social recognition is vital to the discoursive configurations and reconfigurations of professional expertise, since this call generates images of appropriate work identities and performances. Social-recognized images seem to be shaping, reshaping and justifying the expertise of the four professions studied, both from within and at a distance. One example is the Norwegian teachers' emphasis on the importance and value of school-testing results and their ways of outsourcing vital aspects of their expertise, which may be signs of the renewed focus on ways of building robust knowledge cultures. Because, strangely enough, when admitting the shortcomings of their expertise, the group of Norwegian teachers seems to be strengthening, rather than weakening, the public appeal of their professional expertise. Consequently, a way of promoting robust knowledge cultures is to educate 'hybrid' and 'collaborative' professionals with the capacity to strengthen the quality of their tangible work by moving beyond the limited skills of their profession.

The semiotic model highlights the movable logos—epistemic principles—of the productive expertise of Norwegian nurses, teachers, auditors and computer engineers. However, when speaking of the epistemic principles of such expertise, these principles cannot be associated with a foundational epistemology promoting rigid schemes and procedures of knowledge production and validation. By contrast, the epistemic principles of the contemporary professions should be perceived as complex and fluid, since the symbolic economies of knowledge-intensive societies invite a rejection of rigid schemes in favor of complex, processual and creative models. Such a perspective goes well with a semiotic outlook, which helps to highlight the ways in which the epistemic principles of a profession are being transformed in the intersection of generative symbolic economies and the *knowledge ties* of this profession. One example is how the group of Norwegian nurses now depicts a work culture permeated by the orderly, systematic and productive 'logic of science', which may be a sign of an altering epistementality among Norwegian nurses. Consequently, a way of promoting robust knowledge cultures is not only to educate professionals with the capacity of developing and renewing their productive procedures, techniques, and skills, but also to educate professionals with the capacity to building and renewing flexible, dynamic and creative epistementalities. However, to strengthen educational institutions in their vital efforts to prepare the students for an even more complex workplace and to offer professionals tools to build robust and dynamic knowledge cultures, more knowledge is needed.

Notes

1. The data material consists of questionnaires, learning logs, individual interviews and focus groups. The questionnaires were answered by all participants in the first and the final years of their initial professional education, as well as 2.5 and 5.5 years after graduation; the learning logs were written during the first year of the participants' professional life; individual interviews were performed in 2005 and 2009; and the focus groups early autumn of 2006. Here, we first of all read the individual interviews of 2005 and 2009.

2. "A discoursive outlook" here refers to a realist notion of "discourse", meaning that "discourse" is seen as a particular object with its own properties and powers, which should be studied in relation to other social objects, such as the state, transnational policies, or economic processes.
3. All teachers interviewed were primary school teachers (teaching grades 1–7). To read the interviews, it is pertinent to take into account some important characteristics of the Norwegian school system: In Norway, public education is seen as a vital pillar in the welfare state and, thus, compulsory from the age of six up to sixteen. Primary and lower secondary education in Norway is based on the principle of a unified school system that provides equal and adapted education for all on the basis of a single national curriculum.

References

Becher, T., & Trowler, P. R. (2001). *Academic tribes and territories: Intellectual enquiry and the culture of disciplines*. Buckingham: Open University Press.

Burawoy, M. (2000). Grounding globalization. In M. Burawoy et al. (Eds.), *Global ethnography: Forces, connections, and imaginations in a postmodern world* (pp. 337–350). Berkeley: University of California Press.

Castells, M. (2004). Informationalism, networks, and the network society: A theoretical blueprint. In M. Castells (Ed.), *The network society: A cross-cultural perspective* (pp. 3–45). Cheltenham: Edward Elgar.

Dreyfus, H. L., & Dreyfus, S. E. (1986). *Mind over machine: The power of human intuition and experience in the era of the computer*. Oxford: Blackwell.

Durkheim, E. (1901/1982). *The rules of sociological method*. New York: Free Press.

Durkheim, E. (1957/1996). *Professional ethics and civic morals*. London and New York: Routledge.

Elam, M., & Bertilsson, M. (2003). Consuming, engaging and confronting science. The emerging dimension of scientific citizenship. *European Journal of Social Theory*, 6(2), 233-251.

Evetts, J. (2003). The construction of professionalism in new and existing occupational contexts: Promoting and facilitating occupational change. *International Journal of Sociology and Social Policy*, 23(4/5), 22–35.

Evetts, J. (2006). Short note: The sociology of professional groups. New directions. *Current Sociology*, 54(1), 133–134.

Fournier, V. (1999). The appeal to 'professionalism' as a disciplinary mechanism. *Sociological Review*, 47(2), 280–307.

Hartelius, E. J. (2008). The rhetoric of expertise. Unpublished doctoral dissertation, University of Texas at Austin.

Knorr Cetina, K. (1997). Sociality with objects: Social relations in postsocial knowledge societies. *Theory, Culture & Society*, 14(4), 1–30.

Knorr Cetina, K. (1999). *Epistemic cultures. How the sciences make knowledge*. Cambridge and London: Harvard University Press.

Knorr Cetina, K. (2007). Knowledge in a knowledge society. Five transitions. *Knowledge, Work and Society*, 4(3), 25–42.

Knorr Cetina, K. (2009). The synthetic situation: Interactionism for a global world. *Symbolic Interaction*, 32(1), 61–87.

Marginson, S., Murphy, P., & Peters, M. (2010). *Global creation. Space, mobility and synchrony in the age of the knowledge economy*. New York: Peter Lang.

Nerland, M. (2010). Transnational discourses of knowledge and learning in professional work: Examples from computer engineering. *Studies in Philosophy and Education*, 29(2), 183–195.

Nerland, M., & Jensen, K. (2007). The construction of a new professional self: A critical reading of the curricula for nurses and computer engineers in Norway. In A. Brown, S. Kirpal, & F. Rauner (Eds.), *Identities at work* (pp. 339–360). Dordrecht: Springer.

Noordengraaf, M. (2007). From "pure" to '"hybrid" professionalism. Present-day professionalism in ambigous public domains. *Administration & Society*, 39(6), 761–785.

Norwegian Ministry of Education and Research. (2008). Norge som ledende kunnskapsnasjon [Norway as a leading Knowledge Society]. Retrieved March 3, 2010 from http://www.regjeringen.no/nb/dep/kd/tema/Utdanning_og_kompetanse/Mer-om-kompetansepolitikk.html?id=115314

Nowothny, H., Scott, P., & Gibbons, M. (2001). *Re-thinking science. Knowledge and the public in an age of uncertainty*. Cambridge: Polity Press.

OECD. (2010). Higher education in a world changed utterly. Doing more with less. Discussion paper. Retrieved April 15, **2010,** from http://www.oecd.org/dataoecd/45/42/45925685.pdf

OECD. (2011). Economic policy reforms. Going for growth 2011. Retrieved April 15, 2011 from http://www.oecd.org/dataoecd/25/22/47473811.pdf

Paavola, S., and Hakkarainen, K. (2005). Three abductive solutions to the learning paradox—With instincts, inference and distributed cognition. *Studies in Philosophy and Education*, 24, 235–253.

Peirce, C. S. (1904). New elements. In *The essential Peirce. Selected philosophical writings, vol. 2* (1893–1913) (pp. 300–324). Bloomington and Indianapolis: Indiana University Press.

Peirce, C. S. (1907). Pragmatism. In *The essential Peirce. Selected philosophical writings, vol. 2* (1893–1913) (pp. 398–433). Bloomington and Indianapolis: Indiana University Press.

Sajor, E. E. (2005). Professionalisation or hybridization? Real estate brokers in metro Cebu, the Phillipines, during the boom of the 1990s. *Urban Studies*, 42(8), 1321–1343.

Sassen, S. (2001). *The global city. New York, London, Tokyo*. Princeton and Oxford: Princeton University Press.

Sassen, S. (2006). *Territory. Authority. Rights. From medieval to global assemblages*. Princeton and Oxford: Princeton University Press.

Strand, T. (2011a). Metaphors of creativity and workplace learning. *Scandinavian Journal of Educational Research*, 55 (4), 341–355

Strand, T. (2011b). C. S. *Peirce's rhetorical turn: Prospects for educational theory and research. Philosophy of Education 2010 Yearbook* (pp. 85–92). Urbana: Philosophy of Education Society.

Tynjälä, P., Välimaa, J., & Sarja, A. (2003). Pedagogical perspectives on the relationship between higher education and working life. *Higher Education*, 46, 147–166.

Urry, J. (2002). *Global complexity*. Cambridge: Cambridge University Press.

• CHAPTER THIRTEEN •

Educating the Person for Democratic Participation

R. Scott Webster

According to Sennett (2006) the global economy is largely controlled by "impatient capital". He also identifies that education is clearly connected to economic interests through politics. Therefore a tension exists between such global economic interests seeking private short-term gains and the political intent of democratic states which seek more public long-term goods (Deetz, 1992). Schooling and other educational institutions are located within this tension as their purposes include serving private interests via *training* to compete in the economy and serving the public good through *education*.

As Dewey (1916, p. 103) argued, *education* "has no definite meaning until we define the kind of society we have in mind". Before one can speak of *education* rather than just training, one must first make explicit the political dimension regarding the sort of society being worked towards. Since Dewey's time our current societies in the West have become predominantly capitalistic and corporate. Consequently the ontology of such societies, that is, the way of life which young persons are initiated into via their schooling and education, encourages them to primarily seek entry into an economic world. Dewey (1929) described this sort of ontology or individualism as a "perversion". Through sociocultural theories we can appreciate that human nature is indeed largely influenced by the cultural environment in which we find ourselves. In this chapter I shall be drawing mainly on the works of Dewey to explore this connection between culture and our nature in order to examine how a focus upon the ontology of education, that is, what sort of personhood is encouraged through educative experiences, in order to address how education might contribute towards the prevention of such crises from reoccurring. The particular focus to be argued for is for a democratic way-of-being or character as the recommended ontology for education.

The Economic Crisis and Human Nature

In his analysis of the global economic crisis Posner (2009, p. 75) identifies some "immediate causes" such as "risky lending with inadequate personal savings...the housing bubble...very low interest rates...and the withering of regulation of financial services". His main focus however is given to the political dimensions and specifically to the ideology of capitalism. He concludes that the economic crisis was due to the failure of capitalism itself and was not primarily a failure of government. He therefore recommends that there ought to be better regulation by government in the so-called free market and justifies this because such intervention is specifically for the financial stability of the public good where the public now is understood to be global in its dimension.

While Posner (2009, p. 105) argues that the main culprit of the recent economic crisis was cheap credit and not any sort of "irrational behaviour" performed by economists, businesses or consumers, he does indicate that our nature, the way we have learned to 'successfully' conduct ourselves in our culture, is oriented to be individually self-interested to the detriment of the greater good. Failure to give consideration to others beyond our immediate selves is reflective of the short-term profiteering approach of a corporate society. Posner (pp. 83–84) argues that consideration should be given to the character traits (not flaws) which are responsible for people acting in such a way where 'successful' persons demonstrate "a below-average aversion to uncertainty and...an above-average love of making money". He clearly regards that persons working in corporations and in economic science are very intelligent and do not indicate that they are acting irrationally. This makes some sense *only* when we limit their activities to operating in closed systems which centre the interests of businesses and consumers. However Posner warns that such capitalistic schemes are not in the interest of the community at large, which runs the risk of a depression. This is because such risky behaviours can be considered only as 'rational' and a 'private virtue' when limiting the scope of analysis to individual firms who are to benefit their bottom line. But these same behaviours are clearly 'irrational' and a 'public vice' for the community. He concludes this tension with the following statement.

> In sum, rational maximization by businessmen and consumers, all pursuing their self-interest more or less intelligently within a framework of property and contract rights, can set the stage for an economic catastrophe. There is no need to bring cognitive quirks, emotional forces, or character flaws into the causal analysis. This is important both in simplifying analysis and in avoiding a search, likely to be futile, for means by which government can alter the mentality or character of businessmen and consumers. (Posner, 2009, pp. 111–12)

It is here that I wish to take up a point of difference with Posner in his assertion that it may not be beneficial to pursue the notion of character flaws because of the assumed rational 'good' that is being exercised for the self-interested individual and business. Exercising a particular way-of-being which is, according to Posner, simultaneously rational as well as irrational—depending upon what perspective one chooses to adopt—is argued here to be demonstrative of a problematic character and one which contributes significantly to the possibility of contributing towards economic crises. The point being asserted here is that any character trait, irrespective of whether it is capable of producing short-term gains for a limited closed-system of consideration, *is* necessarily problematic and a 'flaw' if it contributes to an unjust crisis for some or all of the global community once one recognises that economic systems are not closed systems but are open in nature and are thoroughly integrated with all other social and environmental systems.

To refer to human nature as essentially self-interested and particularly adept at 'succeeding' in a capitalistic system described as being a rational nature and, therefore, as having some value is difficult to justify once we consider how it simultaneously affects the greater community. It is argued here that the value of the character or nature of persons can be ascertained only by giving consideration to *all* of the impacts its actions have on the environment as a whole. Such a holistic approach to evaluating personhood is critical especially when addressing how education may contribute to its formation. Dewey is well known for transcending the many divides and dichotomies which are often taken for granted in our society—including the one to which Posner refers where a self-interested rationality can be both a private virtue and a public vice. Dewey argued that

> the business mind is not itself unified. It is divided within itself and must remain so as long as the results of industry as the determining force in life are corporate and collective while its animating motives and compensations are so unmitigatedly private. A unified mind, even of the business type, can come into being only when conscious intent and consummation are in harmony with consequences actually effected. . . . Proof of the existence of the split is found in the fact that while there is much planning of future development with a view to dividends within large business corporations, there is no corresponding coordinated planning of social development. (Dewey, 1929, p. 9)

We might add to Dewey's analysis that some environmental factors are now being included by business firms today, such as responding to carbon emission taxation, but nevertheless we continue to witness very little overall social development being included. Dewey very clearly lays out the need for us to consider character or human nature in a holistic sense without fracturing our existence into different realms such as the private and the public as if these existed quite separately from each other. Quite clearly, in order to address the sort of character which ought to be possessed in order to avoid contributing towards another economic crisis, we must engage with how our activities impact upon the environment in a public and global sense. This entails that we no longer deem actions 'good' just because of their apparent rational benefits in a closed system such as self-interested economics. If any character trait is to be considered 'good' it must be demonstrated as such via its impact upon the global community as an open system.

Richard Sennett (1976) reported in his *The Fall of Public Man*, published thirty-five years ago, that people were losing the orientation to think about and act towards the public and social good, and instead were becoming myopically focussed upon themselves as private individuals. In his more recent work, *The Culture of the New Capitalism*, he explains that our current capitalistic culture encourages short-term relations, promotes a freedom to get rich quickly and a lifestyle of instant and selfish gratification, mainly through a desire to consume. What is being lost is a sense of the social where an increasing individualism leads to a sense of isolation and as a result our societies experience greater inequality. Sennett (2006, pp. 54–55) observes that "inequality has become the Achilles' heel of the modern economy" and that "inequality translates into distance...the less a felt connection on both sides". So consequently while persons participating in this current capitalistic culture are pursuing short-term consumptions and gratifications, they are perhaps missing out on some of the more profound aspects of what it means to be human. According to Sennett this deeper and more significant aspect of a good life has an intrinsic social nature.

In Sennett's (1998, p. 10) analysis he argues that 'character' by definition, involves long-term projects, including emotional experiences, mutual commitment, long-term goals and, therefore, a willingness to delay gratification. Such a way-of-life involves cultured habits developed through self-control and self-discipline exercised with a conscious orientation to the others who compose society. By referencing Anthony Giddens, Sennett (1998, p. 44) describes a life without such cultivated habits of character based instead on momentary impulses and short-term actions and relations as "a mindless existence". Consequently Sennett notes that the qualities which are esteemed in the work environment which rewards individuals and businesses with 'private goods' are not necessarily the same qualities of good character which focus instead on 'public goods', which are more appropriate for society at large.

Similarly to Sennett, Eric Fromm (1990, p. 110) notes that the social character of twentieth -century capitalism tends to display insatiable consumption based upon standardized tastes by individuals who "can be easily influenced" and yet contrastively "feel free and independent". He argues that this feeling of individual freedom is largely illusory. However what concerns him is that the private desire of consumption and freedom which is strictly asserted as a personal good or even personal right is, unfortunately, "stronger than all other moral considerations" (Fromm, 2001, p. 98).

If we are to consider such an inclusive and holistic perspective on the sort of character or nature we are enacting as Dewey, Sennett and Fromm advocate, what is becoming apparent is that it is difficult to sustain a private-public divide where activities in the private realm can be 'good' while ignoring their impacts in the public realm. I am not suggesting that the private is somehow to be understood only in terms of self-interest and is therefore of less value that other communitarian concepts such as the public. Rather I am arguing that the private—while valuable—must be evaluated as an intrinsic aspect of an open system which inevitably involves the public to some degree. Paul Fairfield (2005, p. 21) similarly argues that we must pursue the values of the private and the public *together* where the private has an important role for understanding the rights and existential well-being of persons and so therefore "the public and the private are not antithetical values but dialectical counterparts". Social justice and the minimization of economic crises are only possible through the dialectical interplay of both of these aspects in order that neither of them becomes oppressed.

As part of his recommended response following his analysis of the global economic crisis, Posner (2009, p. 321) argues that it is only through politics that we "can adjudicate and mitigate" between various interest groups and their personal interests in light of the public good. This is significant because it is argued here that by focussing on the importance of democracy we are able to give priority to the political rather than to economics. This is also recognized by Deetz (1992, p. 13) and aligns with Sennett's solution for preventing economic hardships by looking to politics if we are to seriously seek justice and fairness. By politics Sennett (2006, p. 84) also includes education in the form a person's *Bildung* or cultivated character. This sort of education is claimed to motivate individuals to participate politically in the democratic sense of actively seeking public rather than only private goods, and would necessarily involve "global dimensions" because citizens, having a "will to know", would be actively interested in finding "out how the world around them works", not just in an intellectual sense but as being active agents able to operate for the greater good as a consequence of understanding global complexities (Sennett, 2006, pp. 160-171).

This connection of education to economics via politics and culture is clearly significant and is often addressed in many of Dewey's writings. His justification for giving special notice to education was because this "is strictly correlative with culture in its inclusive social sense" (Dewey, 1929, p. 103). Dew- Dewey's desire to bring about social change for a better world—just as we are seeking here—is also considered of great potential benefit for innovating a particular approach to education in today's world which is able to contribute to a new way-of-being for persons in order to bring about a more just society. This is characterised by being actively able to seek goods of a more public nature—which or course was Dewey's main interest and he sought this through his notion of democracy, including its ontological dimension of a new kind of individuality.

Dewey's New Individuality

The capitalistic culture of Dewey's time did not appear to differ a great deal compared with what we are witnessing today just over half a century after his death, although the influence of the hidden hand of the free market is perhaps having a much greater global impact. In Dewey's (1929, pp. 24-46) time, which he interestingly described as "a corporate age", he warned against an apparent "complete economic determinism" which significantly influences society's institutions as well as all individuals. Both he and Posner (2009, p. 284) conclude that capitalism is a form of social Darwinism and so we witness unjust consequences for many persons selected by the free market as being unfit to 'succeed'. Bauman (2004, 2007, p. 20) has more recently described such persons as "being disposable" and as "the waste of 'economic progress'". Dewey judged that socially unjust outcomes is a 'defect' of our societies which exercise control by privileging an 'interest in private profit' including economic, material and entertainment dimensions. By identifying this rather Machiavellian character which places personal interest above moral considerations, he concluded that

> there is a perversion of the whole ideal of individualism to conform to the practices of a pecuniary culture. It has become the source and justification of inequalities and oppressions. Hence our compromises, and the conflicts in which aims and standards are confused beyond recognition. (Dewey, 1929, p. 49)

He therefore recommended that what is needed to address this "deepest problem of our times" is a new kind of individuality. His conception of this new individuality takes responsibility in the political domain in order to direct economics in more just directions through personal participation for a common culture for which we all have a right to contribute towards. This of course is a democratic approach involving not only the organisation and structure of governments and institutions but also as a way of life for all individual persons as social beings (Dewey, 1916, p. 93).

It must be made clear that Dewey was not making the claim that first we ought to educate and change individual persons and *then* this will lead to a change in a new unified culture. Such an approach would have to assume that individuals, while being schooled, could exist in a separate realm from the rest of society and be protected from its influence. This certainly is not possible as the mass of the school population spend more time outside of the school grounds in the rest of society rather than within its walls. Dewey sought to transcend any assumption that there could be a division of realms and therefore argued that individuals ought to learn to live well in the current social context—even if it is vague and confused. Even in his day he claimed that society displayed "a troubled and tangled economic scene" which results in "confusion" as individuals attempt to make sense of it and themselves and how they ought to live (Dewey, 1929, p. 80). The way to change this for the better was for individuals to collectively enact changes to their cultural and economic way of life—through their collective agencies.

One site which, according to Dewey, could play a significant part in promoting such a change towards a new kind of individuality was education. The role of education, for Dewey (1929, p. 102), was to change from primarily being oriented towards churning out "efficient industrial fodder" to meet the demands of a pecuniary culture, and to stop evading giving "serious consideration to the deeper issues of social life". Such a traditional approach to individualism results in "mental poverty" because it lacks the capacity amongst students for "resistance, discriminating criticism, or the vision and desire to direct economic forces in new channels" (Dewey, 1929, p. 103). His view of such a transformative education was that it ought to primarily be democratic in nature. While much has been written about the logic of democracy as both a process and as a systematic organisation or structure, much less attention has been given to the ontological dimension regarding what it might mean to *be* democratic as a person—and in particular as an educated person (Biesta, 2006). Irrespective of whether one's role as a citizen is defined and essentialised as being part of a democratic political system or not, I am arguing that one is nevertheless able to *be* democratic in how one lives one's life.

Democracy as a Moral Way-of-Being

It is important to recognise that democracy is as much as moral concept as it is a political one (Kelly, 2009), and consequently its significance for the ontological dimension of education, that is, the way-of-being which is promoted in persons (sometimes recognised as 'character') is readily recognised. Through capitalism there is the promotion of desire and consumption (Sennett, 2006, p. 139) within individuals, while through democracy there is a promotion of moral responsibility. This is because democracy operates as an ideal for the good life of all individuals. Any notion of the 'good' in respect to life for the individual must also make reference to the rest of the community at large—including the environment—which are affected by such an endeavour. Therefore for a particular 'good' to be justified, it must make reference to the public at large and not necessarily involve only anthropocentric views. This is because, as a particular notion of a good is asserted, such as it is 'good' for an individual to protest by publicly burning a copy of the Koran, for example, or for one to obtain the maximum economic wealth as one is able to, then the accompanying justification for such an assertion for a certain way-of-being or character must necessarily include references to the consequences for the relations that such an individual *already* finds himself involved with—such as fellow members of his global community where one's pollution, while perhaps evaporating from one's immediate environment, nevertheless clearly affects the environment of many others.

Being democratic requires the individual to be responsible to the community. This is in contrast to the rather isolationist proposal by the French philosopher Voltaire, who recommended that we ought to just mind our own private business and 'tend our own garden'. Dewey (1922, p. 180) appears to have taken up this analogy and challenges such a self-interested way of life by pointing out that "the boundaries of our garden plot join it to the world of our neighbors and our neighbors' neighbor". Elsewhere (Dewey, 1929, pp. 122–23) he argues that "to gain an integrated individuality, each of us needs to cultivate his own garden. But there is no fence about this garden: it is no sharply marked-off enclosure. Our garden is the world". That is, he clearly pointed out that while some of us may choose to believe we are relatively uninvolved in the lives of others and that our actions—our way of life—doesn't directly affect others, he claims that all of our activities do in fact affect the environment in some way and that others, therefore, necessarily will also share such a changing environment and the associated consequences. Therefore such a moral way-of-being requires us to give serious consideration to how our actions will inevitably affect others with which we are intrinsically involved.

Dewey (1916, p. 105) identified that the society which claims to be democratic must make "provision for participation in its good of all its members on equal terms". Therefore there is an obligation on each and every member to give an account as to how her actions also enable and do not limit the equal participation and opportunities of other members of the community. In one of his most well-known books, *Democracy and Education*, Dewey argues that

> a democracy is more than a form of government; it is primarily a mode of associated living, of conjoint communicated experience. The extension in space of the number of individuals who participate in an interest so that each has to refer his own action to that of others, and to consider the action of others to give point and direction to his own, is equivalent to the breaking down of those barriers of class, race, and national territory which kept men from perceiving the full import of their activity. (1916, p. 93)

Here we see the moral dimension of Dewey's understanding of democracy as a way-of-being. On a superficial reading it might appear that Dewey's approach to morality is one of consequentialism, that is, the merits (or evils) of a particular action or set of actions can only be evaluated in terms of their immediate results or consequences. However, pure consequentialism is never able to be attained because moral judgment, that is, the basis for undertaking particular actions, must be decided upon *before* the consequences are made manifest. So rather than try to label Dewey as a consequentialist we can appreciate that his morality involves constant democratic behaviour where individuals strive to attain some 'good' through inquiry, experimentation and dialogue with others.

This notion of 'the good' is not reflective of the so-called Platonic Forms due to the basic problem of idealism where a universal notion of an absolute good is attempted to be applied to every concrete situation. Rather the notion of 'the good' is something which is very context specific, that is, the agent must be able to make a judgement as to what she thinks will be the most valuable outcome of her actions each "micromoment" (Komesaroff, 2008) that she reflects upon the consequences that her actions appear to be causing. Such a notion of the moral good is not something which pertains to a principle such as 'don't steal' or 'don't lie' which must be simply 'applied'. Such conformity to authoritative rules and regulations is reflective of an ontology which Bauman describes as the 'ethics of obedience', where the individual obeys and conforms to the status quo norms of the particular social group one is a member of. Such an authoritative approach to morality does not align with democracy because by its nature such an authority does not encourage citizens to inquire, challenge and debate possibilities beyond the status quo or the often assumed closed system nature of economics.

Quite clearly, this sort of democracy as being argued for here—as a way of life—is primarily moral and cannot be subsumed as being essentially an aspect of the 'free' market. This is because this latter phenomenon is only economic in nature and does not align with the moral imperative for individuals to be responsible for the community at large. This is an important distinction for Dewey (1941, p. 277), who argued, "The attempt to identify democracy with economic individualism as the essence of free action has done harm to the reality of democracy and is capable of doing even greater injury that has already done". Indeed he considered the climate of his America to have obscured and marginalised "the spiritual factor" of the democratic tradition involving freedom and equal opportunity because the whole notion of what it means to be a human individual is being perverted due to the pecuniary culture of the time (Dewey, 1929, p. 49). While social life in the America of his day might have been narrowly and obsessively focused upon individuals competing for economic wealth, it is considered here that this has now become hegemonic in our day—but on a global scale. Saul (1997, pp. 87-94, p. 139) similarly attacks attempts to equate democracy with capitalism because this latter ideology, which is largely corporatist in nature, "creates a conformist society" in which "the public good is minimized" and which is therefore quite at odds with a democratically free citizenry who are able to freely challenge, debate and experiment with what might be best for the public at large. This is why he argues that national public education which promotes critical ways of understanding is so central to enabling democracy to flourish because democracy is something which the citizens participate in and is not something provided or delivered by politicians.

This conflation of democracy with capitalism and the free market which we witness in our time is largely because, as Goldman (as cited in Deetz, 1992, p. 148) has argued, a "special moral status has been given to business" since it is largely assumed that financial profit enables political freedom. Consequently the political interests inherent in the original movements of democracy pertaining to free citizens in free societies have been conquered by the economic interests of corporations through 'common-sense' notions which portray freedom as being one and the same with a free market. Consequently Deetz (1992) concludes that serious consideration of moral questions are largely surrendered in the face of the seduction of ideology associated with what he refers to as "corporate colonization" which usurps the potential of democratic political ideals.

Similarly Carr and Hartnett (1996, p. 45) have observed that the current redefined and dominant understanding of democracy has been "transformed from a moral concept that incorporated a vision of human nature and a commitment to a particular form of life". As a result of this domination of neoliberal ideology these authors argue that there ought to be a change to our understanding of democracy to once again be more closely aligned with classical democratic ideals which include the moral dimension. They reference the works of Dewey as being most informative for such a project, because he was primarily concerned with humankind's 'social intelligence' first and foremost. Carr and Hartnett (p. 57) claim that "for Dewey, the revitalization of democratically organized public life was the most important requirement for the future development of democracy" because it was one which aspired to enable the growth and a good life for *all* the members involved. Dewey's notion of democracy, as involving collective deliberation centred upon the common good, continues to serve as an exemplar of how democracy necessarily involves a moral way of life which actively seeks the good of all. Consequently it is argued there that the promotion of a democratic way-of-being through education can significantly reduce the chance of economic crises by challenging the often myopic focus of private gains as per the ideology of capitalism to also give consideration to what impacts these can have on other community interests.

Democracy as an Aspiration

In addition to being a moral and political concept it is also contended here that democracy plays an important inspirational role which ought to directly influence the aims and purpose of education. Being a scholar of Plato and Hegel, Dewey was critical of idealism mainly because it represents a two-realm structure of reality where ideas, including aims and end-purposes, are assumed to exist in a separate realm to the physical and concrete existence of living persons in their environment. As a pragmatist he was concerned with how the value of particular ideas and purposes could be actualised in the activities of our day-to-day lives and not in how they might have value only in an abstract and absolutist sense as per idealism. He expressed this concern when he stated:

> To put the intellectual centre of gravity in the objective cosmos, outside of men's own experiments and tests, and then to invite the application of individual intelligence to the determination of society is to invite chaos. (Dewey, 1908, p. 39)

Therefore, while he was wary of ideals being assumed to have an existence *beyond* the here and now, he nevertheless valued the notion that ideals can be very valuable for the practices of living when they are understood as the ideas which inspire us to action. Rather than dichotomise between ideals as *ends* or purposes and the practical activities as *means*, he argued for a holistic understanding to means *and* ends, where end-purposes are evident in giving guidance and direction to how we take action as embodied beings.

The end-purposes which help give direction to how we live our lives can often be considered as inspirational in the sense that they inspire and animate our *raison d'etre*, which is as much an emotional engagement as it is intellectual. It is not a purely rational vision which forms the logical basis of what we might strive towards in order to give meaning and purpose to our lives, but it is something which we also find emotionally appealing. As such these ideals can be understood as being both existential and spiritual (Dewey, 1908, p. 39; Webster, 2009). For Dewey democracy was an ideal which can inspire us in how we might live our lives in our day-to-day activities and, thus, how we might direct economic practices to supporting inspiring visions of the good life for *all*.

Fairfield similarly identifies this aspiration aspect as one of the main reasons why democracy has appealed to so many people throughout history. Many have chosen revolution and made personal sacrifices in order to pursue an ideal of democracy with its promises of a better life for communities. Fairfield argues:

> We may explain the phenomenal success of democracy: neither by its theoretical grounds nor by its practical results, but by its direct connection with deeper existential self-understandings, aspirations, meanings, and passions that are widely prevalent. (2008, p. 59)

Understanding democracy as an aspiration or as an 'animating spirit' as Fairfield describes does not work against understandings which promote democracy as consisting of rational deliberation. Rather it simply recognises that "the basis of rational thought, or a sizeable portion of it, cannot itself be rationally demonstrated" (Fairfield, 2008, p. 61) and so we need to go *beyond* rationality. This does not mean *against* rationality by promoting some form of irrationality, but rather we need to acknowledge that there needs to be an existential connection between the individual and the idea of democracy such that the person becomes moved to action by the ideal. Ideals which are aspirations must necessarily share a deeply personal and existential connection with individuals which are often experienced as being very private.

Dewey (1929, p. 244) argued that the various ideals which are found in morals, politics and religion can only have significance in the lives of existing individuals where they are called "ends-in-view" or "purposes" because they animate and give direction to our activities. He therefore argued that ends and means should not be dichotomised but should find their unity within the being of individual persons. Ends do not exist in an absolute realm but can be changed and adjusted through the practices of activities in concrete experiences. As a sort of *telos* they do not function as unchangeable absolutes but are themselves subject to reevaluation, revision and adjustment. This requires a to-and-fro dialogic between aspirations, initiating activities and evaluating the consequences of actions that may or may not lead to changing how individuals understand the value of their guiding private aspirations and how these impact upon the public. This requires individuals to be willing to share their apparently private end-purposes for why they participate in particular economic activities.

We need to negotiate what we ourselves think we understand by living a meaningful life and what we personally mean by democracy and how such leading ideals are able to add valuable guidance to all of our actions. This is also the position that Dewey appeared to hold as he argued,

> To my mind, the greatest mistake that we can make about democracy is to conceive of it as something fixed, fixed in idea and fixed in its outward manifestation. The very idea of democracy, the meaning of democracy, must be continually explored afresh. (1937, p. 182)

He justified his view here partly because he understood that life itself does not stand still but is under a continuous process of becoming and changing as it adjusts and responds to its environment, which is also constantly undergoing changes. This doesn't mean that we ought to pursue a rigid and inflexible understanding of democracy in an absolute sense, but it does highlight the need to appreciate the ontology of democracy *before* we settle on its supposed logic. If democracy is something which offers value to the way we live our day-to-day lives and is able to challenge capitalism, then its value ought to be made evident in all of the consequences of our actions. As each of our experiences may offer new encounters, the potential implications for democracy in each new concrete situation is something to be discovered. This inability to predict with certainty what an outcome will be in each new situation is not a weakness of being democratic but rather it describes the ontology, which itself is democratic. Dewey acknowledged this when he stated,

> I don't know just what democracy means in detail in the whole range of concrete relations of human life–political, economic, cultural, domestic–at the present time. I make this humiliating confession the more readily because I suspect that nobody else knows what it means in full concrete detail. (1937, p. 190)

This form of living is not like proselytising where one already knows that one's particular understanding of democracy is right and all one needs to do is simply 'apply' it in all situations. Rather to *be* democratic each generation needs to be willing to seriously reconsider how they understand how the value of democracy might be made manifest in each cultural practice–including economics–and in doing so, must be willing to listen to the concerns of others and how they perceive they are being affected by particular actions. This necessarily identifies the ontology of democracy as a moral way-of-being and can be adopted in order for us to address the practices of capitalism. This approach would allow us to examine how both business corporations and individuals are inspired, how they understand the value of their purposes and actions, and then challenge and evaluate these in terms of what might be the best for the public good. Such a way-of-being, or character, offers a potential means for preventing economic crises by continually calling into question how specific perceived private virtues might also simultaneously be public virtues.

Conclusion

In summary, one of the major factors to have contributed to the global economic crisis of 2008 which have been considered in this chapter was that the mindset of businesses and consumers is 'split' as identified through Posner's problematic of private virtue–public vice. Through the ontological aspect of education—the sorts of persons to emerge from the educative process—a healing of such a split has been argued for which can enable persons to transcend this perceived divide between the private and the public. This calls for a focus upon a new sort of personhood, which I claim is somewhat akin to Dewey's notion of his new individuality. This focus upon individuality is argued here to be most suitable to transforming the social character of capitalism which has worked against responsible and critical *individual* initiates to action in the public domain.

Sennett argues that through capitalism we have become conditioned to seeing education only in terms of how it positions us as compliant components for economic advantage. This is a type of black and white—closed systems sort of thinking where the only 'good' which is pursued is understood within the very limited parameters of the immediate and private. This can be challenged through education via critical thinking typical of democratic participation which explores the grey areas of uncertainty as per open systems rather than the more certain blacks and whites associated with closed systems. Consequently such thinking would encourage *individual* learners to actively and critically engage with the public good as all considerations of private goods associated with economic participation must necessarily eventually impact upon the public if carefully and rigorously thought through.

This is considered here to offer quite a paradigm shift to how the entire system of mass compulsory schooling is being practiced. According to Max Weber our schooling has been reflective of militarized capitalism where individuals are trained to become obedient to authorities rather than exercise their own critical capacity to challenge social norms. This is why Sennett (1998, pp. 145-148) claims that "strength of character" is required to be "willing to confront the new capitalism" and it can only do so through exercising critical thought to be cognisant of how we are already embedded in "connection to the world" and therefore all individuals must act responsibly to it. Investing in an education which pursues thinking deeply about the significant networks of relationships we have in the environment requires a slower sort of pedagogy which promotes thinking. Such a slower approach is required to confront the relentless work of 'impatient capital' which works against giving careful and considered thought beyond immediate private personal gains and so this approach can be considered in a high-stakes accountability culture to be quite 'ineffective' (Blake et al., 1998).

Such an approach in education which promotes serious thinking "about deeper issues of social life"—which Dewey called for—requires a certain thoughtful way-of-being or character which has been argued in this chapter to be primarily democratic in nature. Sennett (1998, p. 119) argues that a superficial approach to character as exemplified through a self-interested capitalistic culture is a failure of a "deeper kind" because it incapacitates persons "to make one's life cohere…to realize something precious in oneself…rather than merely exist". This is why he likens such an approach as being essentially "spiritual" because it deals with being able to make our existence meaningful in a significant sense. Such an approach to education, which is able to promote a democratic way-of-being, enables persons to live meaningful lives (Webster, 2009), even in environments which are apparently uncertain and even undemocratic in nature. Such an approach to education is required to resist and challenge the conforming social character which Fromm, Saul and Sennett have argued is characteristic of a capitalistic culture and which all too easily can produce economic crises on a global scale because it fails to constantly deliberate first and foremost about the public good.

References

Bauman, Z. (2004). *Wasted Lives*. Cambridge: Polity Press.

Baumann, Z. (2007). *Liquid Times: Living in an Age of Uncertainty*. Cambridge: Polity.

Biesta, G. J. J. (2006). *Beyond Learning*. Boulder, CO & London: Paradigm Publishers.

Blake, N., Smeyers, P., Smith, R. & Standish, P. (1998). *Thinking Again: Education after Postmodernism*. Westport, CT & London: Bergin & Garvey.

Carr, W., & Hartnett, A. (1996). *Education and the Struggle for Democracy*. Buckingham: Open University Press.

Deetz, S. A. (1992). *Democracy in an Age of Corporate Colonization*. Albany: State University of New York Press

Dewey, J. (1908). Intelligence and Morals. In J. A. Boydston (Ed.), *John Dewey: The Middle Works* (Vol. 4, pp. 31–49). Carbondale and Edwardsville: Southern Illinois University Press.

Dewey, J. (1916). Democracy and Education. In J. Boydston (Ed.), *John Dewey: The Middle Works* (Vol. 9, pp. 1–370). Carbondale & Edwardsville: Southern Illinois University Press.

Dewey, J. (1922). Human Nature and Conduct. In J. A. Boydston (Ed.), *John Dewey: The Middle Works* (Vol. 14, pp. 1–227). Carbondale and Edwardsville: Southern Illinois University Press.

Dewey, J. (1929). Individualism, Old and New. In J. A. Boydston (Ed.), *John Dewey The Later Works* (Vol. 5, pp. 41–123). Carbondale and Edwardsville: Southern Illinois University Press.

Dewey, J. (1937). The Challenge of Democracy to Education. In J. A. Boydston (Ed.), *John Dewey: The Later Works* (Vol. 11, pp. 181–90). Carbondale and Edwardsville: Southern Illinois University Press.

Dewey, J. (1941). The Basic Values and Loyalties of Democracy. In J. A. Boydston (Ed.), *John Dewey: The Later Works* (Vol. 14, pp. 275–77). Carbondale and Edwardsville: Southern Illinois University Press.

Fairfield, P. (2005). *Public/Private*. Lanham, MD: Rowman & Littlefield.

Fairfield, P. (2008). *Why Democracy?* Albany: State University of New York Press.

Fromm, E. (1990). *The Sane Society*. New York: Owl Books, Henry Holt & Co.

Fromm, E. (2001). *The Fear of Freedom*. London & New York: Routledge.

Kelly, A. V. (2009). *The Curriculum*. London: Sage.

Komesaroff, P. (2008). *Experiments in Love and Death: Medicine, Postmodernism, Microethics and the Body*. Melbourne: Melbourne University Press.

Posner, R. A. (2009). *A Failure of Capitalism*. Cambridge, MA & London: Harvard University Press.

Saul, J. R. (1997). *The Unconscious Civilization*. Camberwell, Vic.: Penguin Books.

Sennett, R. (1976). *The Fall of Public Man*. New York: Norton.

Sennett, R. (1998). *The Corrosion of Character*. New York: Norton.

Sennett, R. (2006). *The Culture of the New Capitalism*. New Haven & London: Yale University Press.

Webster, R. S. (2009). *Educating for Meaningful Lives*. Rotterdam: Sense Publishers.

• CHAPTER FOURTEEN •

Remachining Educational Desire: Bankrupting Freire's Banking Model of Education in an Age of Schizo-Capitalism

Jason J. Wallin

In his seminal essay on the logics of integrated world capitalism titled "Plan for the Planet" (2009a), Felix Guattari advances a problem intimate to revolutionary change in contemporary life. Given that nonintegrated or otherwise *minor* revolutionary forces cut across time and place, Guattari asks, why is it that orthodoxy ostensibly prevails? It is this very problematic that inheres throughout Paulo Freire's (1970/2010) polemic against totalizing systems of institutional power. As Freire explicates in *Pedagogy of the Oppressed*, the institutional apparatus functions to capture the consciousness of the subject according to an a priori image that draws pedagogical life into correspondence with dominant forms of state-thought. Internalized through functions of repetition, surveillance, and coerced participation, the transference of state communiqué induces a paralysis for the subject to think or act otherwise. It is in this vein that *Pedagogy of the Oppressed* palpates an image in which the subject of the institution not only remains ignorant to his complicity in the reproduction of state power but, more insidiously, also actively mobilizes his desire to maintain it.

In what constitutes a perennial problem for efforts to liberate education from under powers of hierarchical coding, desire is brought into machinic connection with the very forms of oppression that prevent it from actualizing revolutionary thought or action. While Freire (2010) concedes that the student has access to the minimal freedom of categorizing the communiqué of the institution, ultimately "it is the people that are filed away through the lack of creativity, transformation, and knowledge" (p. 72). Incisively, Freire's designation for this complex apparatus of capture would refer to the socioeconomic reterritorialization of education in the image of the *bank*. This image might not be thought as a metaphor but, rather, a concept through which we might think education's complex imbrication within networks of socio-politico-economic exchange. Such a reconceptualization of the school as a transversal site of economic processes palpates a remarkable rethinking of education, for while images of the school-as-factory or school-as-barracks remain operative in Freire's banking model of education, *Pedagogy of the Oppressed* dilates upon a broader network of forces that intermingle within the school. What the contemporary demonization of public education in North America has failed to register is that the problem is not as much the school as it is that of an entire society, its forms of transmission, the desire of the masses and requirements of industry (Guattari, 2009b).

Reevaluating Taylor's image of the school-as-factory, Freire implicitly palpates alternatives to the familiar idea that subjugation is an effect specific to forces of production alone. That is, although the banking model of education might be detected via specific processes of subjugation exerted upon the institutional subject, these microtactical actions run subjacent to more generalized powers of social control. While Freire evokes the problems of alienated student desire, the segmentation of work-time according to standards of efficiency, and the valuation of the student adaptability to factory-routines symptomatic of Taylorism, the concept of banking dilates such neodespotic (coded) forms of subjugation upon the abstract machines of economic production. The detection of this reterritorialization is crucial for curriculum theory insofar as it begins to demonstrate how processes of institutional subjugation are implicated within a vast socioeconomic rhizome.[1] Further, by detecting the ways in which the school has become a transversal circuit of economic power, curriculum theory might rethink Freire's challenge of liberating education in relation to the emergence of economic formations unthought within *Pedagogy of the Oppressed*. In these ways, we might avoid the analytic failure being perpetrated by those state forces that have resituated the problems of the social squarely upon the object of the school, its structure and organization (Guattari, 2009b). Rather than seeking out new ways of altering the role of the teacher or attitudes of students, our task today should involve the elucidation of how society functions in order to bring about such changes in the first place (Guattari, 2009a, 2009b). As this essay will seek to explicate, the current economic crisis is intimately wed to the ways in which capitalist modellization functions to affect unconscious representation, or rather, the economy of desire 'itself'. Put differently, the social machines of contemporary capitalism are not merely evident via the visible facilities of communication, hierarchized power relations, or the organization of knowledge transmission. Today, what remains largely unthought is the mutation of desire under capitalism and, further, the investment of capitalism's deterritorializing machines at all levels of educational desiring-production.

The current economic crisis to which education is interminably wed is no longer recognizable according to the formulations advanced in the groundbreaking *Pedagogy of the Oppressed*. On this point the stakes are clear: "Inflating an obsolete target...could serve to misdirect critical and creative energies" (Conway, 2010, p. 2). It is this general provocation that will inform the trajectory of this essay insofar as I will attempt to steal Freire's conceptualization of banking education in order to redeploy it in relation to the emerging forces of integrated world capitalism[2] (Guattari & Negri, 2010). Via this general tactic, I will attempt to accomplish two tasks. First, this essay will seek to detect the unthought problematic education faces in this particular moment of economic crisis. In part, this tactic will require that the concept of banking be wrested from Freire in an effort to draw it more adequately into relation with the contemporary function of capitalism and its abstract contact point with education. Second, this essay will seek to redress the problem advanced at its outset. Specifically, how is it that those social impulses that refuse to join dominant processes of cultural production ostensibly fail to fulminate into a full-scale revolution of the educational apparatus?

Decoding Neodespotism

"If one wants to understand how desire is induced, managed, and channeled into socially sanctioned avenues, then one needs to understand how banking works, for it is banks that orchestrate [the]...arrangement of filiation and alliance" (Buchanan, 2008, p. 108). In *Pedagogy of the Oppressed*, Freire denudes the function of desiring-production under state-capitalism. Specifically, the banking model of education exposes a neodespotic impulse within the social-economic circuit. In the banking model, flows of exchange are strictly controlled, emanating from a dominant 'majority', relayed via the teacher-as-bank-clerk and inscribed upon the body of the student. The linearity of this regulated institutional communiqué ensures that educational knowledge–capital conforms to highly coded processes of semiotic exchange. Herein, the student is reduced to a passive relay in the circulation of sanctioned knowledge proffered from above. Yet, more powerfully, the student's position as a passive relay in the circuit of institutional exchange functions to prove this system of exchange. Foucault (1979) would elaborate on such neodespotic processes in his analysis of surveillance and punishment intimate to the highly codified life of the institutional subject throughout industrialization.

Hemmed in by the strict codification of work-time, physical space, and mechanisms of constant evaluation, the institutional subject would constitute a docile object of disciplinarity coerced to adapt its production correspondent to the necessities of state production. Yet, it is not simply the accumulation of proscribed knowledge or skill that acts as a force of subjugation. Rather, the circuit of institutional power is repeated through the highly coded exchange of such knowledge in the first place. The banking model of education ensures that such exchange is imaginable only insofar as the student can function as a repository for watchwords that conscript the subject to accept and repeat the sanctioned speech of his oppressors. This exchange is, of course, intimate to the optimal functioning of disciplinarity in which the subject willingly internalizes dominant forms of enunciation in an effort to access the rewards they proffer. In this vein, Freire's concept banking might be thought as a 'mediator state' through which all institutional thought and action is made to pass. Not only does this situation produce an infantile subjectivity easily dominated by institutional powers but, perhaps more insidiously, it also promulgates a scenario in which it becomes impossible for the subject to think in terms that are not already cathected to coded systems of exchange.

Freire's concept of banking advances an image of life sedimented by institutional coding. Knowledge capital is segmented, apportioned, and regulated irrespective of the students taught; the student-teacher relationship is captured within an asymmetrical image of power that reinforces the infantalization of the student's subjectivity. Pedagogical life is coded into successive levels of academic progression, developmental ordering, and institutional reward. I have hence referred to the banking model of education as a function of neodespotism insofar as Freire's image of oppression is premised upon the totalizing control of social flows within the institution. The role of the banking model, Freire writes, is oriented to regulating the way that the world "enters into the student" (2010, p. 76). Today, the modellization of education in Freire's image of the bank persists via the proliferation of standardized tests linked to funding, opportunities for social mobility, and institutional status. It is in a similar vein that the contemporary marriage of teacher promotion, institutional funding, and standardized-performance testing has effectively produced vast zones of social underdevelopment throughout North America. This dire situation has in turn been substantiated under the familiar notion of 'economic necessity'. However, this popular notion functionally depoliticizes the exertion of state power by obfuscating political investment under the alibi of 'economic requirement' (Buchanan, 2008). Significantly, it is against such forces of necrotic institutional coding that much contemporary curriculum theorizing has oriented its project.

The image of oppression fulminated thus far pertains to only one kind of social machine. Elsewhere, I have dubbed this machine neodespotic insofar as it functions to code social flows within strictly regulated systems of power and exchange. Yet, insofar as this particular social machine constitutes a primary concern within curricular critique, we have failed to attend to another kind of social production intimate to integrated world capitalism. That is, while the curricular reconceptualists of the 1970s were counterposed to the capture of educational thought within the circuits of state capitalism (traditional segmentary capitalism), the reactive answer to unleash social codes would fall into filiation with another form of capitalism altogether. Where the priorities of state capitalism were manifest in the production of forced labor, the accumulation of capital, and delimitation of creative work, contemporary forces of integrated world capitalism feed off of free labor, capital circulation, and creative innovation (Guattari, 2009b). While the neodespotic impulse to codify social codes mark one pole of social production, a second impulse of social production more suited to contemporary capitalism insists. As Deleuze and Guattari develop, "On the ruins of the despotic machine, [society]...is caught between the Urstaat that they would like to resuscitate as an overcoding and reterritorializing unity, and the unfettered flows that carry them toward an absolute threshold" (1983, p. 282). For example, working-class struggles throughout Europe and North America are accompanied by the resurgence of neo-Nazism while the deterritorialization of the sociopolitical sphere by proponents of gay and workers' rights have emerged counterpart to such neodespotic political formations as the Tea Party in America.

While bound to the problem of social codification, the contemporary economic crisis in education must be rethought in relation to the deterritorializing pole of social-economic production intimate to capitalism. Put differently, it is no longer adequate to think that practices of deterritorialization will suffice to save us. Rather, the question of capitalist deterrorialization must be fulminated against the image of social revolution and liberation born out of the 1970s. It is in this way that we might not only avoid regarding the deterritorialization of social codes as inherently liberatory and, further, postulate new images of social liberation that fail to fall into filiation with the decoding impulses of contemporary capitalism. This is not simply to jettison processes of social coding as irrelevant but, rather, to engage with the implications of an economic form that will constitute the more urgent problematic for the future of education.

Economic Control

The machines of contemporary social production no longer function to impose strict forms of social coding. Today, the symptoms of a different kind of social production are becoming evident through the economics of transfer credits, transferable degrees, and the general introduction of corporate interest at all levels of the educational system (Deleuze, 1992). Cut off from the arboreal *telos* of graduation as its ostensible 'root', education is envisioned within the contemporary market's model of flexibility, incompleteness, and modulation (Gregoriou, 2008). Within this model, "education mutates into an open system...of training...where one...is never finished with anything" (p. 102). "Man is no longer a man confined" Deleuze (1995) writes apropos Burroughs, "but a man in debt" (p. 181). That is, man is no longer strictly controlled through processes of segmentation but, rather, through his integration within networks of continuous exchange according to which he must autoregulate and self-discipline.

Contemporary education has entered into filiation with the capitalist deterritorialization of coded limit points. The once coded knowledge associated with highly specialized apprenticeships has become decoded in order to make education available across different locales, times, and spaces. In this vein, the economic modellization of contemporary education is characterized as a project of lifelong learning, permanent retraining, ongoing evaluative and performative registration aptly organized under the lauded pedagogical project of learning how to learn. Under the deterritorializing impulse of contemporary market economics, education functions to both attract and produce vagabond subjects for whom new forms of flexible training and registration (educational "services") can be continuously mobilized. In this vein, a new kind of educational subject is being born from under the image of passivity that remains a potent foil in contemporary curriculum studies. The analogy of the student as a receptacle for institutional knowledge is jettisoned in lieu of an active subject who negotiates, modifies, and unleashes semiotic flows. As many curricularists have falsely assumed, this shift is neither inherently liberatory nor counterposed to the banking complex as it has mutated in an age of integrated world capitalism.

The traditional analogy that schooling functions as a mechanism of accumulation and containment has been superseded by one of perpetual circulation in which the student is more fully integrated into the circuitry of semiocapital exchange. Herein, the interminable flow of information foisted upon the student becomes less an attempt to fill them than to invest the student within a modellized image of capital exchange requisite upon perpetual semiosis. In a similar vein, where the school-as-factory delimited the voice of the student, the mantra of 'giving students voice' by unleashing their capacities for creative production dominates the contemporary imaginary. Sir Ken Robinson's popular polemic against the school's delimitation of creativity points to a general shift away from the containment of the student in lieu of unleashing their creative impulses as a catalyst for the kinds of innovative and flexible high-order production required by an economic apparatus that thrives upon novelty and difference. This is to say that the function of power is no longer exclusively tethered to the transference of specific knowledge contents from the institution to the student. Emphasis has now shifted to reflect an increasing demand for critical, creative, and highly adaptable knowledge workers. It is in this vein that the function of power is no longer adequately conceptualized as a transcendent force of oppression and segmentation.

Rather than controlling from above, systems of power are now immanently activated by our coming to them (Massumi, 2002). Control is now exacted through "miniaturized methods" (Guattari, 2009a, p. 236). The contemporary subject is socially composed through processes of registration triggered when they log into the Internet, modify their bank accounts, query credit ratings, or update academic transcripts. In a manner that must be distinguished from the segmentary function of the traditional banking model, the deterritorializing impulse of contemporary capitalism has promulgated a new logic of control in education. The contemporary institutional apparatus no longer works by inhibiting mobility but by establishing ways to continually register the movement of the subject through the course of her life. Today, institutional registration is effected through the operation of systems of perpetual training, performance assessments, and the conferral of awards and degrees. Such systems of implicit control do not simply function 'from above' but, rather, become immanent to one's insertion within a socioeconomic system in which training, assessment, and awards constitute passwords for one's circulation therein. "The old monetary mole is the animal of the space of enclosure", Deleuze (1992) writes, "but the serpent is that of the societies of control...[t]he disciplinary man was a discontinuous producer of energy, but the man of control is undulatory, in orbit, in a continuous network...[e]verywhere surfing has already replaced the older sports" (p. 1). Institutional passwords are no longer linked to completion, since the very notion of completion constitutes the slowing or termination of exchange. In this vein, the metaphors of classic thermodynamics have been rendered obsolete insofar as the contemporary function of banking works to ward against the stabilization of the socius in the conservative image of the closed-system worldview. Contemporarily, the password functions in concert with the mobile subject as a mutable and immanent mode of data collection, digital tracking, and market sampling. The horizon of completion is erased and superseded by a dromology of access.

The Redistribution of Desire

It is no longer adequate to understand oppression in ideological terms. As Deleuze and Guattari (1983) write, the social machines produced via contemporary economics are not ideological. Instead of functioning as a carrier of ideology invested in the subject, the bank now works to control and manage desire itself. "What matters is not ideology," Guattari (2009a) writes, "but the organization of power" (p. 37). Such organization does not proceed from ideology, since ideology is an effect of the way in which a particular kind of desire *already* invests economics. Significantly, the manner in which desire is invested in economics has mutated in the contemporary period. "A capitalist...does not desire in the same way a slave merchant or official of the ancient Chinese Empire would" (Guattari, 2009a, p. 36). What has changed, Deleuze and Guattari (2009a) aver, is the distribution of desire itself.

This posed inquiry into the distribution of desire has been delimited by an overemphasis on ideology. What ideology is able to obscure, Deleuze and Guattari (Guattari, 2009a) argue, are the ways in which power is organized in the first place. To exemplify this, Deleuze (cited in Guattari, 2009a) refers to the ways in which public professors were called upon to criticize their complicity as agents of bourgeois ideology in the wake of the 1968 student riots in Paris. While professors of the political left engaged in masochistic self-criticism, more conservative professors were able to quickly reorganize their power. The collective struggle against competitive examinations that fueled the 1968 protests was obfuscated under the seemingly liberatory guise of ideological confession. Subjacent to this public confession, new microfascisms and superego groups were already being mobilized. Simply put, a focus on ideology alone does not address the way that desire is already invested in the organization of power. The contemporary crisis in education is hence not simply an ideological one. As Lazzarato (2006) argues, "The state, capital and the various institutions are not the source of social power relations, they derive from them" (p. 173).

Freire's banking model of education is intimately concerned with the ways in which power is organized within the educational apparatus. However, its critique of the educational apparatus remains thoroughly tethered to processes of overcoming conscious indoctrination. Although the interests of oppressors continue to lie in altering the consciousness of the oppressed, this has yet to grapple with the ways in which systems of social production are imbricated with the unconscious. As Attias (1998) writes, "The capitalist system...can be maintained only so long as the vast majority of individuals do not merely share in it, but also give it their unconscious assent" (p. 11). It is here that systems of power function to circuit desire into particular forms of libidinal arrangement. In this vein, desire does not refer to a socially constructed lack that the subject attempts to remediate through the consumption of material or ideological substitutes for lost objects. This conceptualization of lack is already symptomatic of an unconscious binary machine that regulates the libidinal economy in a circuit of scarcity and fulfillment.

To think what desire creates necessitates that we begin by stealing the notion of desire back from classical psychoanalysis. Desire is not essentially enjoined to lack, although desiring production might become caught in circuits of habitual antiproduction. Today, the operation of such antiproduction might be seen in the political economy of the modern school, where a division between necessity and excess captures institutional subjects within a circuit of perpetual debt. In this scenario, surplus value is continually being palpated in such a way as to imbricate students and teachers in a circuit of continual production. In a society driven by perpetual semiosis, there is always more to learn. In an age of rapidly developing technologies and infomatics, there are new skills to be mastered and information to be managed. In a system of global educational rankings, there is always progress to be made. Cleverly, this surplus economy drives education into a process of interminable production and debt. Herein, antiproduction might be detected in the way which the labor of teachers and students never catches up with the motility of social surplus value. This strategy is intimate to the functioning of capitalism, which ensures the interminability of production by realizing antiproduction at all levels of social assemblage.

Thinking of the ways in which capitalism has become invested in modes of production is crucial for the analysis of how life is exploited in contemporary schools. "The capitalist is interested only in the different machines of production that he can connect to his machine of exploitation: your arms, if you are a janitor; your brains, if you are an engineer; your looks, if a cover girl" (Guattari, 2009b, p. 144). It is in this mode of molecular exploitation or, rather, exploitation that takes place at the machinic rather than identitarian (molar) level, that capitalism has already realized desire in terms that do not devolve upon the binary machine of lack or fullness. Systems of control do not singularly function upon the wholly formed subject but, rather, upon its 'molecular' potential to connect with social machines of production. In relation to this machinic image of control, oppression can no longer be adequately thought in terms of oppositional or even dialectic models. Put differently, because desiring machines can be arranged in multiple configurations, there is no longer a need to select from the coded possibilities mobilized by either binary or tertiary-machines of production. As Lazzarato (2006) argues, "In capitalism, it is not a single drama—that of Spirit (Hegel) or Capital (Marx)—but a 'multiplicity of social dramas' which must be taken into account" (p. 172). Integrated world capitalism has realized desire as a force of connection and diversification, utilizing these forms of desiring production to drive the neoliberal aspiration for continually motile designer identities. More powerfully, however, the machinic logic of contemporary capitalism has mutated the social field by producing assemblages that no longer correspond to the segmented distribution of labor and leisure, production and reproduction, life and economics (Lazzarato, 2006).

Today, prior images of social codification have radically shifted. In post-Fordian society, the office "dissolves into society", becoming redistributed in such a way as to radically blur the segmented image of the school-as-factory (Vähämäki & Virtanen, 2006, p. 212). Under the auspices of the edutainment industry, educational labor has collapsed with leisure, while the flexible work-time of online education has dissolved the segmentation of home and work. Against the image of delimitation and repression intimate to industrial society, contemporary capitalism functions to stimulate "the maximal amount of freedom and the breaking of disciplinary relations becomes the absolute foundation of creating wealth" (Negri cited in Vähämäki & Virtanen, 2006, p. 212). While the paradigm of confinement is particular to education throughout industrialization, its logic of oppositional force is too restricted to account for the ways in which power has become multiplied at infinitesimal levels of the social-machine (Lazzarato, 2006). If our analysis of banking is to remain adequate to the powers of integrated world capitalism, the presumption of an economic superstructure insisting beneath the educational apparatus must be rethought.

Where the banking concept of education imagines the exploitation of the student in relation to a particular kind of Oedipal drama wherein desire is forcibly overdetermined by the state, new exploitative processes function to "accelerate [a] process of entry into capitalistic flows" (p. 209). Today, this acceleration is detectable via the radical rethinking of developmental taxonomies in an effort to stimulate and exploit prenatal and neonatal educational markets. Further, in an image of pedagogical life increasingly celebrated for its inversion of the banking concept, many student-centered approaches to education contemporarily imagine the student liberated from the doldrums of the classroom and limits of instructor knowledge via the pursuit of personalized interests and technologically driven self-study. Within this ostensibly liberatory model of decentralized[3] education, the desiring production of the student becomes passively linked to pursuits of individual choice ideally suited to the equally individualistic and personalized character of the designer marketplace. Herein, the deterritorializing impulses of capitalism are enjoined to processes of implicit exploitation insofar as they function to unleash and redistribute desire as a force of schizophrenic production suited to market sensibilities. "Social machines feed off the contradictions they give rise to, on the crisis they provoke, on the anxieties they engender, and on the infernal operations they regenerate. Capitalism has learned this, and has ceased doubting itself" (Deleuze & Guattari, 1983, p. 151). Today we must begin to detect the ways in which the capitalist apparatus does not fear difference but, obversely, the cessation of difference itself.

Economic Capture

"Anything can always be recovered", Guattari (2009a) writes, "the most daring artistic production, the most untimely philosophy, as long as it does not depart from the framework of writing, books, the University" (p. 145). Herein, Guattari points to both an apparatus of capture as well as a line of escape that might be dubbed *absolute deterritorialization*. Before dealing with the extreme case of absolute deterritorialization, however, it is crucial that the analysis of our contemporary educational crisis begin to detect the ways in which desiring production is captured insofar as such processes are crucial for the survival of integrated world capitalism and its ability to control those "collective organizations that contribute to the molding of the collective workforce" (Guattari, 2009a, p. 237).

In a manner qualitatively distinct from the 'private' space and secret watchwords of factory society, capitalism stimulates 'publicity'. It is in this vein, Deleuze asserts, that capitalism appears "democratic" while concomitantly withholding everything from admissibility (cited in Guattari, 2009b). This, Deleuze asserts, marks a special form of delirium induced by economics. That is, while capitalism draws desiring production into the public field, this does nothing to vulgarize economic and financial mechanisms. Briefly, the delirium of capitalism works in the open while warding against an articulation of how desire and reason are already 'abnormally' redistributed in capitalism (Guattari, 2009a). Although we might begin to detect economic forces via the various symptoms they palpate in the social, this does not yet attend to the particular kind of irrationality that runs subjacent to contemporary capitalism. Where the madness of factory society is marked by the overdetermination of reason in instrumentality, capitalism inheres a different kind of dementia corollary to its regulated processes. The capitalist system 'works' and yet is completely delirious (Guattari, 2009a). As Deleuze avers, "There are...investments of desire that cannot be confused with investments of interest, and on which interest depend in their determination and distribution: an enormous flux, all kinds of libidinal-unconscious flows that make up the delirium of this society" (cited in Guattari, 2009a, p. 36). While the symptoms of economic production may be apparent in education, their analysis by means of critical theory often reveals only their calculated influence upon the institutional subject. While such critical approaches illuminate social repression, they may be inadequate for the analysis of the capitalist symptomology. It is in this vein, Guattari (2011) argues, that we might otherwise understand the processes of capitalism by way of its particular schizophrenic redistribution of desire. Briefly put, new conceptual tools and approaches to analytic symptomology must be mobilized in order to grapple with the mutation of capitalism in the contemporary age.

While the banking concept continues to be a productive tool with which to detect deliberate forms of social repression, it does not yet approach the way that banking is itself cut from an irrationality carried throughout its forms of social actualization. Where curriculum theorists have sought to disrupt the economic apparatus by appealing to the delirious semiosis of postmodernism or its impetus to overturn the coded orthodoxies of structuralism, there has been a general failure to understand the ways in which the symptomology of capitalism is entwined with a schizophrenic impulse to push all social codes to the brink of deterritorialization. These modes of capture fulminate into a general problematic for curriculum theory. It is against the image of authoritarian unification that many curriculum theorists have drawn upon postmodernity as a means of overturning the tyranny of state thought. While postmodernity challenges the orthodoxies of signification particular to industrial society, its function as a potential counterpart to capitalist practices of social decoding, cultural hybridization, and the apolitical personalization of desire have remained largely inadmissible within educational thought. Furthermore, the polarization of desire as either a function of bureaucracy or anarchy fails to register how such poles function concomitantly within capitalist processes (Guattari, 2009a).

Guattari writes that one of the most significant forms of contemporary repression extends from the "pseudo-personological siege" of integrated world capitalism (cited in Guattari and Rolnik, 2008, p. 181). In a manner that affronts the ubiquitous celebration of individuality in contemporary education, Guattari argues that the conceptualization of personal desire functions to delimit collective desiring production. That is, the entrapment of desire at the level of the individual represses the emergence of collective forms of revolutionary action insofar desire is conceptualized as a matter of personal will. Implicated in this capture apparatus are those models of developmentalism that focus control at the level of the individual and educational systems of tracking and reward that invest desire at the level of individual production. This distribution of desire stimulates processes of 'flexible' control wherein institutional subjects are impelled to continuously surveil the output and actions of others. This is one unthought underside of institutional merit pay systems, which implicitly rely on mutual surveillance and the delimitation of collective expression. Yet, this particular apparatus of capture has yet to grasp the more insidious function of personalization.

As Guattari and Rolnik (2008) develop, processes of personalization, or rather, of distinguishing oneself as a unique individual through a praxis of customization, are particular to a new form of subjective alienation in capitalism. Specifically, while the character of customization works to provide the individual with the ostensible libratory ability to choose, such choice forecloses upon a radical escape from personal itself. More important perhaps, the focus on personalization in contemporary capitalism already circulates within modellized lines of differentiation that implicitly presuppose the ways in which one might self-identify or, more profoundly, experiment with the ways a life might go. Herein exists what Guattari dubs the "alienated production of subjectivity" (p. 181). That is, the personalized subject is continually captured within a circuit of multiplied yet conservative choices that ultimately crush alternative forms of desiring production. For contemporary curriculum theory, a particular danger inheres the celebration of personalization as it has emerged in certain instances of autobiography and arts-based research. Specifically, where desire is reterritorialized upon the figure of the researcher, the prospect of thinking either the 'molecular' desire of the unconscious or micropolitical forms of collective desire can be significantly reduced, hence demobilizing people from collective political action. In this way, desire becomes too closely registered in terms of ownership, or otherwise, in terms of trying to capture intensities in one's name. How much of what curriculum theory has dubbed autobiographical research is but an attempt to personalize desire? This is my experience!

The general problematic at work here pertains to the way in which the connective force of desiring production is reterritorialized upon the individual. That is, rather than registering the ways in which desiring production is always social, the personalization of desire in contemporary capitalism attempts to constrain forces of connection by reterritorializing them back upon the body of the designer subject (Alliez, 2006). Herein, the diverse array of revolutionary collective arrangements, subject groups, and social libidinal impulses that might be palpated into the social are alienated via their reduction to the singular image of individual desire[4] (Guattari, 2009b). This reduction marks one of the greatest strategies of deterritorialization perpetrated within capitalism. The link between desiring production and the social are radically decoded only to be apolitically resituated upon the individual as a stable category of control and capture. "From the cradle onward," Guattari argues, capitalist relations of production "shape a certain type of producer-consumer individual" (2009b, p. 175).

"The Best Capitalist Drug"

Guattari (2011) argues that capitalism has palpated a new form of pathology within social production. It is this new symptomology that must today inform the reconceptualization of the banking model. To reiterate Buchanan (2008), any understanding of social production necessitates that we are able to first understand banking and the ways in which it is able to redistribute desire in contemporary society. Not only does the reconceptualization of banking support a renewed analysis for the often unregistered functions of schizophrenic social production but, further, it suggests that the 'average' postmodern and poststructural (defined in opposition to foundationalism) answers to factory education may not be as radical as some educational theorists have contended (Guattari, 2009a). Specifically, aspirations to promulgate new fields of knowledge, hybridize social forms, or laud the multiplication of subject positions are not necessarily opposed to the desiring machines of capitalist production. As Guattari (2009a) argues, the "creative discoveries...of fringe groups are taken over by mass media; there is a completely tolerant attitude to some forms of freedom of action...a certain amount of protest, half-tolerated, half-encouraged and absorbed, can be an intrinsic part of the system" (p. 238). This is "the best capitalist drug" (Guattari, 2009b, p. 141).

This scenario leads to a crucial juncture. Insofar as social production is stimulated and captured by the forces of capitalism, is revolution possible? In a sense, this returns to the problem advanced at the outset of this essay. Specifically, given that the social field is populated by forms of nonintegration, why have we not seen a general revolution in education? Perhaps this question was premature insofar as we have entered into a period in which fringe groups and autonomist movements have begun to proliferate in areas of greatest repression. Indeed, new social formations throughout the Middle East have ostensibly begun to take power away from sedimented nation-states (Guattari, 2009a). Yet, amidst this, the continued production of impoverished zones within developing nations and hyperexploitation of Third World countries continues unabated. A parallel to this scenario exists at the micropolitical level of the school. Today, education has become a sociopolitical problem informed by new discourses of social risk management in which delinquent and minority groups find themselves in the position of being administered by new economic and political personas. Yet, even risk management continues to fall short of knowing which fringe groups will be captured within the circuits of capitalist production and which will form authentic "molecular revolutions" (Guattari, 2009b, p. 239). That is, we do not yet know which of the emerging forms of social deterritorialization will bypass their reterritorialization upon the body of capital in the creation of an "ethico-analytico-political attitude" or new social territory (Guattari and Rolnik, 2008, p. 172). Such a creation would ride the deterritorialized schiz-flows promulgated by capitalism for a goal other than that presupposed by capital's desiring machines.

While we might be on the run, Deleuze suggests, we must continue to look for new weapons with which to palpate revolutionary potentials (cited in Guattari, 2009b, p. 47). Put differently, although deterritorialized flows of social production are suited to the function of capitalism, they inhere the potential for the absolute deterritorialization of the internal limit necessary for capitalism to function; namely, that all forms of social production are reterritorialized upon the body of capital itself. In terms of the contemporary crisis in education, this problematic necessitates that curriculum theory continue to survey the social field for instances of disidentification as a means to create different kinds of "referential axes…[that] undermine…production relations, traditional social and family systems, traditional attitudes to the body, to sex, to the universe" (Guattari, 2009a, p. 240). This disidentification must necessarily take place at material levels of production through which we might better analyze how desire is distributed in the first place, beginning with the youngest children with whom the lifelong repression of unique desires begin (Guattari, 2009a). Such an approach might allow us to think the specific challenges of institutional redundancy, delinquency, dropouts, and intentional maladjustment as desiring resistance against an apparatus of ubiquitous institutional exchange and surplus. Today there are groups of youth who continue to refuse their connection to dominant organizations and processes of cultural production (Guattari and Rolnik, 2008).

The transformation of pedagogical life cannot be commenced via molar levels of visible change alone. Indeed, we must begin to register new ways to understand revolution distinct from the image of full-scale social upheaval. More specifically, the contemporary attempt to think educational change must become inseparable from the detection of molecular revolution or, rather, the singularity of revolution birthed from the production of unique enunciative forms and nonnormal behaviors out of sync with the universalizing impulses of contemporary capitalism. This task might entail rethinking the school as a site for collective production and the alternative arrangement of desire. Such a pedagogical machine is evident in A. S. Neill's (1993) *Summerhill School*, wherein student desire is concretely linked to the life of the school rather than abstract forms of economic valuation or exchange. It is in a similar vein that the desiring production of local schools might be machined to alternative or otherwise heterogenic systems of enunciation as prefigured in the work of Celestin Freinet (Acker, 2000), whose use of the printing press as a machine for molecular revolution would link the desiring production of students (as a collective subjectivity) to social production. It is in this vein that contemporary educational thought must go further in its detection and production of autonomist movements whose desiring production is aimed at breaking from the capitalist modellization of the unconscious. After all, Guattari (2011) writes, "We have the unconscious we deserve" (p. 9).

Guattari's provocation requires that pedagogy become intimate to the task of creating "other worlds within this world" as a means to escape capitalism's flattening of desire and, further, to remachine flows of desiring production within the school (Guattari and Rolnik, 2008, p. 16). This posed, the formation of alternative or countercultural forms of enunciation are not inherently liberatory. They must continually be connected to the authentic molecular concerns of group formations. It is no use to create a pirate Internet radio station, for example, if this mode of enunciation is not machined to the aspirations of a collective that seeks to reconfigure their very relationship with daily life (Guattari and Rolnik, 2008). In part, such a reconfiguration might involve the recuperation of unique social territories, collective identities, and traditional value systems made redundant under the universalizing and amnesiatic functions of integrated world capitalism. This is not simply to celebrate the untimely or anomolous 'in itself', but to palpate alternative circuits for the distribution of desire that "capitalism considered to have been completely overcome" (Guattari and Rolnik, 2008, p. 77). This would not necessitate the creation of some oppositional force to capitalism. Rather, it might entail harnessing the decoded flows of capitalism for the production of new social territories that refuse the one dimentionalizing finality of capital itself. That is, alternative forms of social arrangement and desiring production may ultimately demote the ostensible inevitability of capitalist processes and the new forms of illness it has actualized at all levels of social production (Guattari, 2009a, p. 277).

Notes

1. As it is conceptualized in *A Thousand Plateaus* (1987), the rhizome is not simply an image of liberation. Rather, Deleuze and Guattari conceptualize the rhizome in a manner that is already populated by potentials for stratification.
2. Guattari's notion of integrated world capitalism might be briefly summarized in terms of its prioritization of production over both the state and the market. This model is distinct from both liberal capitalism's focus on the market and the privileged position of the state in state capitalism.
3. While the image of schooling fulminated in *Pedagogy of the Oppressed* aspires to the centralization of control, the modern institution does not fear speaking of decentralization insofar as power functions through a rhizome of "collective facilities" (Guattari & Rolnik, 2008, p. 208).
4. As Bonta and Protevi (2004) develop, desire pertains to inhuman processes of geologic, organic, and social processes of connection. The ontological error herein pertains to the way in which desire is disconnected from the inhuman and recentered as a character particular to human will.

References

Acker, V. (2000). *Celestin Freinet*. Santa Barbara, CA: Greenwood Press.

Alliez, E. (2006). Anti-Oedipus—Thirty years on (between art and politics). In M. Fuglsang & B. M. Sorensen (Eds.), *Deleuze and the social* (pp. 151–168). Edinburgh, UK: Edinburgh University Press.

Attias, B. A. (1998). To each its own sexes? Toward a rhetorical understanding of molecular revolution. In E. Kaufman & K. J. Heller (Eds.), *Deleuze and Guattai: New mappings in politics, philosophy, and culture* (pp. 96-111). Minneapolis: University of Minnesota Press.

Bonta, M., & Protevi, J. (2004). *Deleuze and geophilosophy: A guide and glossary*. Edinburgh, UK: Edinburgh University Press.

Bowers, C. (1980). Curriculum as cultural reproduction: An examination of the metaphor as carrier of ideology. *Teachers College Record*, 82 (2), 267–290.

Buchanan, I. (2008). *Deleuze and Guattari's Anti-Oedipus*. New York: Continuum.

Cherryholmes, C. H. (1988). *Power and criticism*. New York: Teachers College Press.

Conway, J. (2010). *Gilles Deleuze: Affirmation in philosophy*. New York: Palgrave Macmillan.

Deleuze, G. (1992). Postscript on societies of control. *October*, 50 (2), 3–7.

Deleuze, G. (1995). *Negotiations 1972–1990*. (M. Joughin, Trans.). New York: Columbia University Press.

Deleuze, G., & Guattari, F. (1983). *Anti-Oedipus: Capitalism and schizophrenia*. (R. Hurley, M. Seem, & H. R. Lane, Trans.). Minneapolis: University of Minnesota Press.

Deleuze, G., & Guattari, F. (1987). *A Thousand Plateaus*. (R. Hurley, M. Seem, & H. R. Lane, Trans.). Minneapolis: University of Minnesota Press.

Foucault, M. (1979). *Discipline and punish: The birth of the prison*. (A. Sheridan, Trans.). New York: Random House.

Freire, P. (1970/2010). *Pedagogy of the oppressed*. New York: Continuum.

Fuglsang, M., & Sorensen, B. M. (2006). Introduction: Deleuze and the social: Is there a D-function? In M. Fuglsang & B. M. Sorensen (Eds), *Deleuze and the social* (pp. 1–18). Edinburgh, UK: Edinburgh University Press.

Gregoriou, Z. (2008). Commencing the Rhizome: Towards a minor philosophy of education. In I. Semetsky (Ed.), *Nomadic education: Variations on a theme by Deleuze and Guattari* (pp. 91–110). Rotterdam: Sense Publishers.

Guattari, F. (2006). *The Anti-Oedipus Papers*. Los Angeles: Semiotext(e).

Guattari, F. (2009a). *Soft subversions: Texts and interviews 1977–1985*. Los Angeles: Semiotext(e).

Guattari, F. (2009b). *Chaosophy: Texts and interviews 1972–1977*. Los Angeles: Semiotext(e).

Guattari, F. (2011). The *machinic unconscious: Essays in schizoanalysis*. Los Angeles: Semiotext(e).

Guattari, F., & Negri, A. (2010). *New lines of alliance, new spaces of liberty*. Williamsburg, Brooklyn, NY: Autonomedia.

Guattari, F., & Rolnik, S. (2008). *Molecular revolution in Brazil*. Los Angeles: Semiotext(e).

Lazzarato, M. (2006). The concepts of life and the living in the societies of control. In M. Fuglsang & B. M. Sorensen (Eds.), *Deleuze and the social* (pp. 171–190). Edinburgh, UK: Edinburgh University Press.

Massumi, B. (2002). *A shock to thought: Expression after Deleuze and Guattari*. London: Routledge.

Neill, A. S. (1993). *Summerhill school: A new view of childhood*. New York: St. Martin's Press.

Vähämäki, J., & Virtanen, A. (2006). Deleuze, change, history. In M. Fuglsang & B. M. Sorensen (Eds), *Deleuze and the social* (pp. 39–57). Edinburgh, UK: Edinburgh University Press.

When No Crisis Is the Real Crisis! The Endless Vertigo of Capitalist Education

Marcus Bussey

The recent killing of Osama bin Laden was a dramatic exercise in public pedagogy and serves as one bookend to this reflection on the relationship between education—the institution of schooling—and crises. This bookend can be thought of metaphorically as the bullet. It provides a rhetorical lens for thinking about how our culture handles dissent and of education's role, as an instrument of culture and enculturation, in a range of violences that are part of its legitimate exercise of power. The other bookend is much more prosaic—it is what I think of as the pen. This metaphor covers the myriad bureaucratic interventions, from marking the role to signing legislation and policy into effect, that characterizes dominant global educational culture. The bullet and the pen are rhetorical devices that help me think about the functions of education today. They define the working context of education which is both a social, even public, display of power and promise (aka the bullet) and institutional performance (aka the pen). The space between the bullet and the pen is one of constant upheaval, negotiation and contestation. It is where life happens and where the social is constantly reinvented, a la Deleuzian theory (1987), as a field of becoming in which the personal and the structural, bullet and pen again, generate ever-new forms for meeting the needs of capitalist culture. This rhetorical starting point for a reflection on education and crisis is important because, as Michael Shapiro has argued, rhetoric can be "not an abdication of analysis but integral to it" (1992, p. 23). The openness of rhetoric can offer a space of indeterminacy for creative engagements with the persuasive forces that demand clarity and so repress the possibilities immanent to all contexts.

Education does not simply manage dissent. More important, and this has already been alluded to above, it manufactures consent[1] by fostering commitment to the current order. As theorists from Bourdieu (1990) and Foucault (1995) to Anyon (2005) and hooks (1994) have demonstrated, education uses a range of seductive methods to do this. There is, for instance, at its simplest level, the promise of wealth and status or the dream that all can join the party. Around both promise and dream the student, as citizen-consumer, is invited to weave habitus and regimes of truth that discipline the subject. Simultaneously it rewards the individual who, as Castoriadis dryly put it (1997, p. 155), "functions adequately" more or less. This educative consensus has been well documented in critical and emancipatory pedagogic circles (Apple, 2006; Giroux, 2005; Kincheloe, 2004; McLaren, 2005). Its manufacture has involved the media, economics, politics, policy and the purveying of a set of values, through accountability and assessment structures, that foster a corporate culture in schools and universities (Bussey, 2009b). In this way they come to (are driven to) emulate capitalist processes of production that normalize competition, accountability, consistency and replicability (Ritzer, 1995). The end result is that education has become an exercise in biopolitical control that embodies the disciplinary logic of late modernity.

These reflections sketch out the rhetorical terrain—a space between the rhetoric of the bullet and that of the pen—for a pedagogy of resistance and possibility. The ground is familiar to many and may invoke assent or dissent depending on where you sit in the ideological spectrum. Yet despite the validity of, or possibilities inherent to, such critique there is a certain vagueness when it comes to operationalising any alternative vision in schools and universities. Of necessity rhetoric is vague and even empty until grounded not simply in action but also in the cognitive landscape of a shared praxis. Without this, we are left wondering what the ringing is in our ears. So critical rhetoric aside, this vagueness may be attributed to the possibilities inherent to such a critique being largely unintelligible within the discursive logic of capitalist classrooms where students, their families and the authorities all expect and respond to specific queues that flag authority, significance, success and failure. There is a self-fulfilling logic to institutionalized education—it proves itself powerful by offering (and delivering) both success and failure to those in its charge. Furthermore, the vagueness of critical rhetoric is also due to the misplaced logic of understanding educational sites as generative of causal chains that reproduce the economic systems of ordering, that is, the crises, that are under consideration in this book.

Though educational sites can undoubtedly be sites of resistance they do not generate the kind of rationality that drives capitalist culture today. The logic of capitalism which is now virtually hegemonic in classrooms and schools is economic and lies, as Deleuze and Guattari would assert, on another plane of activity altogether (1994). Anyon nailed this when she observed of the U.S. system:

> As a nation, we have been counting on education to solve the problems of unemployment, joblessness and poverty for many years. But education did not cause these problems, and education cannot solve them. (2005, p. 3)

As a form of critical futures thinking, we need to sidestep the debate about origins and look instead at processes that work between the rhetoric of the bullet and the rhetoric of the pen. It is here we find the grey land of disorientation (Bussey, 2009a). From a pragmatic point of view, this is potentially a space of dissent though generally it is experienced as a vertiginous place in which crises drive our social systems and the cultural milieu that underpin them. Generally people fixate on the elements that constitute their context—these are the structural forces defining what is possible. In pragmatism, whether it is the formal kind developed by Pierce or Dewey or the dynamic kind offered to us by Deleuze (Semetsky, 2006), it is in the space *between* the structures that human agency is experienced as process. When we focus on structure we immediately accept limits; when we focus on process we become aware of possibilities. Yet process is fluid and unstable, like when you are caught in a large wave at the beach. You cannot fight the wave but have to go with it. So even in process there are historical dynamics and socioecological pressures that constrain action. Crises add to this by amplifying disorientation, increasing the sense of flux and deceasing our ability to recognize or operationalise possibilities. As such they are a core feature of capitalist creativity as they erode limiting structures, force people into the between and into a bewildering array of new contexts that release creativity and energy. This creative ferment is contained by the logic of capital production and is bounded by the theatre of the bullet and the pen.

In this threefold reading of crisis as bullet-between-pen, the bullet represents the random anomalous chaotic flux of the day-to-day. It is the litany that drives the media and consumes huge amounts of our energy and attention at both individual and social levels (Inayatullah, 2004). There is something pedestrian about this kind of crisis for all the drama that attends it. It is the familiar crisis enacted on the world stage—it can have a theatrical quality such as that played out on Wall Street in the closing months of 2008, or in the suburbs around Fukushima, or even, if we take terrorism as a crisis of confidence, in the compound in Abbottabad where bin Laden was finally tracked down and killed. The pedagogy in such contexts is of system failure and retribution mixed with vulnerability and anxiety.

In contrast, the system as pen can pull the trigger by labeling, failing, drugging or expelling those in its charge, but it also seduces by offering pathways into the labyrinth of modernist desire. I suggest that the system needs *crises of the between* to sustain the edgy logic of late modernity that thrives on up-upheaval and the high energy produced at the edge of chaos. This dynamism has a huge human cost that is masked by the drama of crises in domains such as education, health, security and the environment in which the pedagogy becomes one of turbulence, uncertainty and doubt. The edginess of such crises drives a productive form of creativity, yet misses the escape routes always imminent in the between as the zone of becoming from which new human social formations emerge (Bussey, 2012, Forthcoming).

Whether such crises are dramatic or mundane the coverage from the media and the commentary from politicians and public intellectuals alike tend to be insistent and alarming: The whole world is in crisis! Crisis has become the norm, not the exception. It generates spaces—or what Agamben (2005) would call 'states of exception'—where the violence of killing, as in the case of bin Laden, becomes rational and indeed commendable! This is exciting stuff and demands our attention. It drags our focus away from substantive issues of ethics, praxis and sustainable living and holds it transfixed on what Bauldrillard (1998) called 'the spectacle'. In fact, it takes the full panoply of a royal wedding, a wonderful spectacle, to assuage the anxieties of many and invoke a momentary sense of normalcy. It is such a moment—the systaltic pause—that reminds us that life used to be (was it really?) less driven, complex, uncertain and off-centred. This event, of course, fosters nostalgia for the past and for a time when simplicity was the norm and identity was less troubled, thus reinscribing conservative political urges and myths.

Ours is a society addicted to crisis. This addiction is the raison d'être behind late modernity's managerial approach to the grey open, truly dangerous, space between the bullet and the pen. This indeterminate between is the domain of immanence, the culturally creative heartland of all human activity. This is where we live, always struggling as Latour reminds us, to keep the floor clean and the kitchen (aka laboratory) in order (1991). The between is a dangerous space, because it acts as a cultural Tarhir Square that situates and ferments dissent between the violence of the bullet and the structure of the pen. The instability of this space has always been managed by culture via norms, values, and practices that mask the ferment providing individuals and communities with a sense of order amidst the disorder of the Chaosmos. Culture provides a sense of continuity, stability and security. Tradition, bound to identity and reinforced by habit, holds the openness of the between at arm's length. Now that time-honoured traditions are no longer appealing to a modernity that privileges the new and novel (Bauman, 2000), modernist culture markets discontinuity and crisis as the desired alternative to what is perceived as stasis, entropy and decline (Loy, 2002). There is no middle ground. The citizen-student is offered either the vertigo of crisis and growth or the slippery slide of decline. Thus in orthodox economics crisis and growth are closely aligned as both rupture the present while directing attention into a future already ordered with the ongoing logic of both.

Currently education contributes to this process by enacting crisis both systemically through constant change which is accompanied by the drama of speed, acceleration and intensification (Finger and Asún, 2001) and pedagogically through a discourse of uncertainty that destabilises educational objectives, focusing attention on information and content management rather than the deeper synthetic possibilities of critical and holistic learning (Gatto, 2002). The resultant *edu-anxiety* creates stress for those working at all levels of the system: stress for students, their families and teachers, stress for those in educational support systems from the tuckshop to the offices of the Minister of Education. High levels of stress, of course, reduce our ability to learn by generating the white noise that masks the creative possibilities inherent to any moment. If education is to make a contribution to engaging this culture of crisis, it must do so by challenging the prevailing climate of change and uncertainty that afflicts both system and individual alike. Such a change requires a paradigm shift not towards the eternal verities of the past (the conservative response of back to basics), but towards the possibilities of the future. This, in turn, requires the promulgation of practices that inculcate tolerance, resilience and innovation along with the requisite stillness to allow for the affective self-composure of each student around a secure, resilient and open identity.

What I am proposing here is the laying of a foundation for slow education akin to the slow food movement (http://www.slowfood.com/). We need slow education to enhance our ability to respond to the crises and stresses of late modernity. Slowing down will help us think about the processes of education and its relationship with the productive forces of our world. Slowness challenges the speed, disorientation, crisis addiction, and homogenization of current educational practice. Slow education can counter the edu-anxiety that dominates education today. This slowness is about the inner health of the learning system. Like slow food it is interested in the relationships of production—local relevance; social health; the 'taste' of a subject of study; the time students and their teachers have to develop scholarship, meaning, relevance, relationship and rigor; the sense that learning needs to be more than just functional in nature and that scholarship has intrinsic merit (Bussey, 2008). When we approach our complex world in this way it becomes an invitation to creative and proactive engagement rather than the coercive and reactive task-master of a diminished and terrified education system. Such an education can lay the foundation for resilient identity formation. Resilient identities are not easily overwhelmed or goaded into reactionary behaviors and prejudices. They have a critically alive consciousness which understands and nurtures relationship both between cultures and also between the cultural and natural world.

Currently this edu-anxiety is symptomatic not just of education as a system but also of culture as an educative process of becoming. Edu-anxiety flags the instability of identity in the face of capitalist production in which flows of energy recycle, transmute and invert ideas, symbols, and identities in a maelstrom of nuclear-identity fission. The individual, as the primary social unit of modernity, akin to the atom in physics, is the primary source of energy as the alienated ego constantly releases energy into the economic and political domains.[2] This energy is material, restless, economic as well as intellectual, creative and innovative. It is expressed through high mobility, unstable relationships, heavy consumption and also as cultural innovation, psychological and spirit malaise and technological brilliance. It sustains the economic systems of capital and must not be allowed to coalesce in real terms into networks, groups and communities, and where these exist in potential they must be distracted, forever turned away from relationship. In this context we can keep the trappings of family, community and nation, but not the substance. This is why the space between the bullet and the system where becoming, immanence and possibility restlessly work out alternatives is so feared. This is also why education as a central cultural process in identity formation has such subversive potential. Furthermore, education is a key object in the crisis manufacture business.

Education plays an effective role in maintaining a fragile, volatile sense of identity in postindustrial society. Yet through slow education a deeper sense of identity can be fostered. To survive crises, financial or otherwise, requires new stories to emerge that counter 'this feeling of living on the edge' that Hicks and Bord describe (2001 p. 414). I believe education is well placed to offer such stories if only it could shake off the driving logic of edu-anxiety and arrive at a place of stillness in the midst of change.[3] Stories frame issues and cultures all operate, usually unconsciously, according to set narratives that underpin the epistemological lenses framing the paradigmatic terrain that education both maintains and enforces (Thompson, 2004). To understand the core values of any age we need only look at the education systems they generate. This period of edu-anxiety has its roots in acts of cultural, civic and political will in the nineteenth century that set the template for education on the factory model (Hetherington, 1997; Scott, 1998). Similar acts of will now need to be engaged for new, less orderly stories to emerge.

We already know the ingredients for this story as the language, aspirations, and imaginary formations are imminent in the present: relationship; equity—gender, planetary, specist; transdisciplinarity; ethics; ecological outlook; and intercivilisational dialogue. How these are embodied in a system is another matter. The imagination is constrained by dominant models of ordering. At the moment, education is a vehicle for managing the danger of immanence. Yet immanence, the chaos of it—its muddle of possible becomings—always threatens to assert its right to reinvention. So we have that age-old tension between the addiction to order, or sets of orderings that mobilize and stratify the real in time and space, and the fluid juices of the Chaosmos. Capital attempts to harness this fluidity, to brand it in its own image. This is the trick of modernity: to market instability as the flux of capital and to model human processes as capital processes. In this becoming-capital, education must also reflect the order-chaos tension and obey the rhythms of capital process. It does so by enforcing a rational mode of accounting (aka tests) upon those in its care, by representing information as capital and students as clients-consumers and the system as a mode of production that has 'standards, deliverables, outcomes and strategic goals'. Once this is accomplished the constant flux of capital is reinscribed as 'system restructures' and 'curriculum overhauls' that purport to further efficiency and pedagogical outcomes.

Thus financial crisis equates with capital crisis and this in turn becomes educational crisis as the ground for edu-anxiety which demands the response once again of system. This permanent reinvention of system, the endless restlessness of formulations, as the reflection of an equally restless creator-market is currently framing education as a strata of the economic in which calculability, legibility and accountability are driving memes. Market failure, aka learning failure, is punishable as an offence against order. In this way we see that the socioeconomic assemblage of capitalist modernity is in fact committed to the disorders of restless capital formations. Those in the system are never allowed to find their feet, gain their bearings, chart a clear line of flight, nor listen to the whisperings of their own heart. They are perpetually being transported to other strata of the system in order to maintain the endless sense of vertigo that underpins its maintenance. From this perspective the real crisis would be for there to be no crisis at all.

Notes

1. This phrase, of course, is famously used by Herman and Chomsky (1994) to describe the role of the media in managing public opinion. Their analysis relies on a range of literacies

and illiteracies that are grounded in the educational consensus propagated as Western mind.

2. Of course, this relates to the social sphere. It is also worth noting that the individual is also, as Hal and Sidra Stone (1989) show, multiple in nature and, following Deleuze (1993), exists as a folded becoming-being in which identity is only ever provisional and contextual. The work of Ferruci on psychosynthesis is also noteworthy for its contribution to an understanding of the inner possibilities of integrative work (2004).
3. Ananta Kumar Giri's edited text, *The Modern Prince and the Modern Sage*, offers an example of how such stories can be generated—it is inclusive, dialogical, transdisciplinary, and eclectic and even in its structure offers insights into alternative orderings (see Giri, 2009).

References

Agamben, G. (2005). *State of Exception*. Chicago: University of Chicago Press.

Anyon, J. (2005). *Radical Possibilities: Public Policy, Urban Education, and a New Social Movement*. New York & London: Routledge.

Apple, M. W. (2006). Rhetoric and Reality in Critical Educational Studies in the United States. *British Journal of Sociology of Education, 27*(5), 679–687.

Baudrillard, J. (1998). *The Consumer Society: Myths and Structures*. London: Sage.

Bauman, Z. (2000). *Liquid Modernity*. Cambridge: Polity Press.

Bourdieu, P., and Passeron, J.-C. (1990). *Reproduction in Education, Society, and Culture*. London: Sage.

Bussey, M. (2008). Embodied Education: Reflections on Sustainable Education. *International Journal of Environmental, Cultural, Economic and Social Sustainability, 43*(3), 139–147.

Bussey, M. (2009a). Six Shamanic Concepts: Exploring the *Between* in Futures Work. *Foresight, 11*(2), 29–42.

Bussey, M. (2009b). A Utopic Reflection. *Social Alternatives, 28*(3), 57–58.

Bussey, M. (2012, Forthcoming). Forms to Dream By: New Histories, New Research, and a Neo Humanity. In A. K. Giri (Ed.), *Pathways of Creative Research: Towards a Festival of Dialogues*. New Delhi: Primus Books

Castoriadis, C. (1997). *World in Fragments: Writings on Politics, Society, Psychoanalysis, and the Imagination* (D. A. Curtis, Trans.). Stanford, CA: Stanford University Press.

Deleuze, G. (1993). *The Fold: Leibniz and the Baroque* (T. Conley, Trans.). Minneapolis: University of Minnesota Press.

Deleuze, G., & Guattari, F. (1987). *A Thousand Plateaus: Capitalism and Schizophrenia* (B. Massumi, Trans.). London & New York: Continuum.

Deleuze, G., & Guattari, F. (1994). *What Is Philosophy?* New York: Columbia University Press.

Ferruci, P. (2004). *What We May Be: Techniques for Psychological and Spiritual Growth through Psychosynthesis*. London: Tarcher/Penguin.

Finger, M., & Asún, J. M. (2001). *Adult Education at the Crossroads: Learning Our Way Out*. London: Zed Books.

Foucault, M. (1995). *Discipline and Punish: The Birth of the Prison* (A. Sheridan, Trans.). New York: Vintage.

Gatto, J. T. (2002). *Dumbing Us Down: The Hidden Curriculum of Compulsory Schooling*. Gabriola

Island, Canada: New Society Publishers.

Giri, A. K. (Ed.). (2009). *The Modern Prince and the Modern Sage*. London: Sage.

Giroux, H. A. (2005). *Against the New Authoritarianism: Politics After Abu Ghraib*. Winnipeg, Manitoba: Arbeiter Ring Publishing.

Herman, E. S., and Chomsky, Noam. (1994). *Manufacturing Consent: The Political Economy of the Mass Media*. London: Vintage.

Hetherington, K. (1997). *The Badlands of Modernity: Heterotopia and Social Ordering*. London & New York: Routledge.

Hicks, D., & Bord, Andy (2001). Learning about Global Issues: Why Most Educators Only Make Things Worse. *Environmental Education Research*, 7(4), 413–425.

hooks, b. (1994). *Teaching to Transgress: Education as the Practice of Freedom*. New York & London: Routledge.

Inayatullah, S. (Ed.). (2004). *The Causal Layered Analysis (CLA) Reader: Theory and Case Studies of an Integrative and Transformative Methodology*. Tamsui, Taiwan: Tamkang University Press.

Kincheloe, J. L. (2004). The Knowledges of Teacher Education: Developing a Critical Complex Epistemology. *Teacher Education Quarterly*, *31*(1), 49–66.

Latour, B. (1991). *We Have Never Been Modern* (C. Porter, Trans.). Cambridge, MA: Harvard University Press.

Loy, D. R. (2002). *A Buddhist History of the West: Studies in Lack*. Albany: State University of New York Press.

McLaren, P. (2005). *Red Seminars: Radical Excursions into Educational Theory, Cultural Politics, and Pedagogy*. Cresskill, NJ: Hampton Press.

Ritzer, G. (1995). *The McDonaldization of Society: An Investigation into the Changing Character of Contemporary Social Life*. Newbury Park, CA: Pine Forge Press.

Scott, J. (1998). *Seeing like a State: How Certain Schemes to Improve the Human Condition Have Failed*. New Haven, CT: Yale University Press.

Semetsky, I. (2006). *Deleuze, Education and Becoming*. Rotterdam/Taipei: Sense Publishers.

Shapiro, M. J. (1992). *Reading the Postmodern Polity: Political Theory as Textual Practice*. Minneapolis: University of Minnesota Press.

Stone, H., and Stone, S. (1989). *Embracing Ourselves: The Voice Dialogue Manual*. Novato, CA: New World Library.

Thompson, W. I. (2004). *Self and Society: Studies in the Evolution of Consciousness*. Charlottesville, VA: Imprint Academic.

• CONTRIBUTORS •

Stephen J. Ball is the Karl Mannheim Professor of Sociology of Education at the Institute of Education, London. He is the editor of the *Journal of Education Policy* and *Education Foundations and Policy Studies.*

Ana Laura Barudi graduated in Education from Universidad de Buenos Aires and is a master's candidate in Administration and Public Policy from Universidad de San Andrés. She is teaching and a research assistant in the School of Education at the same university.

Marcus Bussey is a futurist, world historian and educator. He works in the faculty of Arts and Social Sciences at the University of the Sunshine Coast, Queensland, Australia. He is also a researcher with the university's Sustainability Research Centre, where he is involved with a number of collaborations with CSIRO on social learning, adaptive capacity and climate change. He has worked for twenty years in a range of public and private schools and has a particular interest in grassroots community schools that focus on whole child pedagogy and experiential learning. He lectures and researches internationally and is currently working on a range of projects involving citizen research and collaborative rhizomic experiments with learning and social change. This work is regularly updated on his Web site, www.futuresevocative.com

Patrick Carmichael is Professor of Educational Research at Liverpool John Moores University, where he is director of 'Ensemble', a major project to explore the potential of emerging 'semantic web' technologies in teaching, learning and research. He is particularly interested in the ways in which networking supports the development of educational and research practice, particularly in interdisciplinary areas and in new fields where disciplinary norms have yet to be established. He has published extensively on subjects including teaching and learning in higher education; participatory research approaches; digital archiving; and technology enhanced learning.

David R. Cole is Associate Professor in English and pedagogy at the University of Western Sydney. David has previously edited three books, *Multiple Literacies Theory: A Deleuzian Perspective* (Sense) with Diana Masny, *Multiliteracies and Technology Enhanced Education: Social Practice and the Global Classroom* (IGI) with Darren Pullen, and *Multiliteracies in Motion: Current Theory and Practice* (Routledge) with Darren Pullen. He published a novel in 2007 called *A Mushroom of Glass*; his latest book is *Educational Life-forms: Deleuzian Teaching and Learning Practice* (Sense). David uses his knowledge of Deleuze and multiple and affective literacies to investigate areas of educative interest.

Mike Cole is Research Professor in Education and Equality and Director of the Centre for Education for Social Justice at Bishop Grosseteste University College, Lincoln, UK. He is the author of *Marxism and Educational Theory: Origins and Issues* (Routledge, 2008); *Critical Race Theory and Education: A Marxist Response* (Palgrave Macmillan, 2009); *Racism and Education in the UK and the US: Towards a Socialist Alternative* (Palgrave Macmillan, 2011); and the co-author (with Sara C. Motta) of *Constructing Twenty-first Century Socialism in Latin America: The Role of Radical Education* (Palgrave Macmillan, 2012). He is the editor of *Equality in the Secondary School: Promoting Good Practice Across the Curriculum* (Continuum, 2011) and *Education, Equality and Human*

Rights: Issues of Gender, 'Race', Sexuality, Disability and Social Class (3rd edition, Routledge, 2011). He is the co-editor (with Curry Malott) of *Teaching Marx Across the Curriculum: The Socialist Challenge* (Information Age, 2012)

Jim Crowther is Senior Lecturer in the Institute of Education, Community and Society, at the University of Edinburgh's Moray House School of Education. He is currently the editor of *Studies in the Education of Adults* and is the coordinator of the international popular education network (PEN). He has various publications in the area of popular education, adult literacy and the politics of educational policy.

Abraham P. DeLeon is an assistant professor at the University of Texas at San Antonio in the Department of Educational Leadership and Policy Studies. His critiques are grounded in radical social theories and have been influenced by cultural studies, anarchist theory, critical discourse studies, the postmodern tradition, critical pedagogy, and postcolonial studies. He has articles that appear in journals such as *Educational Studies, Urban Review, Critical Education, Equity & Excellence in Education*, and upcoming in the *Journal of Curriculum Theorizing*. He has also authored numerous book chapters in various edited collections. He also was a member of the editorial collective that produced *Contemporary Anarchist Studies: An Introductory Anthology of Anarchy in the Academy* (Routledge, 2009) and has co-edited *Critical Theories, Radical Pedagogies, and Social Education: Towards New Perspectives for the Social Studies* (Sense Publishers, 2010).

Victor H. Diaz is a doctoral student at Arizona State University, whose research interests include teacher education, social justice education and liberatory pedagogy. He received his master's degree in Educational Equity and Social Justice from San Francisco State University, and has taught both high school and middle school English/Language Arts for eight years. He has also spent the past four years training and supporting middle and high school teachers in Teach For America.

Gustavo E. Fischman is Professor in the Mary Lou Fulton Teachers College and Transborder Studies at Arizona State University. His research background is in comparative education and critical policy studies. He is the editor of *Educational Policy Analysis Archives/Archivos Análiticos de Políticas Educativas* and *Education Review/Reseñas Educativas*, and author of four books and numerous articles on higher education, teacher education and gender issues in education.

Dr. Silvia M. Grinberg is a researcher at the National Committee of Science and Technology in Argentina (CONICET), Professor of Pedagogy and Sociology of Education, Director of the Centre for Contemporary Pedagogical Studies (National University of San Martín, UNSAM), and Coordinator of the Socio-Pedagogic Division (National University of the Patagonia, UNPA). Silvia's interests include questions of educational inequality, specifically processes of subjectivation related to the ways of operating, procedures and mechanisms by which certain local, regional and global dynamics take shape in school life. Her work concerns governmentality, biopolitics and education. Recently, she has been developing research in the contexts of extreme urban poverty and hyperdegraded territories (shantytowns). The research is specifically oriented toward pedagogical devices *(dispositifs)* and processes of subjectivation.

Silvina Gvirtz has a doctorate in Education and is Director of the master's degree in Education at Universidad de San Andrés, researcher at the CONICET (National Council for Scientific and Technical Research), vice president of Foundation CIPPEC's Board of Administration, editor of the journal *Revista de Política Educativa*, and General Director and Founder of the program *Escuelas del Bicentenario*. She has published eighteen books (the latest, *Partnerships for*

Educational Improvement. State and Society at Escuelas del Bicentenario) and numerous articles for international journals. In 2003, she received the Guggenheim fellowship, and the following year she won the National Academy of Education 20th Anniversary Award.

Robert Haworth is an Associate Professor in Multicultural Education at University of Wisconsin–La Crosse. He currently serves as the director for the *Research Center for Cultural Diversity and Community Renewal*. He teaches undergraduate and graduate courses surrounding diversity and education, globalization and neoliberalism. He has published and presented internationally on anarchism, youth culture, informal learning spaces, as well as critical social studies education. He co-founded *Regeneration TV*, along with other research collectives that have been directly involved in contesting neoliberal policies. He is currently working on an edited book titled *Anarchist Pedagogies*.

Ana Inés Heras has participated as coordinator for the Jujuy action research project and is also a member of Familias por la Escuela Pública, a self-managed, autonomous collective of families supporting Buenos Aires public education (see http://www.familiasxlaescuela.org.ar/). She earned her Ph.D. and master's degrees in Education, with an Emphasis on Sociolinguistics and Ethnography, at the University of California, Santa Barbara, with the support of the Fulbright Fellowship for International Students. She is currently a researcher in the National Career Track in Argentina, as well as an independent researcher at the Institute for Social Inclusion and Human Development, a self-organized, autonomous NGO.

Eduardo Langer has a BA in education from UBA and an MA in social sciences from FLACSO. He is currently a doctoral candidate at UBA. He received a research grant from the National Committee for Science and Technological Research (CONICET) and is a researcher of sociology of education (National University of San Martín, UNSAM; National University of the Patagonia, UNPA). Eduardo's concerns include questions of governmentality and education in the framework of the critical sociology of education. He is developing research around the study of pedagogical devices, linked to the process of regulation of conduct and the practices of resistance in everyday life in secondary schools.

Kate Litherland is currently a researcher on the Ensemble Project at Liverpool John Moores University, which is investigating the potential applications of semantic technologies to case-based learning. Prior to this she completed a PhD in contemporary Italian language and literature and a short post-doc on the language of the Italian media at the British School at Rome, which was followed by a series of session-lecturing posts in that subject. Her current research is focussed on the discourses around 'authenticity' in learning technologies in higher education, the pedagogical affordances of technology in this context, and the theoretical implications of this.

Michael A. Peters is Professor of Education at the University of Waikato, New Zealand, Emeritus Professor at the University of Illinois at Urbana-Champaign, and Adjunct Professor in the School of Art, Royal Melbourne Institute of Technology (RMIT). Previously he was Excellence Professor at the University of Illinois (2005–2011), held a personal chair at the University of Auckland (2000–2005) and Research Professor at the University of Glasgow (2000–2005). He is the editor of *Educational Philosophy and Theory* (Wiley-Blackwell), *Policy Futures in Education* and *E-Learning and Digital Media* (Symposium). He completed his PhD on Wittgenstein ("The Problem of Rationality") and co-authored *Wittgenstein: Philosophy, Postmodernism, Pedagogy* (with J. D. Marshall) and *Showing and Doing: Wittgenstein as a Pedagogical Philosopher* (with Nick Burbules and Paul Smeyers). His interests are broadly in educational theory, politics and policy. He has written more than sixty books, including most recently the trilogy (co-authored with Simon Marginson and Peter Murphy) *Creativity and the Global Knowledge Economy* (2009), *Global Creation: Space, Connection and Universities in the Age of the Knowledge Economy* (2010), *Imagination: Three Models of Imagination in the Age of the Knowledge Economy* (2010) (AESA Critics Book Award 2010); *Subjectivity and Truth: Foucault, Education and the Culture of the Self* (2008) (AESA Critics Book Award 2009), and *Building Knowledge Cultures: Educational and Development in the Age of Knowledge Capitalism* (2006), both with Tina (A. C.) Besley.

Mae Shaw is Senior Lecturer in the Institute of Education, Community and Society at the University of Edinburgh's Moray House School of Education. She has been a community worker in a range of settings and now writes extensively on the politics of community development. Her most recent publication is a co-edited collection *The Community Development Reader: History, Themes and Issues* (Policy Press, 2011). She is a long standing member of the Community Development Journal.

Torill Strand is Associate Professor at Østfold University College in Norway. Her competencies range from meta-theory to social epistemologies, educational philosophy and theory, cosmopolitanism and semiotics. Among her most recent titles are "C. S. Peirce's New Rhetoric", "The Making of a New Cosmopolitanism", "Emerging Global Epistementalities" and "Metaphors of Creativity and Workplace Learning." She has just guest-edited a special issue on 'Cosmopolitanism in the Making' (*Studies in Philosophy and Education*) and is currently guest-editing a special issue on 'C. S. Peirce's Rhetorical Turn: Prospects for Educational Theory and Research (*Educational Philosophy and Theory*). Torill is president elect of the Nordic Philosophy of Education Society and secretary-treasurer of the International Network of Philosophers of Education (INPE). E-mail: torill.strand@ped.uio.no; Web page: http://www.uv.uio.no/pfi/english/people/aca/torist/index.html

Focusing on the ethical and ontological significance of 'anomaly' in education, **Jason J. Wallin's** published writing has appeared in such venues as the *Review of Education, Pedagogy, and Cultural Studies, Educational Philosophy and Theory*, the *Alberta Journal of Educational Research, Teaching Education, Journal of Curriculum Theorizing*, and the *Journal of the Canadian Association for Curriculum Studies*. Jason's most recent book, *A Deleuzian Approach to Curriculum: Essays on a Pedagogical Life,* was published in 2010 (Palgrave). In 2009, Jason received the Graduate Student Teaching Award from the University of Alberta for teaching excellence and in 2010 was conferred the Elliot Eisner Award for outstanding doctoral work in education. Jason is reviews editor for the internationally renowned journal *Deleuze Studies*.

R. Scott Webster is a senior lecturer and the coordinator of the curriculum and pedagogy discipline group at the School of Education at Deakin University. He is author of the book *Educating for Meaningful Lives: Through Existential Spirituality* (Sense Publishing) and numerous other articles. His main research areas are philosophy of education, teacher education, critical thinking, ethics, values, meaning of life, spirituality and democracy. In his research he draws mostly upon the works of Dewey, Kierkegaard, Nietzsche, Heidegger and Gadamer.

• INDEX •

•A•

•B•

• C •

• D •

• E •

• F •

• G •

• H •

•I•

•J•

•K•

•L•

• M •

• N •

• O •

• P •

•R•

•S•

•T•

• U •

• V •

• W •

• Y •

A.C. (Tina) Besley, Michael A. Peters,
Cameron McCarthy, Fazal Rizvi
General Editors

Global Studies in Education is a book series that addresses the implications of the powerful dynamics associated with globalization for re-conceptualizing educational theory, policy and practice. The general orientation of the series is interdisciplinary. It welcomes conceptual, empirical and critical studies that explore the dynamics of the rapidly changing global processes, connectivities and imagination, and how these are reshaping issues of knowledge creation and management and economic and political institutions, leading to new social identities and cultural formations associated with education.

We are particularly interested in manuscripts that offer: a) new theoretical, and methodological, approaches to the study of globalization and its impact on education; b) ethnographic case studies or textual/discourse based analyses that examine the cultural identity experiences of youth and educators inside and outside of educational institutions; c) studies of education policy processes that address the impact and operation of global agencies and networks; d) analyses of the nature and scope of transnational flows of capital, people and ideas and how these are affecting educational processes; e) studies of shifts in knowledge and media formations, and how these point to new conceptions of educational processes; f) exploration of global economic, social and educational inequalities and social movements promoting ethical renewal.

For additional information about this series or for the submission of manuscripts, please contact one of the series editors:

A.C. (Tina) Besley: tbesley@illinois.edu
Cameron McCarthy: cmccart1@illinois.edu
Michael A. Peters: mpet001@illinois.edu
Fazal Rizvi: frizvi@unimelb.edu.au

Department of Educational Policy Studies
University of Illinois at Urbana-Champaign
1310 South Sixth Street
Champaign, IL 61820 USA

To order other books in this series, please contact our Customer Service Department:

(800) 770-LANG (within the U.S.)
(212) 647-7706 (outside the U.S.)
(212) 647-7707 FAX

Or browse online by series:
www.peterlang.com